BRITAIN AND THE EUROPEAN COMMUNITY

BRITAIN AND THE EUROPEAN COMMUNITY

The Politics of Semi-Detachment

Edited by

STEPHEN GEORGE

CLARENDON PRESS · OXFORD
1992

Oxford University Press, Walton Street, Oxford OX2 6DP
Oxford New York Toronto
Delhi Bombay Calcutta Madras Karachi
Petaling Jaya Singapore Hong Kong Tokyo
Nairobi Dar es Salaam Cape Town
Melbourne Auckland
and associated companies in
Berlin Ibadan

Oxford is a trade mark of Oxford University Press

Published in the United States
by Oxford University Press, New York

British Library Cataloguing in Publication Data
Data available

Library of Congress Cataloging in Publication Data
Britain and the European community : the politics of semi-detachment /
edited by Stephen George.
p. cm.
Includes bibliographical references and index
1. European Economic Community—Great Britain. 2. European
communities. 3. European federation. 4. Great Britain—Politics
and government—1979– I. George, Stephen.
HC241.25.G7B682 91–35904
ISBN 0–19–827315–0

Typeset by Cambridge Composing (UK) Ltd
Printed and bound in
Great Britain by Biddles Ltd.
Guildford & King's Lynn

Preface

IN 1987 Simon Bulmer and William Paterson published *The Federal Republic of Germany and the European Community*,[1] a book which applied to one member state of the European Community (EC) a model that had been outlined by Bulmer in an article published four years earlier.[2] This 'domestic politics approach' was an attempt to get away from analyses of policy-making in the EC that focused simply on the Community level.

Such analyses divided into those which stressed the process of integration as an autonomous political dynamic at the Community level, such as neofunctionalism, and those which stressed that the process was still dominated by the member states, and were based on the 'realist' characterization of the national interest of the states.

Bulmer's approach was distinct from either of these. He accepted that Community policy-making was still dominated by the member states, but argued that the states could not simply be assumed to pursue rationally chosen national interests. Adopting the pluralist critique of realism, he stressed that the behaviour of states was determined by domestic politics. Policy was not the result of rational calculation: it was the outcome of a political process.

It was this approach that Bulmer and Paterson applied to the Federal Republic of Germany, and the same approach is adopted in this book to understanding the policy of Britain within the EC, in the hope that it will contribute to the cumulative understanding of Community policy through the understanding of the policies of the leading member states.

The papers that make up this volume result from the work of a study-group on Britain and the EC that met over three years, from 1988 to 1990, and was funded by the University Association for Contemporary European Studies (UACES). The views expressed in the individual chapters are in each case those of the author of that chapter, and not necessarily of the group as a whole, let alone those of UACES. However, the opportunity to meet regularly and

---

[1] S. Bulmer and W. Paterson, *The Federal Republic of Germany and the European Community* (London, 1987).

[2] S. Bulmer, 'Domestic Politics and European Community Policy-Making', *Journal of Common Market Studies*, 21 (1983), 349–63.

discuss the work in progress contributed to producing a greater unity of theme than is sometimes evident in edited collections, and for facilitating this UACES deserves great credit.

At one stage it was the intention to include one or two case-studies of British policy in specific sectors, as Bulmer and Paterson included a case-study of the Federal Republic of Germany and the European Regional Fund in their book; but it was finally decided that there was no such thing as a 'typical' sector, and that it would make more sense to allocate the application of the structural analysis to a later round of meetings which would be devoted specifically to explaining British policy in specific sectors.

Finally, the group does hope that other teams of scholars might feel that the approach adopted here is sufficiently fruitful to want to apply it to other member states of the EC. A volume adopting the same approach to France and the EC would be a particularly useful complement to those on the Federal Republic and on Britain, given the central importance of these three states in determining the direction of Community development over the years.

STEPHEN GEORGE

Sheffield, February 1991

Contents

Abbreviations

AUEW	Amalgamated Union of Engineering Workers
BDI	Bundesverband der Deutschen Industrie (Federation of German Industry)
BEUC	Bureau Européen des Unions de Consommateurs (European Bureau of Consumers Associations)
BLG	British Labour Group
BREMA	British Radio and Electronic Equipment Manufacturers' Association
CAP	Common Agricultural Policy
CBI	Confederation of British Industry
CDU	Christian Democratic Union
CECG	Consumers in the European Community Group
CEMR	Council of European Municipalities and Regions
CIAA	Confédération Internationale d'Agriculture Alimentaire (International Confederation of Food Farming)
COPA	Comité des Organisations Professionelles d'Agriculture (Committee of Professional Agricultural Organizations)
COREPER	Committee of Permanent Representatives
CPRS	Central Policy Review Staff
CSD	Civil Service Department
CSP	Confederation of Socialist parties (of the EC)
DEMYC	Democratic Youth Community of Europe
DHSS	Department of Health and Social Security
DTI	Department of Trade and Industry
EC	European Community
ECC	Euro-Constituency Councils
ECOSOC	Economic and Social Committee
Ecu	European currency unit
ECSC	European Coal and Steel Community
ECJ	European Court of Justice
EDC	European Defence Community
EDG	European Democrat Group

EDU	European Democratic Union
EEC	European Economic Community
EHO	Environmental Health Officers
ELD	(Federation of) European Liberals and Democrats
EFTA	European Free Trade Association
EMS	European Monetary System
EP	European Parliament
EPC	European Political Co-operation
EPP	European People's party
ERDF	European Regional Development Fund
ERM	Exchange Rate Mechanism
ESF	European Social Fund
Euratom	European Atomic Energy Community
FCO	Foreign and Commonwealth Office
GMWU	General and Municipal Workers Union
GNP	Gross National Product
HMG	Her Majesty's Government
IEHO	Institute of Environmental Health Officers
IMF	International Monetary Fund
IRA	Irish Republican Army
ITSA	Institute of Trading Standards Administration
IULA	International Union of Local Authorities
LACOTS	Local Authority Committee on Trading Standards
LCE	Labour Committee for Europe
MAFF	Ministry of Agriculture, Fisheries, and Food
MEP	Member of the European Parliament
MP	Member of Parliament
NATO	North Atlantic Treaty Organization
NEB	National Enterprise Board
NEC	National Executive Committee
NFU	National Farmers Union
OEEC	Organization for European Economic Co-operation
OPEC	Organization of Petroleum Exporting Countries
PLP	Parliamentary Labour Party

PR	Proportional Representation
SDLP	Social Democratic and Labour party
SDP	Social Democratic party
SEA	Single European Act
SNP	Scottish National party
TGWU	Transport and General Workers Union
TUC	Trades Union Congress
UKREP	United Kingdom Permanent Representation to the European Community
UN	United Nations
UNICE	Union des Industries de la Communauté Européenne (Union of Industries of the European Community)
VAT	Value Added Tax
WEU	Western European Union

Notes on Contributors

NIGEL ASHFORD is Senior Lecturer in Politics at Staffordshire Polytechnic. He is currently completing a book on the Conservative party and Europe; he has contributed to several books and journals on this subject and also on the politics of the United States of America.

SIMON BULMER is Senior Lecturer in Government at the University of Manchester. His publications include *The Domestic Structure of European Community Policy-Making in West Germany* (1986), *The European Council: Decision-Making in European Politics* (with Wolfgang Wessels, 1987), *The Federal Republic of Germany and the European Community* (with William Paterson, 1987).

ALAN BUTT PHILIP is Senior Lecturer in the economics and politics of the European Community at the University of Bath. His publications include *Pressure Groups in the European Community* (1985), *Implementing the European International Market: Problems and Prospects* (1988), and *European Border Controls: Who Needs Them?* (1990). He has also acted as a specialist adviser to the House of Lords Select Committee on the European Communities since 1980, specializing on issues related to regional policy and the structural funds. In 1989 he won the Charles Douglas-Home Memorial Prize for a study of Britain and the European Community.

GEOFFREY EDWARDS is Alderson Director of Studies at the Centre of International Studies, University of Cambridge, and a Research Associate of the Royal Institute of International Affairs. His publications include *The Council of Ministers and the President in Office* (with Helen Wallace, 1977), *A Common Man's Guide to the Common Market* (with Hugh Arbuthnott, 1979, 2nd edn. 1989), and *The Defence of Western Europe* (with Sir Bernard Burrows, 1982).

STEPHEN GEORGE is Senior Lecturer in Politics at the University of Sheffield. His publications include *Politics and Policy in the*

European Community (1985; 2nd edn. 1991), *An Awkward Partner: Britain in the European Community* (1990), and *Britain and European Integration since 1945* (1991).

NEILL NUGENT is Reader in Politics at Manchester Polytechnic. His publications include *The British Right* (with Roger King, 1977), *Respectable Rebels* (with Roger King, 1979), *The Left in France* (with David Lowe, 1982), and *The Government and Politics of the European Community* (1989, 2nd edn. 1991).

JILL PRESTON is Reader in Business Studies at the Anglia Business School, Anglia College of Higher Education, Cambridge. She is the author of several papers and articles on the effect on local government in the United Kingdom of EC membership.

Britain and European Integration: Of Sovereignty, Slow Adaptation, and Semi-Detachment[1]

Simon Bulmer

THE relationship between the United Kingdom and the process of European integration has been particularly fraught. An overview of the post-war period reveals a succession of difficulties:

1. The refusal to join the European Coal and Steel Community (ECSC).
2. The failure to take seriously the negotiations leading to the establishment of the European Economic Community (EEC).
3. A belated conversion to European integration culminating in two unsuccessful applications for membership in the 1960s.
4. Major political divisions concerning accession following the third (successful) application, under the Conservative Government of Mr Heath.
5. The renegotiation of the terms of entry by the Labour Government in 1975, culminating in their approval by a majority of voters in the June referendum following a hotly contested campaign.
6. Continual wrangling, especially from 1979 to 1984, between Mrs Thatcher's Conservative Government and the other member states over the high level of British net contributions to the European Community (EC) budget.
7. Following the EC's approval of important reforms in the Single European Act, Mrs Thatcher's outspoken opposition to the development of a European super-state, especially if it is to further challenge British sovereignty.
8. The resignation of four Cabinet ministers on European issues

[1] I am grateful, for their comments, to other members of the study group, to Elizabeth Meehan, and Martin Baldwin-Edwards.

over the period 1986–90: Michael Heseltine (1986), Nigel
Lawson (1989), Nicholas Ridley (1990), Sir Geoffrey Howe
(1990).
9. The circumstances surrounding the replacement of Mrs
Thatcher as Prime Minister at the end of 1990.

Against this background it is scarcely surprising that the United
Kingdom continues to be regarded as a 'semi-detached' member of
the European Community. Yet things *have* changed. The EC's
decisions in 1988 to reform the Common Agricultural Policy
(CAP), and the more equitable basis for budgetary contributions in
the period since 1984 have weakened some of Britain's grievances
against the EC. Moreover, the programme for completion of the
EC's internal market has brought a much closer identity of purpose
between the EC's objectives and those of the Conservative Government. Finally, by the end of 1988 the key British political forces,
including the Labour party, the Scottish and Welsh nationalists,
the trade union movement, and industrialists had joined those
already 'thinking European'. Of the established UK parties, it is
the Ulster Unionists which remain as bastions of opposition to
the EC.

This volume examines the relationship of Britain and the European Community over the period since 1973. Clearly, in doing so,
it cannot neglect the importance and substance of British history:
of former colonial interests and world-power status. However, our
objective is not to present a narrative account of Britain and
Europe but, rather, to offer some kind of analytical interpretation.
So what kind of interpretation is to be used? Our basic approach
is to take a 'domestic process' approach: to assume that governmental policy is not simply the result of important exogenous
European and international developments. Instead, it is assumed
that Britain's particular economic and political relationship with
the world system is mediated by its national political system. Hence
Britain's role in the EC cannot be understood fully by a mere
account of the activities of successive central governments. The
forces underlying governmental policy must also be examined.
British politics matters.

In fact, such an interpretation is, in many respects, a standard
one for Britain, due to the history of party-political differences over
European policy. However, two points need emphasizing here.

First, of the larger member states, Britain is unique in having a continuing aversion or scepticism towards integration. This contrasts with the Federal Republic of Germany, for instance, where a broad consensus has existed amongst the two major party blocks for three decades. Secondly, the party-political debate has had a close relationship with other political forces in the form of public opinion and interest groups (through the Labour movement, for example). The impact of these two factors in the period since 1973 has been that the government in office has sought to play a gatekeeping role in controlling Britain's relations with the EC. However, such a centralizing role has not always been possible. The attitudes of interest groups, public opinion, political parties, and local government all affect policy, as do the interests of Scotland, Wales, and Northern Ireland. Moreover, it must not be assumed that central government's policy is itself a coherent and integrated whole. Whether it emerges from a Government seemingly dominated by 'Thatcherism' or from the preceding Labour Governments so internally divided by the whole issue of continued membership, policy has reflected different ministerial responsibilities and interest group sensitivities.

By placing governmental policy in this wider context, our study seeks both to give an account of, and to explain, Britain's role in the EC. How far has Britain actually accepted membership of the EC? What constraints are there upon a more committedly pro-European policy on the part of the British Government, given its extensive awareness-raising campaign on the programme of completing the internal market? How far is Britain prepared to go along with the programme itself? What about the agenda 'after 1992': economic and monetary union, the 'social dimension' of the EC, and moves towards closer political union?

In this introductory chapter four components of Britain's relationship with the EC will be examined. The first section deals with the historical background to Britain's belated involvement in the supranational integration practised in the European Communities. Moving on to the present, the following two sections deal with the importance of the EC to Britain as well as with the obverse, namely Britain's importance to the EC. The fourth section discusses the analytical approach that lies behind the study as a whole and outlines the arguments of the volume.

FROM ISOLATION TO 'SEMI-DETACHMENT'?

A historical perspective is of course vital to setting the scene for this study of Britain and the EC in the period since 1973. However, because many analysts regard Britain's foreign and European policies to be the product of a failure to adjust to the changed circumstances of the post-1945 period, it is especially necessary. Various arguments have been advanced to account for the slow adaptation. Common to most of these historical interpretations is a view that, even if British economic decline was setting in at the turn of the century, it was only much later that attention came to be devoted to the reasons for this. Blank takes this economic 'given' of relative decline as the basis of his analysis of British foreign economic policy. He argues that deficiencies in this policy can be explained by 'a series of policy choices, especially in the international arena, that were inappropriate for Britain's resources but to which successive governments adhered with remarkable stubbornness and rigidity'.[2] By extension, then, Britain's failure to become involved in the arguably more relevant process of economic integration was due to a form of 'imperial overstretch'. In order to retain its standing in international politics—and despite adverse economic circumstances—such policies as defending an overvalued pound and maintaining extensive military commitments were pursued: policies which had the effect of exacerbating the pre-existing relative economic decline. By contrast, participation in the process of European integration would merely have confirmed Britain's 'descent from power'.

Hanrieder and Auton examine this maladjusted policy by reference to 'cognitive lag' in the foreign policy élite: policy-makers' failure to recognize the new post-war era of two superpowers, of nuclear arsenals, and of realigned world economic forces.[3] They also draw attention to the continuities of policy through both Labour and Conservative Governments. They argue, however, that

---

[2] S. Blank, 'Britain: The Politics of Foreign Economic Policy, the Domestic Economy, and the Problem of Pluralistic Stagnation', in P. Katzenstein (ed.), *Between Power and Plenty: Foreign Economic Policies of Advanced Industrial States* (Madison, Wis. 1988), 89.

[3] W. Hanrieder and G. Auton, *The Foreign Policies of West Germany, France and Britain* (Englewood Cliffs, N J, 1980), 179–80.

'cognitive lag' is an incomplete explanation. Other commentators have extended responsibility even further in the premise that 'Britain is a society in which historical thinking is particularly important and prominent'.[4]

It is dangerous, however, to overstate historical determinism, for the fact is that there have been adjustments to British foreign policy. The early recognition of the inability to continue as guarantors of stability in the Eastern Mediterranean (resulting in American commitments through the Truman Doctrine) was one example. Another was the realization that the former British strategy of playing continental powers off against one another was no longer appropriate in a bipolar world. These two cases illustrate the point that, whilst there have been changes in British European policy, they have often been reactive in nature. The decision to apply for EEC membership is a case in point, influenced as it was by the negative experiences of the Suez crisis (from which the French drew a more positive response) and by the contrasting economic performances of Britain and the EEC member states.

It is thus necessary to follow a more refined, discriminating approach to the impact of historical influences on Britain's present relationship with the EC. In this context it is useful to adopt the differentiation offered by Hill, who argues that there are three levels of historical impact.[5] First, there are 'those legacies from the past which are . . . almost indistinguishable from the present'. Second, there are historical influences with a major influence but which, ultimately, are amenable to change. Finally, there are constraints of a more limited nature. After an overview of Britain's relationship with European integration, therefore, an attempt will be made to differentiate between various historical influences.

An important distinction that needs to be made at the very outset of an historical overview is the distinction between *co-operation* and supranational *integration*, i.e. where sovereignty is transferred to a level above the nation state. Britain was prepared, in the 1940s and 1950s, to contemplate co-operation but not the transfer of sovereignty associated with the projects for integration. Thus Britain was a prime mover behind the co-operative arrangements set

---

[4] C. Hill, 'The Historical Background: Past and Present in British Foreign Policy', in M. Smith, S. Smith, and B. White (eds.), *British Foreign Policy: Tradition, Change and Transformation* (London, 1988), 24–5.

[5] Ibid. 33.

down in the economic sphere through the Organization for European Economic Co-operation (OEEC) created in 1948; in the military sphere through the Brussels Treaty Organization of 1948, the North Atlantic Treaty of 1949 and Western European Union of 1954; and in the broader political sector through the Council of Europe of 1949. In the case of the first four organizations, Britain can justifiably claim to have played a prominent role. In the case of the Council of Europe, Britain, through its post-war prestige, proved able to undermine completely the integrative aspirations of many gathered at the 1948 Congress of Europe at The Hague, perhaps the high point of federalist aspirations. However, this was to be the last time that Britain was to deflect those countries most in favour of integration from their desired goal. Its consistent reliance on the OEEC as the framework for economic co-operation was a particular irritation to Monnet and to those countries favouring integration.

The Schuman Plan of May 1950, leading to the Treaty of Paris establishing the European Coal and Steel Community (ECSC), which became the first of the three European communities, was rejected by Britain because of its supranational challenge to sovereignty. The Pleven Plan of October 1950 for a European Defence Community (EDC) was also opposed by Britain, with the sovereignty issue again constituting the major concern. However, the EDC treaty failed to be ratified despite having been signed by the six ECSC members. This failure also led to the demise of the proposed European Political Community, which similarly failed to interest Britain.

It is not surprising, therefore, that the British reaction to the calling of the Messina Conference of the foreign ministers of the six ECSC states in 1955 was of a low-key nature. The fact that recent sponsorship of the *co-operative* WEU was regarded as a major British contribution to European unity compounded the reluctance to go further. The effort to relaunch supranational integration, following the EDC set-back, through a broadly-based common market was set down in detail in the Messina Resolution. One paragraph of the Resolution declared that 'The Government of the United Kingdom, as a power which is a member of the WEU and is also associated with the ECSC will be invited to take part . . .'[6] The British response was to send to the resultant Spaak

[6] Quoted in M. Camps, *Britain and the European Community 1955–63* (London, 1964), 520–2.

Committee a senior official from the Board of Trade but he was withdrawn by the end of 1955. The political nature of the committee's work had been recognized by the British Government but had not been allowed to take precedence. The Government's two main objections were an unwillingness to go beyond a mere free-trade area to the greater economic integration of a customs union, as envisaged in the Spaak Report, and an opposition to the proposed supranational nature of the institutions.

Thus the signing of the two Treaties of Rome—one setting up the European Economic Community (EEC), the other the European Atomic Energy Community (Euratom)—took place without British involvement. Instead Britain pressed on with the aim of creating a European free-trade zone under the auspices of the OEEC. In the event, the six states which had signed the EEC Treaty saw no attraction in this scheme; indeed it was regarded as an attempt to undermine the EEC. Nevertheless, a scheme along British lines was established in 1960 in the form of the European Free Trade Association (EFTA) and consisted of the 'outer seven' (Britain, Sweden, Switzerland, Austria, Norway, Denmark, and Portugal). EFTA represented no threat to national sovereignty.

To those analysts who regard British foreign policy and in particular its European dimension as being entrenched and backward-looking, the rapidity with which élite attitudes towards the EEC changed in the late 1950s and early 1960s is not easily explained. To be sure, there was an element of opportunism. In other words, it was the better *economic* performance of the six EEC states and the impact of the Suez crisis that influenced thinking in the Macmillan Government rather than a sudden conversion to supranational integration. At the same time, the economic importance of the EEC might well endow it with a political authority in Europe that could overshadow Britain's foreign policy aspirations. And the role of the United States should not be underestimated. During Prime Minister Macmillan's visit to Washington in March 1960 the American administration made plain its opposition to British attempts to develop an alternative trade block to the EEC. For a range of reasons, therefore, policy was changed and on 31 July 1961 the Conservative Government announced in the House of Commons its decision to apply for EEC membership.

The problem areas in the subsequent negotiations are quite revealing. The compatibility of the common market with continued

Commonwealth trade patterns revealed an understandable concern not to make an abrupt severance of long-standing commercial arrangements. The question of the compatibility of the British agricultural system of deficiency payments with French interests for the emergent Common Agricultural Policy also proved to be a major sticking point at this stage (as indeed agriculture did more generally for much of the period since membership in 1973). The concern about adequate arrangements for trade with EFTA—which had only just come into being—was out of a sense of obligation to other member states but suggested opportunism in that venture. What was most striking, however, was that the basis for non-participation at an earlier stage, namely the political opposition to supranational integration, seemed to be avoided. Yet President de Gaulle's rejection of the British application was precisely on political grounds. It is of course a supreme irony that the rejection came from a political leader whose own commitment to national sovereignty was second to none. However, in seeking to move the EEC away from its declared supranational path, de Gaulle wanted to turn it towards French interests and French leadership. There was no place for British membership in his vision: hence the rejection of 14 January 1963.

The second British application, announced by the Labour Prime Minister, Harold Wilson, on 11 May 1967 was rather more short-lived. De Gaulle clearly still regarded British membership as a Trojan horse, facilitating American influence. After expressing scepticism as early as 16 May, de Gaulle definitively rejected the application on 27 November 1967. It was not until de Gaulle's resignation in 1969 that the path was opened for a further application, tendered in 1970 by the Conservative Government of Edward Heath, resulting in membership from the start of 1973.[7]

What elements of continuity and change can be detected over the period up to 1973 in Britain's attitude towards participation in European integration? Do they offer insights into the period after 1973?

Continuity

The greatest degree of continuity and consistency in British views is to be found on the question of national sovereignty. British

[7] On this see S. George, *An Awkward Partner: Britain in the European Community* (Oxford, 1990), ch. 2.

involvement in European organizations can be judged by this criterion alone in the period prior to 1973. And even with membership, it must be remembered that the practice within the EC had in fact shifted from the 'Community method' set down in the Treaties of Rome towards intergovernmental co-operation: thanks to de Gaulle's insistence on unanimous voting in the 1966 Luxemburg Compromise.

Why has this question of sovereignty been of such importance to British policy? There are numerous historical explanations: the continuity of institutions since the English Civil War; former world-power status; the successful avoidance, as an island, of full-scale invasion; the position of having 'stood alone' in 1940 together with the prestige gained as a victor; the myth of parliamentary sovereignty; pride in national identity as an aversion to 'homogenization' by European social integration (arguably a variant of public concerns about immigration); and perhaps even popular loyalty to the Crown.[8] As William Wallace notes,

> it has been the formal and visible *transfer* of sovereignty embodied in the issue of UK membership of the European Community which has provided the main focus for public concern . . . Successive British governments have taken a pragmatic, even a relaxed attitude to the informal processes of international interdependence, and the consequent erosion of national autonomy.[9]

This is an important distinction between the British and French positions; France having agonized over the issues of interdependence, such as American multinational capital.[10]

In view of the diversity of origins of the sovereignty issue, its echo amongst the public, Parliament, and the media is scarcely surprising. And this echo was certainly strongly in evidence in the debate surrounding accession, and again at the time of the 1975 referendum campaign. It is interesting, however, that the limited tranfer of sovereignty associated with the Single European Act did not develop into a major issue in Britain, even though it did in Denmark (a fellow sceptic on matters supranational). This being

---

[8] The notions of national sovereignty and parliamentary sovereignty can be separated out, although in practice they are often closely connected (and confused). This issue is dealt with below.

[9] W. Wallace, 'What Price Interdependence? Sovereignty and Interdependence in British Politics', *International Affairs*, 62 (1986), 367.

[10] Ibid. 368.

so, if one deduces from this that the sovereignty issue has eventually succumbed to change, then Mrs Thatcher's 1988 'Edict of Bruges' and significant scepticism concerning economic and monetary union require some explanation!

Closely related to the British aversion to ceding national sovereignty has been the pragmatism that characterized foreign policy discourse. Due in part to isolation from the upheavals of nineteenth- and twentieth-century continental history, successive British Governments have failed to recognize the powerful *political* attraction, to other states, of European unification.

Too often the British, untouched by so many of the horrors and humiliations of war—1914–18 as well as 1939–45—that inspired the Community ideal, still find it hard to comprehend the sentiments that in some countries underlie and underpin it and to which politicians both appeal and respond. It is against this background that the 'Euro-rhetoric' in those countries must be judged.[11]

In practical terms this may boil down to little more than the aversion—already discussed—to supranational integration. However, there are serious problems in attempting to find definitive statements of long-term British foreign or European policy objectives. This was illustrated by the response to the developments in Eastern Europe in 1989. The pro-active nature of West German diplomacy was most striking, although Bonn could least afford to be reactive, due to the centrality of the German question to the developments. French proposals, not only for closer integration but also for the European Bank for Reconstruction and Development and even economic aid to the Soviet Union demonstrated an active approach.[12] By contrast, British policy emphasized historic rights, as a victorious power, to participate in the resolution of the German question; a reluctance to reconsider international defence strategy; and a (convenient) wish to reconsider rapid progress towards supranational integration because of the scope for pan-European *co-operation*. Against this background it is worth noting that Churchill's declaration in 1950, that Britain's interests lay in being the point of intersection of three circles of influence—the

[11] C. Tugendhat, *Making Sense of Europe* (Harmondsworth, 1987), 21–2.
[12] The latter initiative was reported to be dismissed in Whitehall 'as a typically French agenda-grabbing stunt' (*Independent*, 20 June 1990): a response which itself captures the aversion to active policy-making.

relationship with the USA, the Commonwealth, and Europe—has been termed 'the last explicit conceptual framework for British foreign policy'.[13]

Hence, just as there has been an aversion in British élite and public opinion to ceding sovereignty, so there has been an aversion to perceiving integration as a *political* process. This is a major contrast with the other large EC member states, which make great play of the grand ideals of European Union and still manage successfully to embody national interests in their vision! For Britain, by contrast, national interests and political integration are regarded as diametric opposites. Thus once the Conservative Government succeeded in influencing the EC's agenda towards deregulation and liberalization of the internal market (in the Single European Act), Mrs Thatcher and her ministers went on to attack the parts of the programme which have political implications, namely the removal of fiscal barriers to trade and the removal of customs posts. This rather schizophrenic approach to the politics/economics of integration is reminiscent of the way past debates about membership have been assertive about the economic benefits but defensive about the political costs.

A further element of continuity derives from the perception of the United States' relationship to European security. Contrary to Churchill's 'three circles doctrine', which sees the special relationship with the USA and the relations with Europe as separate circles, they have in fact been intertwined. Britain has sought to guarantee its own security in a European context by ensuring the involvement of the USA, for example in NATO. Thus, for Britain, its participation in European integration might eventually risk decoupling the American defence guarantees by demonstrating European self-sufficiency. This was, albeit under different circumstances, as much of a concern for Bevin's foreign policy in the post-war Labour Government as for the post-1979 Conservative Government, and in particular for Mrs Thatcher, on proposals for Franco-German military co-operation. Regardless of the validity of this fear—and

---

[13] C. Tugendhat and W. Wallace, *Options for British Foreign Policy in the 1990s* (London, 1988), 2. In fairness it should be pointed out that the Conservative Government did produce a document entitled 'Europe—The Future', as a British perspective on the future evolution of the EC. H M Government, 'Europe—The Future', *Journal of Common Market Studies*, 23 (1984), 74–81. For an assessment of this, see George, *Awkward Partner*, 174–7.

in the 1950s the Americans themselves wanted British involvement in integration in order to promote European unity!—it consistently ran counter to the logic of French thinking on integration. Northedge has argued that one of the reasons for British opposition to integration was that so many initiatives came from the French.[14] What seems more tenable than this interpretation is the fact that French attitudes on European defence have been based on a two-pillar system, whereas Britain has encouraged a more active American role, right up to the breakdown of the party consensus on defence from 1979. So, whether it was the Schuman Plan's goal of ensuring Franco-German security, or de Gaulle's efforts to turn the EEC into a European bloc mediating between the superpowers, there was a clash with British European and security policy due to different perceptions of the role of the USA.

The final continuity lies in Britain's inability to confine itself to a European sphere of economic and political interest. Although the extent of global influence has declined from the situation in the 1940s and early 1950s, when Britain was still a major force, traditional maritime concerns and imperial interests were slow to disappear. Nuclear weaponry, the role of sterling, defence of the Bretton Woods monetary system: these were all part of wider international interests. 'Britain's own demography, financial system, trading needs and political contacts are now so diversified that a falling back into European parochialism is hardly an option.'[15] This situation is as true whether it is applied to the refusal to participate in supranational integration in the 1950s or to a rejection of the notion of 'fortress Europe' in the context of completion of the internal market.

Indeed, under Mrs Thatcher, de Gaulle's earlier fears about Britain acting as a 'Trojan horse' in the EEC can be seen in a new light. To a present-day Gaullist, UK membership would in any case be interpreted as a conduit for some American foreign policy ideas especially during the Reagan presidency: as the whole question of terrorism and the Middle East showed. However, the policy of attracting inward investment from Japanese and American corporations has arguably been more significant. Designed initially as

[14] F. Northedge, 'Britain and the EEC: Past and Present', in R. Jenkins (ed.), *Britain and the EEC* (London, 1983), 15–37.
[15] Hill, 'The Historical Background', 29.

a domestic industrial policy aimed at shaking up British labour and management practices, its significance since the Single European Act has become much more European in nature.[16] Having observed the broadly favourable reception which Japanese companies have had in Britain, others are investing in Britain in order to be best placed to take advantage of completion of the EC's internal market. Britain's role as 'Trojan horse' is now in the economic sphere and characterized by EC disputes over the local 'European' content of Nissan Bluebird cars manufactured in the north-east of England for export to France and the continent. Ironically, French claims that these cars are not sufficiently European in content merely alerts more Japanese manufacturers to the need to be on the inside of the single European market rather than being confronted by a potential 'fortress Europe'. The result is further Japanese inward investment, particularly into the United Kingdom.

The obverse of this is the fact that 'the UK [is] second only to the United States in the absolute size of its foreign direct investment assets'.[17] Tugendhat and Wallace go on to point out that 'British investment abroad has continued to flow most strongly towards the United States ... It has been estimated that some 60% of Britain's total direct overseas assets are located in North America ...'[18]

The significance of these points is twofold. First, it indicates that Britain's global trading orientation continues and indeed is being reinforced. Anglo-American and Anglo-Japanese economic diplomacy (including at ministerial level) is likely to give Britain special interests in EC trade policy and these may be the source of further conflict. The importance of non-European multinationals to Britain's industrial core is distinctive amongst the four larger EC states: in recent years the UK has been the main location for Japanese inward investment in the EC, for example. Secondly, rightly or wrongly, Britain's preoccupation with maintaining political sovereignty in preference to economic autonomy—as identified earlier by William Wallace—is underlined very firmly. And no matter how much the opposition parties may disapprove of the undermining of Britain's industrial base, their ability, in government, to

---

[16] G. Thompson, *The Conservatives' Economic Policy* (London, 1986), ch. 7.
[17] Tugendhat and Wallace, *Options for British Foreign Policy*, 36.
[18] Ibid. 38.

ignore the interests of this important foreign source of industrial investment is likely to be severely limited. If Britain's continuing global economic and political interests have influenced its attitudes towards European integration throughout the post-war period (as argued here), they have certainly been reinforced under the Thatcher Governments. Andrew Gamble's analysis of Thatcherism emphasizes this point: 'the accumulation strategy the Thatcher Government pursued did not ignore Europe, but at no time did the needs of European capital become its focus.'[19] The Government's preference in 1986 for an American rather than a European solution for the troubled Westland helicopter concern is the evidence most frequently quoted on this point. Britain's vested interest in global rather than European capital seems likely to continue for the foreseeable future.

Changing Influences

Apart from these major elements of continuity, there are a number of other influences on Britain's post-war European policy that have gradually given way to change. These must be identified in order that an impression of historical determinism is avoided.

It should not be forgotten, first of all, that the traditional pattern of British European policy had been to attempt to maintain domestic security through playing the continental powers off against each other. At the end of the Second World War British foreign policy-makers swiftly adapted to the two-bloc system and involved the United States in assuring peace on the continent. This was a rapid change in policy, undermining any generalizations of 'cognitive lag', although it did lead to a new continuity in the form of transatlantic defence sensitivities.

Political and economic relations with the Commonwealth were until the 1960s 'givens' influencing British European policy. However, they have gradually declined until they now have a largely residual character. British trading patterns had been tilting in favour of European markets well before membership of the EC in 1973. Hence, whilst it has been argued that Britain does not confine its interest to the European arena, the role of the Common-

---

[19] A Gamble, *The Free Economy and the Strong State: The Politics of Thatcherism* (London, 1988), 113.

wealth has none the less declined. The situation is fairly similar on the political front, too. Commonwealth politics rarely constrains European policy. To be sure, many colonial or ex-colonial issues have come on to the agenda of European Political Co-operation (EPC). However, since in most cases other member states have no particular axe to grind, British policy is often simply multilateralized. The Rhodesia—Zimbabwe problem was one example of this. In Commonwealth trade relations the Lomé Convention has served to give a broader base to residual British links. The main area of tension has arisen with policy towards South Africa, where Britain's particular ethnic and commercial links, the Commonwealth's interest, and the Conservative Government's policy have combined to create persistent problems.[20]

Other earlier difficulties have also now been overcome. British agriculture has adjusted to EC membership; the CAP has eventually adjusted somewhat to the more financially oriented British approach. Perhaps, too, the most enduring feature of British foreign (and foreign economic) policy—the failure to subordinate it to reform of the country's industrial structure—has begun to change. The massive industrial restructuring under the Conservative Governments since 1979 has led to much change. It is true that defence commitments as a share of GNP remain high compared with Britain's competitors. It is true that sterling has been kept high over periods in order to control inflation (or achieve some other monetary policy objective). It is true that Britain's true economic performance has been obscured by the benefits accruing from North Sea oil. However, despite these and other factors, there has been a much greater awareness of the need to adapt to international circumstances rather than blindly subordinating stop-go economic policies to the defence of sterling and other international commitments. The much greater—but not exclusive—focus of British foreign policy upon Western Europe is part and parcel of this development. In fact, EC membership has itself become an established component of Britain's foreign and domestic policies.

Britain's European policy 'heritage' has therefore comprised elements of continuity and change. The 'givens' have acted as constraints upon Britain's role in Europe from 1945; other factors have declined in importance. What is equally important to remem-

---

[20] M. Holland, *The European Community and South Africa* (London, 1988).

ber is the fact that global circumstances are continually changing, as the collapse of communism in Eastern Europe during 1989 demonstrated. None the less, a number of continuing features of Britain's EC membership have their origins in its pre-history: the reluctance or aversion to relinquishing national sovereignty despite the realities of economic interdependence; the slowness of British political forces in adapting to EC membership; and the unwillingness to confine foreign and foreign economic policies to the European arena. These themes, which collectively amount to semi-detachment in the context of the EC, will be re-examined towards the end of this chapter, as a prelude to the analysis in the substantive chapters. However, it is important in the first instance to take a more dispassionate look at Britain's relationship with the EC. Is Britain's semi-detachment more a question of policy style than a measure of its economic and political interdependence with the EC?

THE IMPORTANCE OF EUROPEAN INTEGRATION FOR THE UNITED KINGDOM

European integration comprises two separate strands: the three European Communities (EC) and the foreign policy co-operation process (European Political Co-operation, EPC). The importance of these for the UK has been based on pragmatism rather than principle. With the exception perhaps of Denmark, every other member state has had fundamental *political needs* which have been/are satisfied by participation in European integration. For West Germany these included gaining international credibility, *gaining* sovereignty, supporting its new democracy, and obtaining security and new markets in the divided Europe of the post-war period.[21] For France integration promised an end to recurrent Franco-German hostilities; for Italy it offered comparable benefits to those relating to West Germany; for the three Benelux states supranational integration offered security from their large continental neighbours; for Ireland it offered an escape from the shadow of Britain; and for the three more recent members—Greece, Spain,

---

[21] S. Bulmer and W. Paterson, *The Federal Republic of Germany and the European Community* (London, 1987), 5–14.

and Portugal—it offered an end to periods of isolation, and acceptance into the West European democratic family.

Simplified as these explanations may be, the absence of any equivalent political motivation for British involvement in European integration is of great importance in explaining British reluctance to participate in supranational integration. Indeed, the motives of the original Six were regarded with suspicion as seeking to re-establish some form of Holy Roman Empire, recalling religious divisions of an earlier era. Leaving this aspect apart, for successive British Governments, objectives consisted in achieving European security and outlets for trade; both proved to be possible in the short term without supranational integration. To have adopted an idealistic political commitment to integration would have been a negative step: a questioning of Britain's independent status in international politics.[22]

As is known, and will be explained later in this study, the reservations continue with respect to supranational integration. However, the EC/EPC frameworks *have* assumed importance in British foreign policy. That they have done so is precisely because Britain's independent capabilities in international politics have declined. Britain cannot play the role of superpower, however much the Anglo-American 'special relationship' is employed to give a public impression of Britain's greatness. The fact is that Britain's share of world trade in manufactures has declined over the post-war period, as has its relative standing in Western Europe in terms of Gross Domestic Product. The Commonwealth's value as a diplomatic resource is declining; the South African issue has appeared to be marginalizing Britain's role in the very organization which it created! One of Britain's key diplomatic resources is the extent of its defence commitment: 'Britain's nuclear role remains a vital element in the country's claim to international standing.'[23] The changes in superpower relations and the collapse of communism in Eastern Europe place question marks against sustaining the present level of conventional commitments at the same time as re-

---

[22] It is also worth pointing out that, in the early years, there was a reluctance to participate in what was seen as a Catholic- or Christian Democratic-based movement towards integration. Echoes of this position are to be found in the Conservative party's failure to work with the European People's party (the Christian Democrats) in the European Parliament.

[23] Tugendhat and Wallace, *Options for British Foreign Policy*, 77.

equipping with the Trident nuclear system and, more fundamentally, suggest a review of the reliance upon defence commitment as a diplomatic resource.

What is striking, therefore, is that the EC and EPC are continuing to assume a core position in Britain's international role and yet there is a reluctance to embrace this within the innermost circles of the Conservative Government (just as was the case with its Labour predecessor). For instance, Mrs Thatcher's replacement of Sir Geoffrey Howe as Foreign Secretary in the July 1989 Cabinet reshuffle was interpreted as being motivated by a dislike of his espousal of Europeanism. Mrs Thatcher's own view of European integration appeared to be much more immediately utilitarian in nature. European integration should be subordinated to the goal of restoring Britain's greatness and the EC be treated as a wider arena for the pursuit of the liberalizing and deregulatory economic policies associated with 'Thatcherism'. But, whilst governmental policy has given little rhetorical support for the process of European integration, it is important not to fall into the trap of confusing rhetoric with reality. The EC and EPC have assumed importance to Britain because many of the other reference points of British policy are in doubt and, with the moves towards global regionalism in the international system, a policy of isolationism is unrealistic. Moreover, precisely at a time when European integration is in a dynamic phase, following the Single European Act, and where it is at the forefront of the moves towards global economic regionalism with the internal market programme, there are increasing political and diplomatic resources opening for Britain. That these have not been exploited to the fullest extent bears testimony to the continuing influence of the historical factors outlined above.

Economic Importance of the EC

The British economy has always been oriented towards foreign trade. In 1987 19.7 per cent of British GNP was accounted for by exports.[24] However, over the post-war period the pattern of British trade has shifted considerably so that by 1988 49.8 per cent of British exports were to member states of the EC, while 49.2 per

---

[24] Organization for Economic Co-operation and Development, *OECD Economic Surveys: The United Kingdom* (Paris, 1989).

TABLE 1.1 *Structure of the United Kingdom's trade with the member states of the European Community (as a percentage of total UK trade), 1958 and 1988*

Destination/origin	Exports		Imports	
	1958	1988	1958	1988
Belgium, Luxemburg	1.9	5.2	1.6	4.3
Denmark	2.4	1.4	3.1	1.8
West Germany	4.2	11.6	3.6	15.8
Greece	0.7	0.6	0.2	0.3
Spain	0.8	3.3	1.0	2.1
France	2.4	10.1	2.7	8.5
Ireland	3.5	4.9	2.9	3.5
Italy	2.1	5.0	2.1	5.3
Netherlands	3.2	6.8	4.2	6.8
Portugal	0.4	1.0	0.4	0.8
Total EC	21.7	49.8	21.8	49.2

Source: 'Statistical Annex', *European Economy*, 42 (Nov. 1989), 257.

cent of imports originated from them (see Table 1.1). The figure of 49.8 for British exports, compared with 21.7 per cent in 1958, represents the biggest shift in trade towards the EC for any of the member states over this period.

These figures are an indicator of how important the EC is to Britain in economic terms. There are two main aspects of this economic importance. First, there is the simple fact that the British economy is closely enmeshed with that of the EC through trade flows. The basic British principles of market economics have been broadly in line with the practice of the EC. Some politicians on the left of the Labour party have argued that the EC would represent an intolerable constraint upon a socialist policy programme but, hitherto at least, no Government has sought to implement such a programme. Indeed, under the Conservative Governments of Mrs Thatcher, the EC's economic principles have been moved towards a more liberalized and deregulated approach than that traditionally advocated by the economic liberals in the Federal Republic of Germany.[25] Second, the EC is a significant force in international

[25] Prior to the internal market programme the West German claim to be

trade diplomacy. Consequently it is an important arena for promoting British interests in world trade. These two indicators of the
EC's importance have not presented British Governments with
major difficulties. However, in three economic areas difficulties
have arisen.

First, there has been the poor 'match' between British agriculture
and farm policy with the patterns inside the EC. Due to the form
and timing of industrialization, together with the access to cheap
food supplies of the Empire/Commonwealth, domestic agricultural
policy has tended to be oriented towards the cheaper prices
prevalent in the world market. This pattern was different from that
in the original six member states, where the agricultural share of
Gross National Product and of employment was much greater in
the post-war period. The resultant clash of philosophies between
the 'cheap food' deficiency payments scheme and the more protectionist and producer-oriented Common Agricultural Policy served
to overshadow Britain's adaption to a system which is now the
central point of reference for policy. Following the 1988 package
of reforms aimed at limiting the cost of the CAP, the true
importance of this policy may eventually be realized. The second
area of incongruence relates to the EC's budget. Due to its bias
towards spending on agriculture, from which Britain does not
derive major financial benefits, successive Governments have
sought to change the system so that it takes greater account of the
UK's circumstances.

The third area where policy compatibility has been unsatisfac-
tory relates to the service sector. The significance of this situation
has been most pronounced in financial services.

The UK stands out among OECD member states for the size and strength
of its financial sector, which accounted for 7.5% of GDP in 1985
(compared with America's 4.7% of GDP). Britain's share of world exports
of financial services was 8% in 1985, well ahead of its share of trade in
manufactures.[26]

Under these circumstances the EC's very limited progress in creating a common market in services hampered an area of great

---

defenders of free trade was weakened by covert practices restricting market access.
Technical standards—often the result of the self-regulation of industry—represented a significant constraint upon foreign producers.
[26] Tugendhat and Wallace, *Options for British Foreign Policy*, 36.

potential for British interests. Following agreement to completion of the internal market these barriers to the service sector are to be phased out. Responses in City of London institutions indicate the importance which they attach to this development. If the opportunities are seized, the EC could develop into an important market for the service sectors.

Without doubt the EC has assumed central economic importance to the United Kingdom. Industry and agriculture are closely enmeshed in the EC market. However, the geographically wider orientation of the British financial services industry—stemming from Britain's historically global economic interests—is mirrored by a continuing refusal to confine governmental policy to the European arena. Whether this is part of the accumulation strategy of Thatcherism (Gamble) or simply governments/politicians of whatever colour courting electoral popularity on the global stage (economic summitry, the Group of Five, etc.), the EC has not yet assumed a centrality in official policy. The lengthy debate about sterling joining the EMS's Exchange Rate Mechanism is partly explained by this. Whether the Department of Trade and Industry's 'Europe is Open for Business' campaign permeates all other ministries—and most notably the Treasury—remains to be seen.

Political Importance of EPC

Just as global economic interests have obscured the importance to the UK of the EC, so this has also happened in the foreign policy sphere with EPC. A whole-hearted commitment to European diplomacy would, in successive Governments' views, have jeopardized the Commonwealth and the 'special relationship' with the USA as alternative channels of diplomatic interest. Clearly it is in British interests to maximize influence through all available diplomatic resources. Each of the three channels brings constraints and opportunities. Given Britain's dependence on US technology for the nuclear deterrent, it is not possible to abandon the 'special relationship' without fundamental changes to defence policy. On the other hand, it has to be realized that British interests are not central to American foreign policy and clashes of interest are inevitable, such as occurred over the US invasion of Grenada. How important, therefore, is EPC amongst these three channels?

First of all it is important to recognize that by the 1970s Britain had very limited channels for playing a world role.[27] Against this background Hill observes that,

Any suggestion that British foreign policy should, as an alternative to Europe, rely on its traditional bastions of the United States or the Commonwealth, or a combination of the two, would get short shrift these days from the cognoscenti . . . Britain can no long expect to derive much more than moral support from any of its ex-colonies, however large, rich or anglicized. The 'special relationship' with Washington in particular is now little more than a rhetorical flourish . . .[28]

The fact is, then, that European Political Co-operation has become the dominant reference point for British foreign policy but it has not become the exclusive one. That EPC has assumed this importance can be explained by a number of factors. Britain's involvement in EPC started at a time when the system was still 'running in' because it had only started in 1970. In consequence it was possible to influence the form political co-operation took. Further, given the relatively small coterie of foreign policy-makers, who are not subject to the same amount of 'politicking' as their counterparts in home ministries, the assumption of a European focus to foreign policy has not been noticed widely (Mrs Thatcher *did* notice!). There is also the fact that there have been no serious controversies about the structure and process of EPC: a clear distinction from the British disputes over the CAP and the EC budget.[29] In addition, EPC itself has evolved into a dense network of foreign relations: meetings of ministers and diplomats, diplomatic telexes (about 10,000 each year), and counter-terrorist intelligence. Each small advance opens up new opportunities for British foreign policy and Britain has initiated several procedural improvements. Finally, the international political climate on the threshold of the 1990s points towards greater West European self-sufficiency in foreign and defence policy—a situation likely to be reinforced by the closer economic integration of the '1992' programme—and EPC repre-

[27] Permanent membership of the United Nations' Security Council is one continuing special resource for Britain's international role. The partnership between Mrs Thatcher and President Reagan could also be regarded as an attempt to reassert a role 'above' that of the EC.

[28] C. Hill, 'Britain: A Convenient Schizophrenia', in C. Hill (ed.), *National Foreign Policies and European Political Cooperation* (London, 1983), 26.

[29] Whether this comparative lack of controversy is due to British support for EPC, or to an alternative explanation, namely that EPC has not impinged upon the key issues of sovereignty such as defence and security, is open to question.

sents a major channel for its achievement. From the British perspective, therefore, EPC is a central, but not exclusive, reference point in British foreign policy. For third world countries, by contrast, British foreign policy is more likely to be perceived as fully integrated within the extensive machinery of EPC.[30]

THE UK'S IMPORTANCE TO THE EC

If the EC and EPC are coming to assume an increasingly important role in British policy, how important is Britain to them? Here the situation is one of less importance. First of all, it must not be forgotten that European integration proceeded between the original six member states for two decades without British involvement. Second, the record of disagreements between Britain and the EC over budgetary contributions and the CAP has led the other member states to question Britain's commitment. A number of other EC initiatives have been obstructed by the British Government, such as moves towards a uniform electoral system for the European Parliament or, more generally, the strengthening of the supranational powers of the EC institutions.

A variation on this theme obtains in one or two other policy areas where Britain is not a full participant in policy. The reluctance to achieve full participation in the European Monetary System is the most prominent example. Another is Britain's refusal to have the LINGUA programme extend to education at the secondary level. However, the member states agreed that the application to secondary education would be optional, thus creating a tiered use of the programme. Both cases indicate that if Britain has serious reservations about EC legislation, perhaps motivated by sovereignty concerns, then the other member states may not be constrained from pressing ahead regardless, thereby creating patterns of differentiated integration.[31] If Britain too often operates in the lower tier of integration, there is a serious risk of losing influence.

[30] On the extensive institutional web of European Political Co-operation, see A. Pijpers, E. Regelsberger, and W. Wessels (eds.), *European Political Co-operation in the 1980s* (Dordrecht, 1988).
[31] On the question of differentiated integration, see H. Wallace, *Europe: The Challenge of Diversity* (London, 1985).

Those favouring supranational integration may regret that European initiatives have often come from the Franco-German core or the European Council rather than from the Commission. However, despite these realities Britain has only rarely been a source of governmental initiatives. Its main contributions have arguably been in connection with EPC. Here Britain's importance is much greater. Its range of diplomatic resources, for instance its good connections with the United States and the Commonwealth countries, have undoubtedly been important to the development of political co-operation.

The other area where Britain consistently sought positive initiatives is in respect of liberalization and deregulation of the internal market, including in particular of the service sectors. The British Government first set down a marker in this regard during its 1981 presidency of the Council of Ministers. To be sure, the fact that the service sectors have been brought into prominence in the programme to complete the internal market is not due to Britain alone, for the Commission and other states, particularly the Netherlands, have been important. However, the Thatcher Government can rightly claim to be the most prominent of the larger member states to have advocated these measures, since the Germans have closely regulated their service industries. This is, therefore, a policy area where Britain is important even if there is a strong tension between support for deregulation, on the one hand, and invoking the instruments of sovereign statehood (retention of border formalities, fiscal autonomy, etc.) as the basis for derogations from market principles. Gamble's interpretation of Thatcherism—'the free economy and the strong state' is again instructive.[32]

The UK's importance to European integration remains rather limited. Despite having achieved important successes relating to the CAP and the EC budget, and having secured commitments to deregulation and liberalization in the Single European Act, an apparent lack of commitment in other areas has resulted in Britain remaining on the fringes. It is this situation which has led to a number of commentators warning that Britain risks missing out on important new developments.[33]

---

[32] Gamble, *The Free Economy and the Strong State.*
[33] R. Jenkins, 'Britain in Europe: Left Behind Again?', *The Royal Bank of Scotland Review*, 162 (1989), 3–8.

ANALYSIS AND INTERPRETATIONS

These, then, are the background circumstances of the UK's membership of the EC but what of the framework for analysing them? This study, as already mentioned, will argue that British politics matters. The European Community exists as a framework for achieving common solutions to shared problems. Nevertheless, the striking feature of the EC is the continuing extent of diversity in national practices. EC membership has not led to the existence or imposition of uniform political and economic structures across the continent. In fact, the continued importance of national Governments in EC policy-making—even in the changed climate following the SEA—ensures the continued importance of divergent national policies to European integration. Different economic structures, political traditions, institutional forms all culminate in different national patterns of European policy. This is why key EC questions like deregulation versus regulation or national sovereignty versus supranational integration elicit a different 'mix' of responses in each member state. It is why the nature of the responses may also differ between policy sectors within member states. This study gives primacy to politics in its explanation of the UK's relationship with the EC; the contributors are political scientists after all! It sees British domestic politics as playing the crucial role in determining policy content, albeit in a European and global environment that is constantly evolving.[34]

Invoking domestic politics as an explanation of British European policy is not sufficient, however. Rather, some interpretations need to be offered which will serve as recurrent themes throughout the study. To this end an institutional interpretation is advocated. In political analysis institutions have come to be seen as being more encompassing than the organs of the state. Beyond this 'traditionalist' approach to institutions, some analysts regard the organization of finance, business, and the labour market; the structure of the political system; and the country's position in the international economy as part of an institutional web mediating national policy

[34] For more on 'domestic politics' interpretations, see S. Bulmer, 'Domestic Politics and European Community Policy-Making', *Journal of Common Market Studies*, 21 (1983), 349–63; and Bulmer and Paterson, *The Federal Republic of Germany and the European Community*, 2–4.

formulation.[35] The 'new institutionalists' thus extend the purview
of institutions to the broader conflicts within politics and regard
procedures as being as much of the institutional framework as the
formal provisions of constitutional government. This volume does
not pursue this approach in full but it is largely organized by
'institution'. It also offers three possible interpretations of Britain's
role within the EC, each having an institutional dimension.

First, there is the preoccupation with the retention of national
sovereignty that is often merely a fig-leaf for central government's
wish to maintain control over national attitudes and policy on the
EC (a gatekeeper role). Second, there is the argument, which has
also been advanced by David Allen, that the institutions of British
Government have adapted to EC membership, whilst the wider
British political system has failed to build a domestic consensus for
this.[36] Third, there is the more encompassing claim that Britain
remains a semi-detached member of the EC. Each of these can be
given an institutional explanation.

The national sovereignty/governmental gatekeeping argument
has several institutional aspects to it. British territorial integrity,
the sovereignty of Parliament, the UK's former great-power status,
the absence of a consolidated, written constitution, the unitary
structure of government, the aversion to power-sharing inherent in
the two-party system: all these mainsprings of the first theme find
their expression in British politics in institutional form. Small
wonder, then, that national Governments of both major political
persuasions have sought to secure their own position and have
resisted as far as possible the 'snares' of giving up sovereignty.
During the Thatcher Governments it occasionally appeared as if
the gatekeeper was located at the very door of 10 Downing Street.
Again, the institutional procedures of prime-ministerial government offer some explanation: prime-ministerial gatekeeping
appears entirely consistent with the centralizing trends of the
governmental system during the 1980s.

It is worth emphasizing that the sovereignty issue has both an
internal and an external dimension. The former relates to parlia-

---

[35] For an authoritative exposition of the new institutionalism, see Peter A. Hall, *Governing the Economy: The Politics of State Intervention in Britain and France* (Cambridge, 1986).

[36] David Allen, 'Britain and Western Europe', In Smith, Smith, and White (eds.), *British Foreign Policy*, 168–92.

mentary sovereignty and dates from the struggle between King and Parliament of the English Civil War onwards.[37] The latter concerns British (or English) territorial integrity since 1066. The distinction is often blurred. The EC's supranational body of law is a challenge to the tradition that Parliament cannot be bound. EC law can also constrain national Governments. However, when initiatives launched in 1989 to strengthen parliamentary scrutiny procedures (see Chapter 4) appeared to gain the support of government, the distinct impression was one of the executive seeking to strengthen its own hand in the Council of Ministers rather than of it supporting an increase in parliamentary powers more generally. The national gatekeeper argument, which recurs in this study, places greater emphasis upon government seeking to retain *its* powers, although the link with the parliamentary sovereignty issue is recognized.

The argument that 'government has adapted whereas politics has not' similarly can be traced to institutional circumstances. One possible explanation is that this situation has prevailed precisely as a result of central government's gatekeeping role. The two arguments *could* be seen as amounting to much the same thing.

Here, however, it is argued that the maladjustment of British politics is due to a rather separate set of 'institutional' features associated with the political system (rather than the governmental one), for instance the form of oppositional politics in Great Britain. Adversarial politics—i.e. the idea that the British party system's dynamics tend to produce ritualized party conflict—cannot serve as an adequate explanation of party attitudes to the EC, for divisions within parties have also been significant. However, for much of the 1970s and 1980s it can help to explain why no party in government could embrace EC membership fully, given the mismatches between Community policy and British interests. Moreover, it has not been possible for British Governments, of whatever persuasion, easily to abandon the institutions of world-power status, be they the maintenance of forces East of Suez, the aspirations to an Anglo-American special relationship, the Commonwealth, or the defence of national sovereignty itself. In this respect public opinion has tended to be a drag on the adaptation of politics to EC membership. No party in government has had sufficient courage—due to the pressures of the party system—to

---

[37] Wallace, 'What Price Interdependence?'

commit Britain fully to the European cause for fear of appearing unpatriotic and disloyal to the traditions of being 'above Europe'. The Labour party's commitment to withdrawal from the EC during the period 1981–7 acted as a similar drag on the debate. The Conservatives could not fully embrace the EC because, under Britain's adversarial political system, this would risk giving Labour electoral capital due to public dissatisfaction with the budgetary costs of membership.

It is perhaps no longer appropriate to refer to the *non*-adaptation of British political forces, for the 1989 elections to the European Parliament revealed considerable 'Europeanization' of political issues. Further, following the SEA, interest groups have taken on board the necessity to think European. That political forces have taken a decade and a half to adapt to the implications of joining in 1973 is a striking feature of the British experience, especially since it is almost thirty years since the first bid for membership.[38] In the past political forces certainly lagged behind government in adapting to the EC but there is now some evidence, for instance in respect of the Labour party and the trade unions, that political forces are perhaps even moving ahead of government. Again this may be seen as the exploitation of the conditions of adversarial politics, with the Labour party exploiting the internal divisions within the Conservative party on EC policy. It is perhaps more accurate, then, to point to the different European 'learning curves' of the various parts of the British political system and explain these differences by the absence of a domestic consensus on EC policy.

The third theme—that of British semi-detachment—is the most encompassing in nature and thus finds many institutional expressions. Like sovereignty—see above—it has both internal and external aspects. Internally, it is partly an extention of the previous theme, since semi-detachment is due in large part to the slow adjustment of British political forces. But semi-detachment is also related to Britain's external context. The UK's enmeshment in the international economy has never been oriented towards 'just' the European market. The Treasury's economic diplomacy has been structured around Anglo-American or global arrangements such as the International Monetary Fund rather than being confined to the

---

[38] Britain is not entirely unique in this respect because the process of adaptation has also been slow in Denmark.

European arena. Successive Governments throughout the post-war period have arguably followed the interests of City financial institutions rather than those of industry.[39] Finally, the *acquis communautaire* institutionalized in the EC a policy balance that scarcely heightened Britain's attachment to membership.

Continuing British semi-detachment is not, then, some (mistaken or correct) policy dreamt up in Whitehall. It is, rather, the product of a strong institutional logic permeating the political system, economic markets, and public administration. However, it must be emphasized that this argument relates to *semi*-detachment, indicating that there will be areas where Britain has played a full role: its record on implementing EC legislation for instance.

These three themes then inform our examination of the United Kingdom and the EC. All three find expression in the broader institutional features of the British political system, which are examined separately in the following chapters, after a general review of the nature of British policy in the EC.

[39] See Blank, 'Britain: The Politics of Foreign Economic Policy' for the argument on Government—City relations; also Hall, *Governing the Economy*, for an institutional interpretation of this.

The Policy of British Governments within the European Community

Stephen George

WHAT have been the characteristics of the policies followed by successive British Governments towards the EC since membership? How consistent have policies been over time, and under Governments of different political persuasions? How far does the record lend support to the idea of Britain as a 'semi-detached' member of the Community? These are the questions that are considered in this chapter.

The period covered begins with membership in 1973, under the Conservative Government of Edward Heath, and looks at the Labour Governments of Harold Wilson (1974–6) and James Callaghan (1976–9) and the Conservative Governments of Margaret Thatcher (1979–90).

In contrast with the argument of Bulmer and Paterson that in the Federal Republic of Germany, 'European policy has been formulated overwhelmingly at the technical level with limited involvement of ministers',[1] British policy towards the EC has frequently been influenced by political considerations. Some policy in relatively non-controversial areas has emerged from administrative responses to technical problems; but frequently EC matters have had implications in the party-political and electoral arenas. Because the prevailing consensus on the EC has until recently been predominantly one of suspicion and hostility to attempts to move to closer European unity, this politicization has produced a good deal of continuity across Governments of different political persuasions.

After some introductory comments on the economic and political context of policy-making, the rest of this chapter will examine first

---

[1] Simon Bulmer and William Paterson, *The Federal Republic of Germany and the European Community* (London, 1987), 43.

the broad pattern of British government policy on European integration, then a number of different policy sectors.

THE CONTEXT OF POLICY

The context within which policy towards the EC has been formulated includes developments in the wider international system, of which the EC and Britain are part. The onset of a world recession in the early 1970s, just at the time when Britain finally achieved membership, had important implications. It blew the Community itself off course, and contributed to greater tension between Britain and its new partners than might have appeared in a context of economic growth.[2]

Economic problems endemic to the British system meant that Britain suffered more in the recession than other member states of the Community, and the consequent social tensions became entwined with the debate on the advisability of membership which continued after 1973. The Community was blamed by opponents of membership for adverse developments that owed more to the world recession and to the underlying lack of competitiveness of British industry than to membership of the EC.

This uncompetitiveness is an aspect of the second contextual factor: the condition of the domestic economy. Prior to the onset of the world recession the British economy was losing ground to its main competitors, and one consideration in the British application for membership of the EC was the realization that the Six were benefiting from the common market economically, and were outstripping Britain in rates of growth and in expansion of trade. For the Heath Government membership of the EC was an integral part of a programme for economic revival which also involved the reform of industrial relations and the reduction of Britain's increasingly high levels of inflation.[3] But the Wilson Government had an economic programme in which the only part for the Community was as a market for British exports; and the Callaghan Government

---

[2] Stephen George, *An Awkward Partner: Britain in the European Community* (Oxford, 1990), 42–6, 71–4, 107–12.

[3] Andrew Gamble, *Britain in Decline: Economic Policy, Political Strategy and the British State* (London, 1981); Nick Gardner, *Decade of Discontent: The Changing British Economy since 1973*, (Oxford, 1987).

pinned its hopes for economic revival on the adoption of a co-ordinated international approach involving the United States and Japan as much as the other EC members.[4]

Under Margaret Thatcher hopes for economic revival were based on reducing the role of the state in the economy and on allowing market forces freer play than at any time in the post-war era.[5] The result of this policy was a remarkable revival in the performance of the British economy as a whole, but a revival which was extremely unbalanced both geographically and by economic sector. The financial services sector prospered under the Thatcher Governments, while British industry experienced a high level of bankruptcies and continuing difficulties as a result of high interest rates and the high value of the pound sterling, which acted as a barrier to the growth of exports. These difficulties were reflected in large deficits on the balance of payments in the late 1980s and early 1990s, although the deficits did not bring down the value of the pound, which was buoyed by high interest rates.

Geographically, the south-east of England benefited most from the prosperity, reflecting its proximity to the rest of the EC, the influx of 'hi-tech' industries into the Thames valley, and particularly the spin-off effects from the success of the City of London. In the north of the country, where traditional industries were allowed to run down, the economic record was much more mixed.

There was a noticeable increase in investment in Britain by US and Japanese companies, although these did not generate enough new jobs to counteract the effect of the decline of indigenous manufacturers, plus the increase in the work-force brought about by demographic factors. Nevertheless, inward investment from these other parts of the capitalist world became an important feature of the British economic structure.

The social upheavals caused by painful economic adjustment generated political tensions, and domestic political considerations were important in shaping policy to the EC. During the premierships of Harold Wilson and James Callaghan, the hostility of the rank-and-file of the Labour party to membership interfered with the ability of the Governments to pursue reasonable and co-

---

[4] Martin Holmes, *The Labour Government, 1974–79: Political Aims and Economic Reality* (London, 1985).

[5] Andrew Gamble, *The Free Economy and the Strong State: The Politics of Thatcherism* (London, 1988).

operative policies within the Community, a point that is taken up by Nigel Ashford in Chapter 6.[6]

Under Margaret Thatcher the pace of economic and social change increased, threatening at times in her first term of office (1979–83) to weaken the position of the Prime Minister within her own party, where she relied on the support of the right wing, who tended to be nationalistic in outlook rather than Europeanist, and whose ideological sympathies lay more with the conservatism of President Reagan of the United States than with the Social Democratic or Christian Democratic views of a majority of the leaders of other member states of the Community.[7]

These, then, are some of the main contextual factors that helped to shape British policies within the EC: a world recession which hit Britain harder than it did most other developed capitalist states; a revival from recession in the 1980s which involved a restructuring of the British economy to make it particularly dependent on the success of its financial sector and on inward direct investment from the USA and Japan; a political climate shaped by a low level of public sympathy for the EC; party-political pressures on leaders which often ran counter to attempts to forge closer European unity.

INTEGRATION POLICY

Britain did not join the European Communities when they were first created for a number of reasons, prominent amongst which was a degree of hostility to the idea of the supranational integration of the member states. The British commitment to national sovereignty was common to both the major political parties, and was in

---

[6] See also Raphaella Bilski, 'The Common Market and the Growing Strength of Labour's Left Wing', *Government and Opposition*, 12 (1977), 306–31; John Grahl and Paul Teague, 'The British Labour Party and the European Community', *Political Quarterly*, 59 (1988), 72–85; Michael Newman, *Socialism and European Unity: The Dilemma of the Left in Britain and France* (London, 1983); L. Robins, *The Reluctant Party: Labour and the EEC, 1961–75* (Ormskirk, 1979).

[7] Stephen George, 'Nationalism, Liberalism and the National Interest: Britain, France, and the European Community', *Strathclyde Papers on Government and Politics* (Glasgow, 1989); Jim Bulpitt, 'Rational Politicians and Conservative Statecraft in the Open Polity', in Peter Byrd (ed.), *British Foreign Policy under Thatcher* (Oxford, 1988), 180–205.

marked contrast to the prevailing sentiment in the original six member states. The difference may be explained by reference to the different experience of the Second World War: for the Six it was a war that underlined the dangers of nationalism, and that brought defeat at some stage for all of them; while for the British it was their 'finest hour', a matter for national pride.

Nationalism never disappeared from the French political scene, and revived after 1958 under the leadership of General de Gaulle. But with this important exception, it is probably true to say that in continental Western Europe nationalism was no longer available as a legitimating and unifying ideology following the abuse of the idea by the Fascist and Nazi parties. Post-war conservative parties in the Federal Republic of Germany, in Italy, and in the Benelux countries turned not to nationalism but to the other traditional support of conservatism, religion. Christian Democrat politicans were instrumental in the creation of both the European Coal and Steel Community (ECSC) in 1950 and the European Economic Community (EEC) in 1957. Although these steps were taken because they were believed to be in the national interests of the states concerned, the setting up of the Communities was sold to the electorate in terms of a step away from a discredited national-ism towards a new European unity which would guarantee peace and prosperity. The achievement of both objectives served to strengthen the commitment of the electorate to the ideal as well as to the reality of the Communities.

In Britain it was different. Fascism never managed to expropriate nationalism, which remained the doctrine of the respectable politi-cal parties, with Labour attempting to outdo the Conservatives in the strength of their commitment to it.[8] Despite Churchill's criti-cisms of the Attlee Government's refusal to have any part in the negotiations that set up the ECSC, it became obvious soon after he himself became Prime Minister again in 1951 that he was more pro-integration in rhetoric than in practice.

When Britain did come to apply for membership, it was for pragmatic reasons. Both Harold Macmillan, whose application was blocked by de Gaulle in 1963, and Harold Wilson, whose applica-tion suffered the same fate in 1967, came reluctantly to the conclusion that Britain could not afford to be outside the EC, for

---

[8] Tom Nairn, *The Left Against Europe?* (Harmondsworth, 1973).

economic reasons and (decisively in both cases) for Britain to maintain its influence in the world.[9] It was this difference in approach to the idea of European unity that was to form the basis of the British reputation for being a 'semi-detached' member of the Community.

Yet, when Britain eventually managed to achieve membership in 1973, it was under a Prime Minister who did have a strong personal commitment to the idea of European unity, Edward Heath. The Heath Government followed a policy of trying to strengthen the Community by encouraging the concentration of its institutions in Brussels, pressing for an improvement in the quality of the staff of the Commission, and supporting the formation of a common foreign policy. Yet on two important issues it was not prepared to act as a good European: sterling was not included in the joint float of EC currencies, which was seen as a prelude to economic and monetary union; and Britain consistently prevented agreement on a common energy policy, a particularly important issue given the context of rising energy prices and potential shortages during the Arab—Israeli war of 1973. In the end the Heath Government managed to alienate many of the other member states by its aggressive pursuit of its own national interest, combined with a tendency to lecture the original members on how they ought to be running the club.[10]

Harold Wilson came to office in February 1974 committed to a complete renegotiation of the terms of British entry to the Community. His premiership was dominated by the renegotiation of the terms of entry, which was carried out for Britain mainly by the Foreign Secretary, James Callaghan. It was the tone adopted by the Labour Government that offended the other member states of the Community more than the actual demands that it was making. The main items on the renegotiation agenda were the size of British contributions to the Community's budget, the right of the British Government to operate a national industrial and regional policy

---

[9] On the reasons for the 1961 application see Elisabeth Barker, *Britain in a Divided Europe* (London, 1971), 168–71; Miriam Camps, *Britain and the European Communities: 1955–63* (London, 1964), 274–80; Michael Charlton, 'How and Why Britain Lost the Leadership of Europe (III): The Channel Crossing', *Encounter*, 52/4 (1981), 22–33. On both applications see George, *Awkward Partner*, 28–37.

[10] George, *Awkward Partner*, 96–8.

without interference from Brussels, the establishment of favourable terms for the association of former Commonwealth states in Africa and the Caribbean with the Community, and preferential access to Britain for New Zealand lamb and dairy produce. On all of these issues new terms were eventually agreed which Wilson considered acceptable and which he felt able to recommend to the British people in the referendum that followed.[11]

In fact the budgetary settlement was far from adequate, as later became apparent; and the issue of industrial and regional aid was solved only by Britain accepting assurances that exemptions would be allowed to it in light of its special economic problems rather than by any repudiation of the principle that such policies were subject to monitoring and control from Brussels in the interests of fair competition.

After the referendum Wilson disappointed those who may have hoped for a change of approach by continuing to adopt a policy that amounted to special pleading. For example, Britain did not accept that it ought to have to apply common rules on the industrial pollution of rivers which were expressed in terms of the quantity of pollutants that could be emitted, because as an island its rivers were faster-flowing than those on the mainland of Europe, and effluent was cleared more quickly. The British Government insisted that standards be set in terms of the overall level of pollution in the water. Although technically this argument was correct, in business terms it meant that British industry would have to spend less than its continental competitors in cleaning up its production processes, as it would be allowed to emit more effluent. The issue was therefore seen as a case of Britain trying to gain an unfair competitive advantage.[12]

By far the most serious issue of dispute during the Wilson premiership, after the referendum, was the argument over representation at the Conference on International Economic Co-operation in Paris. The EC was scheduled to have a single delegation, but Callaghan objected to this on the grounds that energy was a major issue on the agenda, and Britain was the only member state of the

---

[11] On the renegotiation and referendum see David E. Butler and Uwe Kitzinger, *The 1975 Referendum* (London, 1976); Philip Goodhart, *Full-Hearted Consent: The Story of the Referendum Campaign—and the Campaign for the Referendum* (London, 1976); George, *Awkward Partner*, 80–95.

[12] George, *Awkward Partner*, 96–8.

EC that was about to become an oil-producer, so it could not agree to be represented by oil-consumers. The line represented a continuation of the awkwardness of the British on energy, which had been a feature of the Heath Government, but also a reversal of the Heath Government's policy of promoting a single voice for the Community in international forums. Eventually a compromise was reached which allowed British officials to form part of a single EC delegation with a right to enter reservations on any issue related to energy that Her Majesty's Government could not accept. It was also agreed to allow Callaghan to address the inaugural meeting of the Conference for two minutes, although in the event he took twelve minutes and thereby caused further ill will, especially as he stated that the failure of the EC to agree a common energy policy was the basis for the British demanding a separate voice, without mentioning that it was the British that had persistently blocked progress on such a common policy.[13]

Perhaps this episode illustrates one of the themes identified by Simon Bulmer in his introductory chapter: the slowness of the political level of government to adapt to membership. Callaghan had a valid point in challenging the competence of the EC to handle these negotiations. However, it may well have been the influence of Tony Benn as Secretary of State for Energy that pushed Callaghan into taking such a high-profile stance against the EC representing Britain. Party-political considerations may well have been leading the way and helping to determine the stance of the Government towards the EC, as they did throughout Wilson's premiership.

Callaghan's central part in the dispute made him a less than ideal choice as successor to Wilson in the eyes of the advocates of European union. During his premiership three issues in particular demonstrated that Britain continued to adopt a semi-detached position within the Community. First there was the question of direct elections to the European Parliament, then the question of British membership of the European Monetary System (EMS), and finally the resurrection of the argument over British contributions to the Community's budget that had been such a controversial feature of the renegotiation of the terms of entry.

Direct elections to the EP were a commitment in the Treaty of

[13] Ibid. 99–104.

Rome, but no progress had been made in implementing the commitment prior to British membership. Agreement from Britain to proceed to direct elections may have been part of a tacit deal between Wilson and Giscard d'Estaing, to secure French acceptance of the renegotiation agreement on New Zealand agricultural produce and on budgetary contributions.

At his first European Council meeting as Prime Minister, Callaghan accepted that the elections should be held in 1978, but he did nothing to introduce the required legislation into the British Parliament until it was too late for it to be enacted in time for the elections to be held as scheduled.

Here was a clear example of the policy of the British Government towards the EC being driven by domestic political considerations. Callaghan's reluctance to introduce the enabling legislation was based on the hostility towards direct elections of a majority of the Labour party. At a time when the Government's parliamentary majority was slender, and the relations of the leadership with the party were strained because of what the rank and file saw as the abandonment of the programme of social welfare measures on which Labour had been elected in 1974, another piece of legislation that would be controversial within the party was the last thing that Callaghan wanted. He eventually agreed to introduce the legislation, and personally to support the holding of the elections under a system of proportional representation (PR), because his majority finally disappeared altogether in the course of 1977, and in order to remain in office he had to conclude a pact with the Liberals, a condition of which was that every attempt be made to get the legislation through in time for the elections to be held on schedule in 1978. PR would have made this possible because it would not have required a boundary commission to spend time drawing up European constituencies, which would inevitably slow down the process. In the event Parliament did not accept PR, and consequently the elections had to be put back a year because of Britain.[14]

The second issue that demonstrated Britain's semi-detached stance was membership of the EMS, the brain-child of the German Chancellor, Helmut Schmidt. It was an attempt to relaunch the

---

[14] David Steel, *A House Divided: The Lib-Lab Pact and the Future of British Politics* (London, 1980), 39; George, *Awkward Partner*, 117–21.

project for European economic and monetary union which had foundered on the exchange rate instability of the 1970s and the divergence between the rates of inflation of the EC member states. Although Italy and Ireland expressed some reservations, and had to be given financial inducements to enter the system, all the other member states did eventually agree to put their currencies into an exchange rate mechanism which tied their values together within narrow bands of fluctuation. Britain did not. Callaghan had serious doubts on economic grounds about tying the value of sterling to that of the German mark, doubts that were fed by Treasury advice; but he had also developed a good working relationship with Helmut Schmidt, and was anxious not to sabotage Schmidt's pet scheme. In the end political considerations again came to the fore. When speaker after speaker at the 1978 Labour Party Conference attacked the scheme, Callaghan stopped wavering and decided against membership.[15]

On both these issues British policy indicated a less than whole-hearted commitment to the idea of European integration, as in the view of some member states did the third major issue of the Callaghan years, the size of British contributions to the Community's budget. In 1978 Britain came to the end of its transitional period of membership, and discovered that it was set to become the largest net contributor to the budget, despite being only fifth in terms of average share of the EC's total gross domestic product. Both Callaghan and his Foreign Secretary, David Owen, indicated publicly that this was an unacceptable state of affairs and that something would have to be done about it. To the other member states this looked uncomfortably like a bid to reopen the renegotiation. In fact the rebate mechanism that had been agreed in 1975 had never been as generous as Wilson had maintained, although Owen caused uproar when he said as much to the Brussels press corps. In addition inflation had eroded the value of the maximum rebate permitted under the scheme, and the boost to the British balance of payments resulting from exports of North Sea oil had reduced Britain's eligibility for rebates.

It was this issue that Margaret Thatcher made the centre-piece of her first Government's policy towards the Community. From

---

[15] Peter Ludlow, *The Making of the European Monetary System: A Case Study in the Politics of the European Community* (London, 1982), 217.

1979 to 1984 Britain fought a hard and sometimes bitter battle for a system of rebates on its contributions to the Community's budget, and in the meantime blocked progress in other areas of Community activity. This phase was settled at the Fontainebleau meeting of the European Council in June 1984, when a rebate mechanism acceptable to Britain was agreed.

At that same meeting the Government presented a paper entitled 'Europe—The Future' which mapped out a route for the development of the EC based on the twin objectives of closer co-operation on foreign policy and the freeing of the internal market from non-tariff restrictions on cross-national economic activity.[16] From this point forward the policy of the British Government became much more positive, culminating in its signing in 1986 of the Single European Act (SEA), which involved a commitment to majority voting in the Council of Ministers on issues directly related to the creation of the internal market, and an increase in the legislative powers of the EP on those issues.

But negative elements remained. In October 1988 Thatcher, in a speech to students of the College of Europe in Bruges, attacked the attempts of other member states, and of the Commission, to link the freeing of the market with reforms to strengthen the central Community institutions (specifically the powers of the European Parliament) and with the creation of a 'social dimension' to the project.[17] This social dimension would involve the harmonization of national social welfare measures; the institutionalization of a role for trade unions in the taking of Community decisions on economic policy; and the introduction of a European company statute which would grant employees rights of consultation within firms and the right to receive information on the future investment plans of companies.

On a number of other issues the British Government also found itself out of line with the understanding of other member states on what was involved in the 1992 project. At the same time as most states were preparing to remove customs formalities at their borders with other EC states, Britain was planning a customs hall as part of the Waterloo terminal for the trains from the Channel

---

[16] H M Government, 'Europe—The Future', *Journal of Common Market Studies*, 23 (1984), 74–81.
[17] Margaret Thatcher, *Britain and Europe: Text of the speech delivered in Bruges by the Prime Minister on 20th September 1988* (London, 1988).

tunnel, the Government insisting that the removal of customs checks would make it too easy for terrorists and drugs dealers to operate within the Community, as well as opening up the possibility of rabies spreading from the mainland through unquarantined pets smuggled into Britain.

Plans for a monetary union, involving the tighter linking together of Community currencies and the creation of a European central bank, were treated with scorn by Thatcher, who insisted that such moves were not necessary, and that her fellow Heads of Government would not be prepared to accept the loss of sovereignty involved even if she were.

Fiscal harmonization was another issue where the British Government raised objections, although here it was far from alone amongst member states. The Commission wanted to harmonize VAT and excise duties within narrow bands. Britain insisted that this was not necessary, and produced its own plan that would solve the problem of differing rates acting as a disincentive to free economic activity by allowing the market to harmonize the rates. Removal of restrictions on cross-border shopping would mean that where higher rates of indirect taxation applied in one state compared to its neighbour, people would shop across the border in the state where duties were lower and therefore goods cheaper. This would force the states with higher rates to lower them, or accept the implications of their retailers being driven out of business. Where significant cross-border shopping did not occur, there was no problem. However, this solution was less popular with member states that had high rates of VAT or excise duty, and were more liable to experience the downward pressure from cross-border shopping than was the United Kingdom.

On all of these separate issues Britain continued to be an awkward partner within the Community after 1984. But in general it is probably true to say that 1984 did mark a turning-point. Before 1984 the policies of successive British Governments, certainly post-Heath, could be characterized as essentially negative, whereas after 1984 the policy was positive with respect to the objective of freeing the internal market, if still negative with respect to what most other member states saw as being the essential complements to that process of liberalization.

It does seem that the British Government has been steadily learning how to operate as a normal member of the EC, and may consequently have become more effective in achieving its objectives; it may also have been learning the lesson of interdependence, and the limits on effective sovereignty, which other member states absorbed much earlier. However, the slowness with which party politics has adapted to the realities of interdependence and EC membership continued to act as a constraint on politicians in office, forcing them to speak in more negative terms than they otherwise might.

SPECIFIC POLICY SECTORS

1. *The EC Budget*

Britain's long-running dispute over the size of its contributions to the EC budget did as much as anything to gain it the reputation of being only partially committed to membership, of being a semi-detached member. While the other member states were prepared to admit that there was a problem, which arose out of agreements reached before Britain became a member, the tone in which successive British Governments handled negotiations over the issue was never *communautaire*, and goodwill frequently seemed to be lacking on the British side in the search to find a mutually satisfactory solution.

The problem for Britain was that it emerged as a large net contributor to the budget, despite being one of the poorer member states of the Community of nine, because of low receipts from the budget and relatively high payments into it. On the expenditure side, the Common Agricultural Policy (CAP) caused the problem; on the revenue side it was the agreements reached in 1969 on the 'own resources' system of financing.

As a net importer of food at the time of entry, with a small but efficient agricultural sector, Britain stood to receive little from the CAP when compared with major exporters of food such as France. Payments are made from the CAP for three purposes: to bring the price of food up to agreed levels above its market price; to subsidize exports going outside of the Community so as to bridge the gap between the price that the exporter receives on the world market and what the receipts would have been at the guaranteed internal market price; and to assist inefficient farmers to improve their productivity. British farmers benefited from the first form of expenditure, but not from the second or third. As the CAP dominated the budget, accounting for over 70 per cent of expenditure in the late 1970s, Britain's receipts from the budget were low.[18]

On the other hand, the system of 'own resource' financing agreed in 1969 ensured that British contributions to the budget would be high. This agreement allocated to the Community as its own resources all revenues from levies on agricultural imports to the EC, and tariffs collected on industrial imports (just 10 per cent being retained by the importing state to cover collection costs), plus up to one per cent of the revenue from a notional harmonized rate of Value Added Tax. This system boosted British payments to a high level because of the high propensity of the country to import goods from outside the EC, which in turn was a function of its late entry and the fact that it had therefore maintained a very different pattern of trade.[19]

Heath recognized the existence of a problem during the negotiations on entry, but in accordance with his policy of securing entry and sorting out problems later, he accepted the system that had been put in place in 1969. The Prime Minister's hopes for correcting any imbalance in payments seem to have rested on securing the creation of a substantial regional development fund from which Britain would benefit.[20]

Wilson rejected this approach, and argued instead for the introduction of a corrective mechanism that would give a rebate to Britain if its payments into the budget became excessive. Although a mechanism was worked out during the renegotiation of the terms of entry, and was presented to the British people in the referendum as a significant achievement, it was in fact, a far from generous formula, as became clear as Britain approached the end of its transitional period of membership in the latter months of Callaghan's premiership. In particular, even if Britain fulfilled all of the complex requirements of eligibility for a rebate, which it was not certain to do, it became apparent that the maximum limit set in 1975 would form an insignificant sum in comparison with the size

[18] Geoffrey Denton, *The British Problem and the Future of the EEC Budget* (London, 1982), 24–5.
[19] Denton, *The British Problem*, 24.
[20] Ross B. Talbot, *The European Community's Regional Fund* (Oxford, 1977).

of the full British contribution. At 1978 prices the maximum rebate translated into sterling as approximately £160 million, compared with transfers in excess of £800 million.[21]

In the traditional Prime Minister's speech to the Lord Mayor of London's banquet in the Guildhall in November 1978, Callaghan reacted publicly to a confidential prediction by the EC's Economic Policy Committee that the UK, already in 1977 the second largest net contributor to the Community's budget, would by 1980 be the largest net contributor, doubling its 1977 deficit of £423 million. He said the Government could not accept this when Britain was seventh in the Community's economic league table; but he suggested that his Government might have been prepared to accept a solution to the problem along the lines favoured by the Heath Government, of accepting higher EC expenditure as a means of offsetting the deficit.[22]

The Thatcher Government, which took over the problem from Callaghan, was also prepared to accept redress in the form of increased EC expenditure in the United Kingdom, but in line with the ideological orientation of her premiership, Thatcher insisted that the overall size of the budget should not be increased. Since other member states were not prepared to accept the inevitable implication that CAP expenditure must be cut, the British demand came increasingly to focus on straight cash-rebates. As the Prime Minister put it on one notorious occasion, what she wanted was Britain's 'own money back'.

The British demands were not generally couched in terms that could easily be accepted by the other member states. It would have been possible to argue that anomalies such as those produced by the existing system were not in the interests of the Community. Instead the argument was couched in nationalistic terms, of what Britain considered was fair and reasonable. Beyond that the tone adopted was of financial orthodoxy: that the Community must end its profligate ways. Since that amounted to an attack on the CAP, it was not likely to find favour in a Community where the Governments of many member states were dependent on the agricultural vote for their political survival beyond the next election.

---

[21] Malcolm Crawford, 'The Billion Pound Drain: What it Costs Us to Be in Europe', *Sunday Times*, 23 July 1978.

[22] *The Times*, 14 Nov. 1978.

After accepting *ad hoc* rebates for 1980 to 1983, Britain achieved an agreement on rebates that Thatcher felt able to accept at the Fontainebleau meeting of the European Council in June 1984. In achieving this, Britain was considerably assisted by the imminent exhaustion of the budget. To prevent the Community plunging into permanent deficit it became necessary to raise the ceiling on VAT contributions from one per cent to 1.4 per cent. Such a move required the unanimous agreement of the member states, agreement that Britain threatened to withhold unless the question of its own budgetary contributions was solved first.

Despite the impression given by Thatcher, the eventual settlement involved concessions on both sides. The British concession was to agree not to count customs duties and levies on agricultural imports as part of its contribution. This met a long-standing insistence by the original member states that only VAT contributions could legitimately be regarded as 'national contributions'. The acceptance of the principle of a permanent rebate mechanism was the concession on the side of the other member states, although it was one that they had been prepared to make in principle earlier in the negotiations, had Britain shown the same willingness to make concessions on its side.

There was room for disagreement over how favourable the settlement was to Britain, although the formula of a rebate of 66 per cent of the difference between its VAT contributions and its receipts from the budget did produce rebates in the region of the £1 billion that had been Thatcher's demand ever since 1979.[23]

That was not, however, the end of the story. In July 1984 Sir Geoffrey Howe, the Foreign Secretary, blocked a supplementary budget designed to bail the Community out of its temporary financial crisis, arguing that such an irregular and possibly illegal measure ought not to be taken unless agreement could be reached on binding rules to ensure future budgetary discipline. The problem with such an apparently reasonable demand was that budgetary discipline inevitably meant bringing the CAP under control, a theme that had run alongside Britain's demands for a rebate on its own contributions throughout the 1979–84 negotiations.

---

[23] George, *Awkward Partner*, 148–61; the case that the rebate mechanism was not entirely a victory for Britain is argued in *Le Monde*, 28 June 1984.

2. *The Common Agricultural Policy*

The CAP was never popular in Britain. Compared with the previous British system of support for agriculture, which allowed prices to find their own level and compensated farmers directly for any deficiency in income that resulted, the CAP was seen in Britain as a policy that imposed high prices on the consumer. This factor was played on by those opposed to membership, and made it difficult for any politician to defend the policy. Yet until the Thatcher Government came to office, no effective campaign was conducted to get reform of the CAP. Previous Governments protested about the high prices, but allowed them to continue in return for special concessions to Britain on things such as butter subsidies, assistance to hill farmers, and preferential cheap access to the British market for Australian and New Zealand agricultural products.

The Thatcher Governments tackled the issue directly, making control of agricultural expenditure part of the campaign for effective budgetary discipline. This approach combined with the rapidly escalating cost of the policy to produce reforms. In September 1984 agreement was reached on a system of budgetary control that set maximum limits on budget commitments for the following year on 1 March, before the Ministers of Agriculture negotiated increases in agricultural prices. Any overshoot on the agreed limits would be overruled, or clawed back over the next two years.[24] Under the British presidency of the Council of Ministers, in December 1986, agreement was reached on a package of structural measures, including financial incentives for less intensive farming. These arrangements were hailed by the British Foreign Secretary, Sir Geoffrey Howe, as 'the most important measure of reform ever achieved in the common agricultural policy'.[25]

In February 1988, in the face of slippage on the earlier agreements, a deal was reached that put a legal limit on CAP expenditure and on its annual rate of increase, which was set as 75 per cent of the growth of Community GNP. In addition production ceilings were set for each commodity, which if breached would trigger price decreases in future years. Some £420 million was set aside in a

---

[24] *The Economist*, 22 Sept. 1984.
[25] Ibid., 20 Dec. 1986, 69–70.

scheme to encourage arable farmers to leave land fallow or convert to grazing.[26]

In all of these reforms Britain was the prime mover. This was probably necessary because the strength of the agricultural lobby in Britain, although not inconsiderable, was not as great as in most other member states; and even those states that had less of a vested interest in the CAP were reluctant to attack a policy that was seen as the biggest single achievement of the Community.

The prevarication of the Germans on the issue of reform of the CAP forms an interesting contrast with the fixity of purpose shown by the British Government. Caught between a strong desire to bring down the cost to West Germany of the EC budget on the one hand, and a politically influential farming lobby on the other, German policy swung between support for reform and blockage of proposed reforms.[27]

The British overcame this blockage by making agreement on effective budgetary discipline, including control of agricultural expenditure, a condition for allowing the Community to escape the financial crisis into which it had been plunged by the swollen agricultural expenditure.

In this way Britain performed a service to the Community as a whole, and away from the glare of publicity their position was supported by other member states that would have found it difficult to front the attack themselves, particularly the French and the Dutch. Constant British criticism of the CAP was seen as evidence of a semi-detached relationship to the Community, because of the status of the CAP as an icon of integration. In fact the British position was instrumental in clearing the way for the future development of the EC.

3. *Industrial and Competition Policy*

EC industrial policy has consisted more of schemes than achievements. Hodges describes it as having 'a somewhat chequered history',[28] but it is possible to question whether it actually has any history at all. Competition policy, on the other hand, has a much

---

[26] *Independent*, 15 Feb. 1988; see also the statement by the Prime Minister to Parliament, *Hansard* (Commons), 15 Feb. 1988, cols. 705–6.

[27] Bulmer and Paterson, *The Federal Republic of Germany*, 71–7.

[28] Quoted in Bulmer and Paterson, *The Federal Republic of Germany*, 53.

stronger record of success, and to some extent has even absorbed industrial policy.

In the 1960s and early 1970s there was a scheme to build up cross-national European firms that could provide an effective counter to what was seen in some quarters as the American challenge to European economic independence. One important aspect of this was the idea of a European company statute, which would make cross-national mergers easier to effect; another was the idea of a European technological community, involving jointly funded public-sector research into the technological areas of most relevance to industry, with the aim of putting European industry ahead of the United States.

With the onset of recession in the aftermath of the 1973 rise in the price of oil, these objectives, although they never disappeared entirely from the agenda, had to give way to a holding action against an increase in subsidies by individual Governments to their own national companies, so that industrial policy came to be conflated with competition policy. By 1978 Shanks could reasonably say that: 'The basis of the Community's industrial policy is ... the establishment of equal competitive conditions between enterprises: the removal of artifical distortions, the destruction of cartels and discriminatory practices.'[29]

As the recession began to bite, and in the face of a fierce blast of competition from the newly industrializing countries of Asia and Latin America, the Community also found itself having to deal with the problems of traditional industrial sectors that had gone into rapid decline, such as steel, shipbuilding, and textiles. Here the Commission felt the need to attempt a Community response because uncoordinated national responses threatened to make problems of overcapacity even worse, and to damage both the Community's internal common market and its common external trade policy. In this respect also, EC industrial policy melted into competition policy.

The attitudes of British Governments to EC industrial and competition policy has varied considerably. Broadly speaking, Labour Governments have been keen to follow an interventionist policy for restructuring the British economy, but have not wanted an

---

[29] Michael Shanks, 'Why is the EEC more interested in lame ducks than industrial winners?' *The Times*, 20 Jan. 1978.

EC dimension, and have seen EC competition policy as an interference with their ability to carry through their restructuring programme. Conservative Governments have been less interventionist at national level, and have consequently not been enthusiastic about EC-level interventionist industrial policy, but they have increasingly recognized the Community dimension to ensuring fair competition.

The Heath Government might have been an exception to this second generalization. Both pro-Community and, in its later phase, interventionist, it might have supported a Community industrial policy; but it did not make this a priority issue, preferring instead to concentrate on getting agreement to a regional development fund. The creation of a common company statute to encourage the emergence of large-scale European companies which could compete with the US giants was an objective supported by Heath in his 1967 Godkin Lectures at Harvard University, although he was sceptical about the merits of a European technological community, arguing that, 'the real breakthrough in depth in European technology has to come through the activities of larger European firms'.[30]

The Wilson and Callaghan Governments had to deal with the domestic effects of recession, and to respond to the Commission's attempts to combat the rising tide of covert national protectionism, in which Britain was one of the offenders. Wilson made the freedom of his Government to pursue its own policies without interference from Brussels an issue in the renegotiation, but eventually the Government was forced to phase out its Regional Employment Premium and its Temporary Employment Subsidy. Towards the end of the Callaghan Government, the National Enterprise Board (NEB) was also under scrutiny by the Commission on the suspicion that it was obtaining capital from the British Treasury at preferential rates of interest and passing the advantage on to the companies that were the subject of its industrial interventions. A system of surveillance was instituted, although it had scarcely begun to operate when the Thatcher Government came to office and abolished the NEC.[31]

---

[30] Edward Heath, *Old World, New Horizons: Britain, the Common Market, and the Atlantic Alliance. The Godkin Lectures at Harvard University, 1967* (London, 1970).
[31] Denis Swann *Competition and Industrial Policy in the European Community* (London and New York, 1983), 49–52.

An indication of how far EC interference in the conduct of national industrial policy was a sensitive political issue came in a letter from Callaghan to Ron Hayward, General Secretary of the Labour party, prior to the 1977 Party Conference. In support of his argument that Britain was not suffering unduly from membership of the EC, Callaghan listed four examples of British firms—British Leyland, Chrysler, Meriden, and Albert Herbert—that had been supported by the Government in breach of EC rules on fair competition; in each case the breach had been overlooked by the Commission in the interests of avoiding confrontation with the Government.[32]

Such problems were resolved by the arrival in office of a Conservative Government committed to ending domestic industrial interventions of this sort. But other issues of dispute arose under the Thatcher Governments. These have concerned interventionist moves by the Commission to deal with distressed traditional industries; the insistence by the Delors Commission that the project for freeing the internal market must be accompanied by the assumption of the control of mergers from Brussels; interventions from the Commission to prevent the Government giving exceptionally favourable financial terms to public-sector industries prior to privatization; and British opposition to the revival of the idea of a common European company statute.

On intervention in crisis sectors, the attitude of the Thatcher Government has belied its free-market orientation, which ought logically to have led it to oppose such moves. In the case of steel, for example, the weakness of the British industry was such that even under Callaghan cut-backs in capacity and rationalization were being pursued, a process that the Thatcher Government tried to accelerate as a prelude to privatizing the industry. In this situation the attempts of the European Commission to organize a regulated and controlled reduction of excess capacity in the European steel industry met with support from Britain. The role of the Commission in setting minimum price levels for sectors of the industry with the greatest overcapacity was seen by the British Government as a legitimate response to the subsidization of their national steel industries by other member states, and the setting of production quotas as an essential means of forcing

---

[32] The full text of the letter is reproduced in *The Times*, 1 Oct. 1977.

other member states to rationalize rather than protect their industries. In October 1980 Britain gave its support to the declaration of a state of manifest crisis in the industry, which allowed the Commission to take more effective measures to end national subsidies.

This example illustrates nicely a dilemma that is likely to become more acute for the British Government in the future. To minimize supranationalism, the first reaction of the British is always to resist any increase in the powers of the Commission. So when the steel rationalization issue first arose after the change of Government, Britain voted with Italy against the declaration of a state of manifest crisis in the industry. Britain's vote was clearly intended as a vote of principle against supranational solutions; Italy's may have been less principled, since Italy subsequently emerged as the member state least inclined to co-operate with the rationalization effort, continuing to produce steel at levels well above the quotas set by the Commission, and flouting the rules on minimum prices. Faced with blatant cheating on the rules of fair trading, the British Government found that it was really on the same side as the Commission, and moved to support for Commissioner Davignon's efforts to bring Italy, and other offenders, into line.

A similar dilemma arose in connection with the transfer to Brussels of responsibility for the vetting of industrial mergers. The initial reaction of the Department of Trade and Industry was to reject the Commission's attempts to take regulation out of its hands. But early in 1989 the DTI reluctantly acknowledged that if Britain attempted to exercise national control over mergers, while other member states adopted less rigorous procedures, the result would be for the mergers to be registered in the states with lax control. Potential jobs would be lost from Britain, and with the onset of the free internal market the British Government would be unable to prevent the products of the merged company from being freely sold in Britain. Again the British Government found itself in an objective alliance with the Commission, and obliged to support a transfer of power to Brussels because it could not rely on its partners within the Community to act disinterestedly for the common good.

At times Britain could be accused of the same fault. In 1987 the Government came into conflict with the Commission over its proposal to write off the debt of the state-owned Rover car group prior to privatization. This was seen from Brussels as unfair state aid, and after an acrimonious dispute between Lord Young of Graffham at the DTI and Peter Sutherland, the Commissioner for Competition Policy, the extent of the £800 million debt cancellation had to be reduced by some £330 million. Although this interference with its policy was clearly resented by the British Government, it eventually accepted that if it wanted EC competition law to ensure that its partners played fairly, it had to be prepared to abide by the same rules itself.

Finally, an issue still unresolved at the time of writing was that of a Community company statute. The Commission, with the support of most of the other member states, made this a fundamental part of its programme for 1992; but the British Government insisted that no such statute was necessary, and that the approximation of national rules would suffice. The essence of the disagreement was that several member states, notably the Federal Republic, had national rules concerning the participation of employees in the decision-making process of large companies, and the provision of information to employees on investment plans; Britain had no such rules, and the Thatcher Government was ideologically opposed to their introduction. The Governments of the states which already had such rules were concerned that their companies would suffer in the post-1992 open market were the regulations not generalized; for them the common company statute was part of the process of creating a 'level playing field' for internal EC competition. Britain's reluctance to accept this argument therefore reflected self-interest as well as ideology.

In summary, then, British Governments have never accepted EC interventionist industrial policies, Labour Governments because they were opposed to Community involvement in their domestic industrial programmes, Conservative Governments since 1979 because of their general opposition to interventionism. On competition policy, the Labour Governments resisted the restraints that the EC imposed on their interventions to restructure the British economy, although they eventually had to bow to them; the Conservative Governments since 1979 slowly and pragmatically came to realize that a Community competition policy was necessary to prevent other member states from excessive interventionism.

4. Research Policy

In the area of research policy the British lack of enthusiasm has been consistent across Governments, and has contributed to the image of Britain as a semi-detached member of the Community. Indeed, similar arguments can be seen being employed by British Governments some thirteen years apart over the funding of EC research.

Literally within days of taking up full membership of the EC at the start of 1973, Britain was involved in blocking agreement on a budget for the Euratom research programme into nuclear energy. Commission proposals for a budget of £110 million over five years were opposed on the grounds that the sum involved was too large, and the period of funding without review too long. The British backed a much smaller budget with funds committed for only three years. Eventually, in early February, a sum of £70 million over four years was agreed. Although the period covered by the budget was longer than the British wished, there were serious doubts over whether four research centres—in Italy, the Netherlands, West Germany, and Belgium—could be maintained for four years on such a modest level of funding. As a basis for comparison, the United Kingdom Atomic Energy Agency was preparing to spend £80 million over four years at its Harwell research establishment, in addition to which Harwell was expected to make a commercial profit of some £35 million which would also be ploughed into its programme.[33] This parsimonious approach was in line with the reservations expressed by Heath in his Godkin Lectures, and quoted above, about the proposals then current for a European technological community.

Very similar arguments were employed in the latter part of 1986 and early 1987 when the Thatcher Government blocked the proposed budget for the framework programme of research into advanced technology areas. In March 1986 the Commission proposed that expenditure on a whole range of projects should be set at 10.3 million Ecu over five years; this was scaled down to 7.735 million after negotiations within the Council of Ministers, but Britain, France, and West Germany refused to accept this figure. Subsequently the Belgian presidency suggested a compromise of

[33] George, *Awkward Partner*, 198–200.

6.48 million Ecu, which first France and eventually West Germany accepted, leaving Britain isolated in opposition.

The British Minister for Information Technology refused to budge from a figure of 4.2 million Ecu as a maximum, an increase of only 10 per cent on the budget for the previous four-year period, and therefore a decrease in real terms, for a budget that would now have to cover twelve, not ten member states. Eventually Britain gave way on this, but the arguments that were deployed were remarkably similar to those used thirteen years earlier over the Euratom budget; that too much money was being committed for too long with inadequate procedures for monitoring how effectively it was being spent.[34]

In contrast, Britain was an enthusiastic supporter of the Eureka programme, launched by President Mitterrand in April 1985 as a counter to the United States' Strategic Defence Initiative (SDI). The SDI, although a military research programme, was widely seen in Europe as a device for further extending the technological lead of the US over Western Europe. Mitterrand's proposal was for a civilian research programme on the industrial application of research advances in the fields of high techology and biotechnology, to involve not just the EC states, but all the states in Western Europe that wished to participate. The scheme appears to have appealed to the British because it was designed to encourage co-operation between private companies rather than involving a high level of public-sector research; because it was more concerned with the application of research than with pure research; and because it was not intended to be a Community programme, the British having always favoured a variety of different forums for European co-operation in preference to increasing the functional competences of the Community.

5. *Monetary Policy*

Achievement of an economic and monetary union has been a long-standing objective of the Community, but not one that has been embraced by British Governments. The Heath Government put sterling into the joint float of European currencies for a few weeks in 1972, but then was obliged by speculative pressure to take it

---

[34] Ibid. 200–1.

out, and resisted suggestions that it should be put back in during
1973. Even more significantly, the Callaghan Government did not
put sterling into the Exchange Rate Mechanism (ERM) of the EMS
when it was set up in 1978. This move has been explained above,
but the continued absence of sterling from the ERM until October
1990 was one of the main factors contributing to Britain's reputation as a semi-detached member of the Community.

The failure of the Thatcher Governments to put sterling into the
ERM is at first sight surprising, given the ideological orientation of
the Governments and given the anti-inflationary bias of the system.
One objective of the EMS, which was largely achieved, was to
create a 'zone of monetary stability' in Europe. That phrase had a
double meaning. It obviously meant stability in the exchange rates
of the different currencies; but it also meant stability in the sense
of bringing down average rates of inflation, which was a pre-
requisite of the system holding together, since widely divergent
inflation rates would lead to irresistible pressures for exchange
rates to diverge.

Whereas the first attempts to move towards economic and
monetary union were bedevilled by the split between what Tsoukalis called the 'economists' and the 'monetarists',[35] the success of
the EMS was based on the convergence of economic policy around
a priority of low inflation. When France attempted to go against
this trend, under the Socialist Government that was elected in
1981, it found that it could not successfully follow a policy that
ran counter to those of its main trading partners and retain the
stability of its exchange rate. After three devaluations between
1981 and 1983, involving a loss of some 30 per cent in the value
of the French franc against the Deutschmark, it became necessary
to change direction and accept the German priority of low
inflation.[36]

This effect is one that the Thatcher Government ought to have

---

[35] Loukas Tsoukalis, *The Politics and Economics of European Monetary Integration* (London, 1977).
[36] On the record of the French Socialist Government see: Peter Hall, *Governing
the Economy: The Politics of State Intervention in Britain and France* (Cambridge,
1986): 'Broken Dreams: Economic Policy in Mitterrand's France', in Sonia Mazey
and Michael Newman (eds.) *Mitterrand's France* (London, 1987), 33–55; 'The
Evolution of Economic Policy under Mitterrand', in George Ross, Stanley Hoff-
mann, and Sylvia Malzacher (eds.), *The Mitterrand Experiment: Continuity and
Change in Modern France* (Cambridge, 1987).

welcomed given its antipathy to inflationary policies. But the EMS also went against the then Prime Minister's strong conviction that markets should be given free rein. Despite the difficulties with this position in an era when speculative flows of capital distort markets to such an extent that sterling could remain high while Britain ran a balance of trade deficit in the billions of pounds each month, it was the line that Mrs Thatcher consistently supported. When her Chancellor of the Exchequer, Nigel Lawson, 'shadowed' the EMS throughout 1987 and the first quarter of 1988, attempting to treat sterling as though it were in the ERM, and therefore responded to upward pressure on the currency by intervening to stabilize its value, his position was undermined by the Prime Minister declaring in Parliament that 'excessive intervention' was unwarranted and risked undermining the battle against inflation.[37]

In addition to her ideological objection to membership of the ERM, Thatcher was also widely believed to have found distasteful the idea that should adjustment to the value of the pound become necessary, she would be obliged to ask the permission of other European states to make the adjustment.

By the end of 1989 it appeared that only the Prime Minister really opposed putting sterling into the ERM. There were, however, grounds for doubt about whether the move was wise for Britain. First, there was a genuine problem about the level at which the pound should be tied into the mechanism. In 1989 it could be argued that from the point of view of ensuring the competitiveness of British exports, the pound was somewhat overvalued; yet there were very real risks involved in trying to bring down the value of the currency. Any such move could lead to a collapse in value to well below the desired level, as investors responded to the reduction by withdrawing funds and thereby precipitating the collapse. This is what happened to Callaghan in 1976, when an attempt by the Bank of England to reduce the value of the pound led to a slide that could only be halted by borrowing first from other central banks, and ultimately from the IMF.[38]

A second problem was that tying the value of the pound to the strongest currency in Europe, the Deutschmark, while the British

---

[37] Mrs Thatcher's statement is recorded in *Hansard*, 8 Mar. 1988, col. 184; the episode is recounted in George, *Awkward Partner*, 191.

[38] Gardner, *Decade of Discontent*, 60–4.

rate of inflation was considerably higher than that in Germany, could exacerbate the inflation. This was the main argument against membership advanced by Sir Alan Walters, who was for a time the Prime Minister's personal adviser on economic affairs. He argued that higher inflation meant higher interest rates; if investors were guaranteed that they could switch their money back into Deutschmarks at any time with no loss of value, they would transfer their funds into sterling to take advantage of the higher interest rates; the Bank of England would be obliged to sell pounds in order to retain the parity with the Deutschmark in the face of high demand, thereby increasing the money supply and fuelling the inflation; reducing rates of interest in order to choke off the influx of funds would also damage the fight against inflation by stimulating domestic demand. For all of these reasons the Prime Minister made it a condition of sterling joining the ERM that the British rate of inflation should be falling and should be near to the average rate prevailing in the EC.

The example of the EMS illustrates the caution of British Governments about entering into far-reaching commitments without being sure of the full consequences. It was precisely the hope of Jean Monnet and his followers that national Governments would enter into such commitments without realizing quite what they were letting themselves in for. The 'expansive logic' that Ernst Haas described as being inherent in the integration project which Monnet set in train,[39] relied on states being prepared to take the first apparently innocuous step on a road that then turned into a slippery downward slope to a destination that they had never originally envisaged. This is what Britain has not been inclined to do, and its reluctance has been the basis for some of its reputation as a semi-detached member of the EC. However, it could be that the 1992 project will prove to be just such a step.

6. *The Internal Market*

Freeing the internal market of the Community from non-tariff barriers to trade and freeing the market in financial services have been declared objectives of the British Government since the British

---

[39] Ernst B. Haas, *The Uniting of Europe: Political, Social and Economic Forces, 1950–1957* (Stanford, Calif., 2nd ed. 1968), 283–317.

presidency of the Council of Ministers in 1981, although they have only been pursued vigorously since the settlement of the dispute over budgetary contributions.

The Heath Government was more concerned with the development of common redistributive policies at the Community level; and the Wilson and Callaghan Governments had little sympathy for internal liberalization, being quite prepared to breach common rules on fair competition and to maintain non-tariff barriers, although they were by no means alone in this among member states.

The Thatcher Government came to office in 1979 committed to the idea that the involvement of the state in economic affairs should be minimized. This approach was extended to the Community level, and Britain proved to be an enthusiastic advocate of the removal of existing barriers to free economic activity. In particular the Government championed the removal of restrictions on capital movements and on financial services, and the liberalization of air transport.

In principle this orientation brought Britain alongside the Federal Republic, which had long advocated the removal of non-tariff barriers to trade. In practice the British Government proved more thorough in its commitment to economic liberalism. In particular the German Government was never happy about the freeing of financial services, where Britain appeared to have a considerable comparative advantage, nor of air transport.

This extension of 'Thatcherism' to the European level became a stronger feature of British policy once the dispute over budgetary contributions was resolved in 1984, and formed the central plank of the programme that the Government put forward for its tenure of the presidency of the Council in 1986. The achievements of that presidency were not outstanding in this respect. Britain broke ranks with its Dutch and Irish allies on the deregulation of air transport, proposing a compromise that fell far short of the 'open-skies' policy that it had been supporting, and even then failed to get acceptance within the Council of Ministers. There was, however, some progress on the freeing of financial services, and Thatcher was able to boast at the end of the presidency that more measures had been agreed on the freeing of the market in the preceding six months than under any previous presidency.[40]

---

[40] George, *Awkward Partner*, 185–9.

7. *External Economic Relations*

International economic relations are one area where national sovereignty has unquestionably been reduced by membership of the EC. All matters relating to tariffs and quotas on trade are legally the responsibility of the Community, not of individual member states. Within the EC Britain has consistently supported an open trading relationship with the rest of the world.

This orientation became stronger under Thatcher. It represented, though, a traditional British commitment to the idea of global economic integration rather than regional integration. Successive British Governments tended to be suspicious of what they saw as tendencies towards regional protectionism amongst some EC member states, particularly France and Greece at various times. This difference of orientation reappeared in the debate over the relationship of the EC to the outside world post-1992. British insistence that the single market must not become a 'fortress Europe', putting up walls against other trading blocs, was stronger than that of other member states. Despite an explicit rejection of protectionism in the communiqué following the Rhodes European Council in December 1988, there remained a suspicion in the rest of the world, and possibly also in Whitehall, of whether some members, particularly France and the Mediterranean states, were genuinely determined to keep the EC open to the outside world.

In their globalist orientation to economic affairs the British sometimes appeared to other Community states to be the mouthpiece for the United States, which also objected to regional blocs and advocated global solutions. This was not the case under Heath, who was perhaps the least Atlanticist of British Prime Ministers, while under Wilson there was really no occasion on which the issue arose. But Callaghan as Prime Minister clearly associated himself with global solutions to the economic problems of combined inflation and stagnation that were afflicting the capitalist world in the aftermath of the OPEC price-rises of December 1973. His 'convoy' approach to floating the world out of recession involved co-ordinated action by the United States, Japan, Germany, and Britain.[41] Callaghan's doubts about Helmut Schmidt's proposal for a European Monetary System also involved concern that the 'zone

[41] Ibid. 105–12.

of monetary stability' which Schmidt hoped to create within the
EC would make trade easier between the member states, but more
difficult with the outside world, and that it might undermine the
influence of the IMF in the management of international monetary
affairs.[42]

8. *European Political Co-operation*

Although the domestic debate on British membership of the EC
was conducted predominantly in terms of the economic advantages
and disadvantages of joining, there are indications that the decisive
considerations for Macmillan and Wilson when they made their
abortive applications were political: the conviction that Britain
would only be able to exercise real influence in the world by acting
in conjunction with the other states of the EC. De Gaulle's proposal
for co-operation on foreign policy in the early 1960s, the so-called
'Fouchet Plan', both attracted British policy-makers, and served to
convince them of the dangers of remaining outside a European
organization that might be about to emerge as a single actor in
international affairs.

Following this line of thinking, British government policy has
always been strongly supportive of European Political Co-operation (EPC), which started in 1970, and which involves the member
states of the Community in a continuous process of attempting to
find common positions on questions of foreign policy. The intergovernmental nature of EPC has been an added attraction for
British Governments which, with the exception of the Heath
Government, have been uniformly suspicious of the ideas of
European union and of the Commission assuming too strong a
role.

Although EPC was given the highest political profile under
Heath, and has been less frequently stressed in public by subsequent
Governments, the policy of co-operation has been enthusiastically
embraced by the Foreign Office, and a high degree of co-ordination
of policy has been achieved. The British Press has given most
attention to this dimension of Britain's relationship with the
Community when co-ordination has failed, as over sanctions

---

[42] Jocelyn Statler, 'British Foreign Policy to 1975. The European Monetary
System: From Conception to Birth', *International Affairs*, 55 (1975), 206–25.

against South Africa in 1986, or when Britain has failed to vote with other EC member states in the United Nations, as on the vote of censure on the United States in 1989 for refusing Yasser Arafat a visa to enter the country to address the UN General Assembly. These highly publicized instances (of what the British Press treat as the EC stepping out of line with Britain) should not be allowed to disguise the fact that on a high percentage of all votes at the UN the EC states do vote as a bloc, Britain included; and at the Conference on Security and Co-operation in Europe in Helsinki in 1974, and at the various follow-up meetings, the EC has similarly emerged as a unified actor. In the latter forum, the EC initially took a more accommodating line towards the Eastern European states than did the United States, and Britain associated itself fully with that approach even during Margaret Thatcher's 'iron lady' phase of strong anti-communist rhetoric. Similarly Britain's much-vaunted closeness to the United States in international affairs did not stop Britain from associating itself fully with EC efforts to bring about peace in the Middle East on the basis of a more even-handed approach to the Palestinians and Israelis than that normally pursued by the pro-Israeli United States.

The importance attached to political co-operation by the British Government was evident in the papers on the future of Europe that it presented at the Fontainebleau European Council in June 1984 and at the Stresa meeting of Foreign Ministers in June 1985. In both cases the path mapped out was for the freeing of the internal market combined with strengthening EPC. That commitment was reaffirmed in the discussions that opened in May 1990 on the next phase of institutional reform. From the viewpoint of the British Government, EPC has been one of the major success stories of EC membership, and one of its most unambiguous benefits.

CONCLUSION

What general themes emerge from this review of the attitude of successive British Governments to the EC? Does it vindicate the impression of Britain as a semi-detached member of the Community? To a large extent it does. With the exception of the Heath Government there has been a notable lack of enthusiasm for the idea of European union, which still holds some sway over the

Governments of the original six member states, and of some of the newer members, notably Ireland. Perhaps linked with this, and owing something to a suspicion of the motives of the original Six, there has been a marked reluctance to enter into new commitments without exhaustive examination of the implications for national sovereignty. Any extension of the competences of the Community has had to be justified to British Governments on pragmatic grounds.

In financial matters, the record appears equally negative if viewed from the perspective of those committed to extending the competences of the Community. Britain has been reluctant to agree to allocating large amounts of money to Community research projects, and has fought long and hard to achieve effective budgetary control. This last has involved arguing for reform of the CAP, which has finally been achieved, but which was resisted by other member states both because of the political influence of their national agricultural lobbies, and because the CAP stood alongside the customs union as a major achievement of the original Six. In economic matters the British have persisted under all Governments since Heath's in viewing the purpose of the Community as being the achievement of a common market, rather than seeing the common market as a step on the road to European union.

Against this, British Governments have consistently and even enthusiastically supported the co-ordination of national foreign policies through EPC. This has perhaps not been unconnected with the fact that EPC operates alongside the EC rather than being incorporated within it. Although a section of the Single European Act deals with EPC, thereby giving it a legal status which it did not previously have, it remains an intergovernmental procedure and a model of the form of co-operation which the British have long advocated as being the best way to move forward.

The same British preference for varied and loose forms of West European co-operation may have prompted the Thatcher Government to give a warmer welcome to Eureka than to the Community's own framework programme for research in high-technology industries, and perhaps also lay behind the ready acceptance by Britain of a French proposal for the revival of the Western European Union (WEU) as a forum for the discussion of West European defence co-operation.

This general approach has led to Britain being accused of being a semi-detached member of the Community. In this chapter the main purpose has been to describe the approach, and Britain has frequently been treated as a single unified actor for that purpose. In the following chapters some explanation is offered of that approach, and the concept of 'Britain' as an actor is disaggregated in order to develop the explanation, and to investigate the other themes identified by Bulmer in Chapter 1.

3

Central Government

Geoffrey Edwards

As the chapters in this volume suggest, one of the primary concerns of successive British Governments has been the issue of national sovereignty. Certainly, as those chapters show, there have been loud lamentations over loss of sovereignty, particularly parliamentary sovereignty. It might therefore have been expected that the impact of Community membership on central government was profound, that structures and processes were being changed and modified in order to meet the 'incoming tide' of legislation from Brussels. Somewhat surprisingly perhaps few non-political circles have discussed the issue. As Young and Sloman suggested when they discussed the Civil Service and the 'hidden' arm of Whitehall across in Brussels: 'It is "hidden" not because of any great secret about British membership of the European Community but because hardly anyone understands how deeply this fact has imposed itself on the way our governing classes spend their time.'[1] Despite the challenge, little academic attention has focused on the impact made; indeed, it has frequently been ignored.[2]

Inevitably, of course, any assessment of the impact of Community membership on central government poses a number of problems and not simply in the way Young and Sloman present it. It is not always easy, for example, to distinguish the changes that have been brought about in Whitehall by the need to adapt to the Community from those created by other new demands, whether external or internal. It has, indeed, been suggested that, at the 'machinery-of-government' level, the Community has had little impact, at least during the initial period of British membership. Pollitt, for example has written:

[1] Hugo Young and Anne Sloman, *No, Minister: An Inquiry into the Civil Service* (London, 1982), 73.
[2] One of the few and still highly relevant pieces of work was that undertaken by Freida Stack in 1983; see F. E. C. Gregory, *Dilemmas of Government: Britain and the European Community* (Oxford, 1983), 4.

The years 1974–79 were very much a period when HMG was learning to 'play the European game', and the whole subject was a particularly divisive one within both the leadership and the rank and file of the Labour Party. In the event, however, such machinery changes as there were took place within the structures of existing departments rather than by departmental reshuffling or major transfers of function.[3]

As we shall see, there has indeed been a largely gradual process of adaptation within departments to the growing range of issues falling within the Community's competence and which therefore have to be negotiated in Brussels.

However, the machinery-of-government level is only one level from which to judge the Community's impact on Britain's central institutions. If central government is defined as 'a complex web of institutions, networks and practices surrounding the Prime Minister, Cabinet, Cabinet committees and their official counterparts, less formalized ministerial "clubs" or meetings, bilateral negotiations and interdepartmental committees',[4] then a variety of different perspectives and levels offer themselves. Britain's participation in the Community has played, and continues to play, an important role in this less mechanistic system, the more dramatic instances being perhaps the resignations from Mrs Thatcher's Government of Messrs Heseltine and Brittan in 1985, Nicholas Ridley in July 1990, and Sir Geoffrey Howe in November 1990 and, most dramatic of all, Mrs Thatcher's resignation later the same month. 'Europe' is inevitably therefore an important variable in the analysis of the British system of government. It is perhaps a significant factor in the debate over whether the British system can still accurately be described as Cabinet government or whether it has now moved towards prime-ministerial government of one kind or another or if it has moved towards ministerial and segmented government.[5]

Inevitably perhaps, one of the problems in assessing the Community's role is the primary focus of any particular study. To examine the impact of the Community from the point of view of its policies on prunes might place MAFF and the DTI in the

---

[3] Christopher Pollitt, *Manipulating the Machine* (London, 1984), 114.

[4] P. Dunleavy and R. A. W. Rhodes, 'Core Executive Studies in Britain', *Public Administration*, 68 (1990), 3–28.

[5] Ibid. Dunleavy and Rhodes, even if only briefly, at least introduce the Community into the discussion in their article.

forefront; to ignore the prunes and focus on issues of national sovereignty, institutional reform, and political integration could lead to a preoccupation with the role of the Prime Minister and the position of the Cabinet Office. The difficulty here is that the Community might seem to endorse either (or any intermediary) position: the sometimes considerable autonomy of the agricultural lobby, for example, brought about a new-found strength for MAFF against the Treasury; the increased significance of the European Council might be regarded as reinforcing the role of the Prime Minister.

The problem is compounded by the question of sources of information. A reliance on, say, parliamentary back-benchers in assessing the impact of Community membership on government accountability would probably lead to different conclusions from work dependent on interviews with successive Leaders of the House and Chief Whips. But a fundamental obstacle to analysing the British system fully and comprehensively is its secrecy: journalists and scholars are frequently dependent on leaks or 'briefings' from rarely wholly disinterested sources.[6] This lack of openness makes the problem of perspective even more acute.

CONTEXT AND CHALLENGE

Enough has been written elsewhere in this volume to provide the context for changes in central government. With varying degrees of intensity, both Labour and Conservative have been divided over Britain's participation in the Community, whether over membership, or over closer integration and the ultimate objectives of the Community. Both have been preoccupied with national sovereignty, as a principle to be cherished or as an instrument of control. Concern over its real or potential loss has tended to suffuse policy formulation, most explicitly perhaps at the political level, but with

[6] An interesting example of how the problem can be manifested was revealed in the debate between Michael Lee and Anthony Seldon on the role of the Cabinet Office, with Lee critical of Seldon's conclusions which were based largely or at least significantly on interviews with past and present Deputy Secretaries from the Cabinet Office. See Anthony Seldon, 'The Cabinet Office and Co-ordination, 1979–87', *Public Administration*, 68 (1990), 103–21; and Michael Lee, 'The Ethos of the Cabinet Office: A Comment on the Testimony of Officials', *Public Administration* 68 (1990), 235–42.

civil servants—whatever their own views—long-attuned to the sensitivity of the issue for their political masters. An extension of the Community's competence and/or an increase in the Commission's authority have tended to be viewed in a number of Whitehall departments and 10 Downing Street as a zero sum game: what 'they' have won, 'we' have lost. What has made matters worse is that the UK has rarely been able to set the agenda, to provide long-term blueprints and shorter-term leadership that could have won support from others. Of course, as many British ministers have been at pains to point out, Britain has been a 'good' European on a whole range of issues such as the establishment of a Regional Development Fund, the completion of the single market (and the implementation of agreed legislation), reform of the common agricultural policy and the Community's budget, and the development of European Political Co-operation. That such issues fall fairly closely in line with Britain's interests is perhaps beside the point; the overall impression has been one of the British reacting (usually negatively) to the initiatives of others, with agreement (usually) only at the last minute.

Such a characterization of UK policy may be somewhat exaggerated; it is far from being a caricature. Other chapters in this collection seek to explain why Britain has taken such a 'semi-detached' position. The point is less that the UK has its own national interests to pursue—all member states have their own interests to pursue and do so with vigour—but that British Governments seem to have such a strong tendency to misjudge the policies and objectives of their partners in the Community, especially their commitment to political integration. Whatever the reasons for this, the results for central government have been significant. If the pursuit of detailed policy objectives has generally been successful (as in the removal of many barriers to trade within the single market), Britain's capacity to pursue a coherent overall strategy in the Community has been more questionable. Where there is little or no political consensus, policy co-ordination and consistency can be pursued only so far.

The ways in which central government has met the Community challenge have naturally reflected the weight of the past as well as traditional values and perhaps some less traditional approaches, with efficiency and effectiveness constant themes. In order to assess their practical implementation, the approach adopted here is one of following through the decision-making process of the Community. This, it is hoped, will bring out the growing intensity of the UK–EC relationship, the demands it makes on the Whitehall machinery and the influence it has on central government more generally.

INFLUENCING THE MACHINE

In the first place, therefore, it is clearly of importance that the UK's interests are clearly known and taken into account within the Commission before it draws up its draft legislative proposals. Much depends on the UK Permanent Representation in explaining Britain's position, but important, too, is the role of British officials within the Commission. Successive British Governments have sought to ensure that the two British Commissioners are in positions of particular relevance to British interests. A considerable degree of success has been achieved, with British Commissioners responsible for External Relations, Regional Policy, the Budget, the Single Market, and Competition at critically important periods since 1973, together with, of course, the Presidency of the Commission under Roy (now Lord) Jenkins between 1977 and 1980. However, while Commissioners are likely to be able to explain the UK's position and provide a useful channel of communication, they are under oath not to take instruction from Governments and need to take care how far they push a national viewpoint. In general, independent-mindedness rather than simple independence has been the more typical characteristic of most of the UK's Commissioners. It has been highly valued, of course, but four years has usually been regarded as long enough in Brussels for British nominees!

In terms of Commission officials, and indeed officials in other Community institutions, the UK has generally been under-represented. In 1973, it had been expected that each of the big four countries would have fielded about 18.4 per cent, a figure reduced with further enlargement to include Spain, Greece, and Portugal to about 15 per cent. In 1974, however, Britons made up only 8.4 per cent of the Commission service,[7] though by 1989 the proportion

---

[7] Virginia Willis, *Britons in Brussels: Officials in the European Commission and the Council Secretariat* (London, 1983), 11.

had increased to 11.7 per cent. Recruitment, as Willis shows, posed a problem during the 1970s primarily because of a reluctance on the part of Whitehall officials to commit resources and people to a venture that the Labour party's opposition might have proved abortive and, more simply, because of ignorance and an initial misunderstanding of the role, function, and status of officials in the Commission.[8] These factors should no longer be relevant and yet under-representation continues, both at senior and especially at recruitment levels.

The issue has not been regarded as unimportant in Whitehall. It has always been recognized that, as in the case of Commissioners, such officials provide a useful and legitimate conduit, introducing British views to the Commission and reporting Commission and other views to the British. Given the importance of the issue, the Civil Service Department set up a special unit to co-ordinate recruitment with the Secretary of the Cabinet holding a watching brief. When the Civil Service Department was abolished in 1981, the Cabinet Office took over full responsibility for recruitment and training.[9]

It seems clear however that while individual efforts may have been made to improve the situation, there has been little consistency and effective direction from the centre. In part this reflects the sometimes uneasy relationship between the Cabinet Office and Number 10 and the individual Whitehall departments engendered by the uncertainties created by increasing financial constraints, frequent studies, investigations and efficiency reports, and the emphasis placed on efficient management within departments. 'Europe' has only gradually featured in such management studies.

None the less, a variety of ways have been adopted by both the Cabinet Office and individual departments to support and encourage recruitment to the Brussels institutions. Whitehall officials have, for example, the right to return to their department within five years (thereafter their return becomes subject to negotiation). But there have been problems of reintegrating those who return after an extended period. The case of Michael Franklin, who returned from the DG VI of the Commission to head the European

---

[8] Ibid. 28–9.
[9] The Management and Personnel Office in the Cabinet Office, which later became the Office of the Minister for the Civil Service. For a résumé of the brief history of the Civil Service Department see the *Financial Times*, 10 Aug. 1987.

Secretariat in the Cabinet Office as Deputy Secretary (and who is credited by Willis as providing a new impetus in Cabinet Office attempts to improve recruitment), was not very typical of those officials who had spent a number of years in Brussels. One of the problems pointed out by Willis was that: 'It was rarely demonstrable to the able and ambitious that service in the Commission actually enhanced career or even immediate job prospects on return to Whitehall, and quite often the reverse seemed to be true.'[10] In some instances, in some departments, there was clearly a suspicion that the official was 'tainted' and had probably 'gone native' while in Brussels. It has taken time for such suspicion to be replaced by an appreciation of expertise and the awareness of an EC dimension to otherwise domestic issues. Nor, given financial constraints, have departments always encouraged 'high-fliers', in whom they have invested a great deal by way of training, to go off to Brussels. On the other hand, a number of departments have supported officials who wish to spend periods of up to two years in Brussels as *agents temporaire*. This has the advantage not only of ensuring a cadre in the department with significant European experience, but *agents* are also paid for by the Commission.

Senior appointments in the Commission are very often the result of intense lobbying. The practice of 'parachuting' in a senior national official remains common if frowned upon. One of the most successful efforts by the British in recent years was the appointment of David Williamson, formerly Deputy Secretary in the Cabinet Office and head of the European Secretariat, as Secretary General. Other efforts have not been quite so successful, in part because of the growing resentment of career officials in the Commission. But promotion itself within such a multinational bureaucracy is rarely easy and there have in the past been criticisms that the British Government has been too reluctant to take an energetic part in the normal process of lobbying for promotion.

British under-representation has been a long-term problem to which central government has been slow to react. One of the most persistent aspects of the problem has been attracting younger candidates. To some extent the latter problem stems from cultural differences between the UK and the rest of the Community— summed up perhaps in the British generalist versus the 'European'

[10] Willis, *Britons in Brussels*, 80.

distinctions between administrator, economist, or lawyer—different recruitment traditions, the Community preferring those with further training or work experience to new graduates, and a process of recruitment that can extend over two years. There have also been problems—laid by British officials at the Commission's door—of poor publicity. While these problems were well known, little was done to counter them—at least until 1989/90 when rather more systematic efforts were introduced. A new enlarged European Staffing Unit was set up in 1990 in the Office of the Minister for the Civil Service in the Cabinet Office in an effort to improve recruitment for Brussels. At the same time a new *European Fast-Stream* scheme was introduced to recruit and train possible candidates for Brussels through experience in the British Civil Service.

NEGOTIATING IN BRUSSELS

Once the Commission has drawn up its proposal, it goes, of course, to the Council of Ministers and thence to COREPER and the relevant working group. Regrettably little academic work has been done on COREPER and even less on the UK Representation. A general conclusion suggested by Philippe Moreau Defarges is that:

The attitude of each national administration to the construction of Europe, be it German or Italian, British or Danish, Irish or French sums up, illustrates—sometimes to the point of caricature—its traditions and its idiosyncracies.[11]

Similarly with the British.

The UK Representation (UKREP) in Brussels has always been one of the largest national representations, with 41 officials listed in February 1990—as compared with 44 in the FRG's Representation, and 34 and 32 in the French and Italian Representations respectively.[12] While the size of the German Representation can be

[11] Colm O'Nuallain (ed.), *The Presidency of the European Council of Ministers* (London, 1985), 135.

[12] *Vacher's European Companion*, No. 71, Feb. 1990. In addition to the Permanent Representative, his Deputy and the Minister (Agriculture), the Representation was divided as follows: Political and Institutional Affairs—6; External Relations—8; Financial and Economic Affairs—6; Agricultural Affairs—4; Industrial Affairs, Energy and Internal Market—5; Social Affairs, Environment, Regional Policy and Transport—6; and Management—3.

explained in terms of the decentralized, federal, and coalitional nature of the German political system, the reasons for UKREP's size doubtless reflect British traditions and idiosyncracies, and, of course, geography. 'Fog Over Channel; Continent Isolated' might have summed up a past age of arrogance, it also points to a problem that will remain with the UK at least until the Channel Tunnel is built; the occasional but potentially critical difficulties of transport. The travel factor can perhaps be exaggerated but it has clearly helped to create general attitude-structures that have been endorsed by the belief that, however clever and skilled Foreign Office officials might be in negotiation, some substantive knowledge of the issues is desirable *in situ*. Given the divisiveness of 'European' issues, it has also been a necessity. Important, too, is the growing conviction that all departments need to build up a cadre of expertise within their ranks. The result has been a Representation usually staffed with 'high-fliers' from a number of departments and with a considerable reputation in both Brussels and London.

The primary role of the Permanent Representation is that of acting as the 'central post box for all documentation and correspondence exchanged between the Community institutions and the Member States . . .'.[13] But it is not simply a question of passing on information and reporting on meetings; officials are called upon to offer advice on subsequent courses of action and to negotiate. Its advice has not always been appreciated. Tony Benn, for example, who has accused the FCO of transferring its allegiance to Brussels,[14] has been highly critical of officials sewing up package deals in Brussels that could not be unpicked in London.[15] Whether justified or not it is a criticism that makes it even more important that UKREP should contain the *crème de la crème* from the relevant home departments. On a multitude of issues, they have to interpret the instructions sent from Whitehall and to do so in the course of sometimes highly complex and interrelated negotiations. The result, as one participant has pointed out, is a tension between negotiating as hard as possible and being seen at home to have

[13] F. Hayes Renshaw, C. Lequesne, and P. Mayor Lopez, 'The Permanent Representation of the Member States to the European Communities', *Journal of Common Market Studies*, 28 (Dec. 1989), 129.

[14] Young and Sloman, *No, Minister*, 79.

[15] Ibid. 74.

won, and wishing to see the particular committee or working group succeed and the dossier sent upwards in good form.[16]

Such a tension there may be, but senior officials have been at pains (sometimes not only metaphorically) to ensure that strong links are maintained with home departments. The use of the telephone is inevitably considerable. A tradition was established early that the Permanent Representative returned to London on Fridays to discuss with the Cabinet Office and other interested departments the strategies and tactics required to meet existing ministerial policies or to advise on new issues. Sir Michael Butler has also reported that during his period at UKREP he also fitted in a monthly meeting in the ECO and 'quite often' a meeting with the Foreign Secretary or the Prime Minister on another day.[17] Nor are such visits confined to the Permanent Representative; the senior MAFF official in UKREP also usually makes a weekly visit to London (on Thursdays) for discussions.[18]

UKREP does not of course have sole responsibility for negotiating within the Community. Despite the size and calibre of the Permanent Representation, it is supplemented by an army of home-based officials who make frequent weekly or monthly visits to Brussels for the multitude of working groups. If in 1982 Sir Brian Hayes estimated that some 200 MAFF officials went to Brussels every month, it was to some extent because of the significance of the Common Agricultural Policy as the only comprehensive policy of the Community. But given the detail involved in so much of the Community's policy negotiations, an influx from an ever-increasing array of departments has been inevitable. From the point of view of the inherent tension involved in negotiation, domestic lines of communication for such peripatetic officials may be more open and direct and positions clearer; even so, the implications of constant interaction among officials should not be underestimated.

The impact of numbers travelling to and from Brussels is to be found in both the knowledge and awareness of European issues each gains. But there is also the expertise demanded of such officials in terms of negotiating skills. As a result there has been a slow decline in the belief that the best training for such officials is

---

[16] Peter Pooley, MAFF's former senior official in UKREP. Quoted in Ibid. 82.
[17] Sir M. Butler, *Europe: More than a Continent* (London, 1986), 115.
[18] Peter Pooley, in Young and Sloman, *No, Minister*, 76.

in the job itself and a considerable increase in both internal departmental training programmes and in the use of the Civil Service College. From the two courses given in 1970/1 in which the EC featured,[19] the Civil Service now runs a whole range of courses from one-day crash courses to intensive residential ones that involve visits to the Community's institutions. There has also been a slow but steady breakdown in the traditional barriers between the Home and the Diplomatic Services as their hitherto separate and separable tasks begin to merge.

THE QUESTION OF CONTROL

In the light of the frequency and number of the visits to and from Brussels, and, indeed the close integration of the UK's negotiating effort in Brussels and London, it remains somewhat surprising that the instructions given to those negotiating on the part of the UK are reportedly among the tightest and most strictly adhered to of all the member states—even more so than the French with their equally centralized system. Geography allows France to keep a smallish Permanent Representation and to send experts from Paris more attune as a result with the demands of Paris rather than those of Brussels. Hence perhaps the French reputation for rigidity and even predictability; the former perhaps in terms of objectives, the latter in terms of tactics.[20]

The British remain strict on both counts with frequently highly elaborate instructions designating preferred and fall-back positions and how to attain them. Such detail is less a question of the Diplomatic Service justifying its continued role than one of wider consequence. An FCO input on at least tactics might still be considered important, for, as Sir David Hannay (a former Permanent Representative) put it:

there are an enormously complex number of tactical choices about how to pursue that policy through the undergrowth, the rather lush undergrowth,

[19] Stack, in Gregory, *Dilemmas of Government*, 134.
[20] See Sir Michael Butler's evidence to the House of Commons Foreign Affairs Committee, 15 Nov. 1989. Published in the Committee *Report on the Working of the Single European Act 1990*.

of the Community institutions and how to influence the other member states in their capitals on it.[21]

But with the growing involvement and expertise of other departments, the FCO can no longer claim exclusive knowledge of the EC, and, indeed, such claims are now more probably put forward with greater (if declining) frequency by the FCO's critics than by the Office itself.

Suspicion of the FCO and its 'European' role has run deep in British politics, both to the left and to the right. The Office's general pro-EC membership position was frequently resented; David Owen, for example, has suggested that during the battle for membership:

Successive governments had allowed them [the FCO] too much leeway. The result was that these Foreign Office civil servants had been acting almost as politicians, making political concessions and judgements, working very closely with ministers and having great influence with ministers . . .[22]

The consequent suspicion persisted in the 1980s during, for example, the frequent conflicts over the Community budget, over British membership of the Exchange Rate Mechanism and over further integration within the Community. And yet, obviously, there has been a need to know what is going on in the Community, the positions being adopted by other member states, and the best way of promoting British interests in David Hannay's 'lush undergrowth'. For Tony Benn the result has been that:

I think the Foreign Office's influence in Whitehall is now quite pernicious because the Foreign Office can properly claim that every bit of economic policy, industrial policy, social policy is now European policy and has to be fed through them. If they think it will interfere with our relations with our partners in the Community they will veto it, if they can, in Whitehall . . .[23]

And he went on to suggest that if they failed in Whitehall, the Office would try again in Brussels—helped there by the Community habit of policy-making by means of package deals. It is not

[21] S. Jenkins and A. Sloman, *With Respect Ambassador* (London, 1985), 88–9.

[22] David Owen, *Personally Speaking to Kenneth Harris* (London, 1987), 110, quoted in P. Hennessy, *Whitehall* (London, 1989), 402.

[23] Young and Sloman, *No, Minister*, 79.

surprising perhaps that some ministers—and not only from the
Labour Party—have sought to ensure a tight rein.

But for others involved, the issue goes deeper still. Peter Pooley
(formerly with MAFF and in UKREP), for example, has suggested
that:

The British have an obsession with consistency which I think stems from
the nature of our politics. Ministers must say the same as civil servants,
civil servants the same as ministers ... And so the British are more
predictable. They are very well briefed, they are very articulate, it's very
easy to get hold of and understand their point of view. It's relatively more
difficult to change it.[24]

Certainly one might conclude from Stephen George's chapter on
Westminster that Parliament is unlikely to be able to change
government's position. The House of Commons especially has had
considerable difficulty in scrutinizing legislation and holding government to account. Such limits to parliamentary scrutiny both
reflect and contribute to changed attitudes towards individual
ministerial responsibility. They also raise important questions over
the extent to which Parliament can any longer control government
collectively—the issue of course that has exercised many reluctant
'Europeans' in British politics. Concern over instructions may be
both a practical response to the complexities of negotiations in the
Community and a logical extension of collective responsibility. It
is also a result of the lack of consensus over the ultimate character
of the Community. In the absence of long-term objectives, there is
a premium on the consistency of immediate reactions.

THE EC AND WHITEHALL

The maintenance of consistent control over the British input into
Community negotiations is based on a highly streamlined decision-
making machine in London. The system that has evolved since
1973 is one which places emphasis on the Cabinet Office and
particularly its European Secretariat. To that extent, 'Europe' has
been a factor reinforcing the trend noted by a succession of
commentators in the 1970s towards the assumption of powers by

---

[24] Jenkins and Sloman, *With Respect Ambassador*, 93.

Cabinet or groups of Cabinet ministers and within the Cabinet Office.[25] How authority is shared out on any particular issue at any particular time will inevitably vary, though much depends on the position of the Prime Minister and the relationship between the Prime Minister, the Foreign Secretary, and the Chancellor of the Exchequer. Despite the occasional consideration of a 'minister for Europe'—as in the summer of 1987 when 'reliable sources in Whitehall' reported Mrs Thatcher's determination to move Community business away from the FCO[26]—no such post has been created. The issue of working relationships has in some respects also been compounded by the rapidity with which ministers have changed departments, the average tenure of office in the 1980s being two years, with the DTI a particular casualty.[27] The political results of this can be seen elsewhere in this volume.

In terms of departments, the then Prime Minister, Mr Heath, together with the Secretary of the Cabinet and Head of the Civil Service, took the decision in 1973 that each department should itself deal with the Community issues arising in its field of responsibilities, with a co-ordinating role being taken by a European Unit in the Cabinet Office responsible to the Chancellor of the Duchy of Lancaster. While elements of the system have been modified—or at least threatened—it has remained very largely intact. Modifications have usually been an intra-departmental rather than an inter-departmental matter and, as a result, have tended to be overlooked.[28] In terms of 'management'—the improvement of which has been at the centre of reform efforts especially since 1979—Europe nowhere appears to have been a factor.

---

[25] For a summary of such commentaries see P. Hennessy, *Cabinet* (Oxford, 1986), particularly ch. 2 and the same author's *Whitehall*, particularly ch. 8.

[26] See *Sunday Telegraph*, 12 July 1987.

[27] Richard Rose, *Ministers and Ministries: A Functional Analysis* (Oxford, 1987), 88. Rose also points out that even when a minister is not reshuffled, few sit particularly easily or are able to identify with the long-term concerns of the ministry to which they are or may be so temporarily attached.

[28] Perhaps the only inter-departmental exception, noted by Pollitt, occurred in 1982 when responsibility for the Common Agricultural Policy regimes of tobacco, cotton, flax, and silkworms was transferred from Industry to MAFF, Wales and Scotland, though Industry retained general political responsibility. Pollitt, *Manipulating the Machine*, App. 1. The fact that Peter Hennessy rarely mentions any changes brought about or influenced by Community membership in his massive *Whitehall* perhaps reinforces the point.

None the less, some departments have been obliged to adapt to Community membership quickly and more substantially than others. Some departments, such as the FCO, parts of the DTI, and the Department of Energy, had of course been in continuous negotiation with the Community since the inception of the Coal and Steel Community in 1952, so that changes could at least be anticipated. For others, such as MAFF, Community membership has meant a radical reorientation. For yet others, such as the Home Office or the Department of Education, the Community remains a peripheral concern, even though one of growing salience as the EC/ Twelve begin to co-ordinate policies in such areas as internal security, the free movement of people, and vocational, language, and other training.

THE FOREIGN AND COMMONWEALTH OFFICE

According to Sir Michael Butler (a former Permanent Representative), the Community has 'galvanised' the FCO.[29] The potentially profound challenge of the CPRS's Review of 1977 seems to have been the last in what seemed to be becoming a regular event.[30] Community membership—including the *de facto* blurring of the distinction between the Diplomatic Service and the Home Civil Service—has contributed to something of a rehabilitation, though at times it might have appeared in doubt, as in 1982 with the threat of a rival source of advice with the appointment of Sir Anthony Parsons as the Prime Minister's special adviser on foreign policy or again in 1987. Despite the suspicions of the FCO, seemingly held to the full by Mrs Thatcher, successive Cabinets have ultimately tended to recognize its expertise and the value of its advice on Community matters. But in terms of European Political Co-operation, the FCO has received a new lease of life. To the relief of many within the Office, here was an area that concerned the FCO above all, for procedurally it involved few other departments since it was all largely a matter of declarations rather than of expenditure, and, since it was intergovernmental in

---

[29] Jenkins and Sloman, *With Respect Ambassador*, 89.
[30] The Central Policy Review Staff's Report under Sir K. Berrill in 1977 followed, for example, the Duncan Report of 1969.

character, it aroused little hostility, even if in substance it some-times threatened to complicate Mrs Thatcher's efforts to restore the Anglo-American special relationship.

The FCO remains the formal channel of communication between Whitehall and UKREP although, inevitably, each depart-ment uses its own links. The Permanent Representative remains an FCO appointment with his Deputy from either the Treasury or the DTI. Within the FCO itself, responsibility for Community policy has evolved from the Mutual Aid set up largely to deal with Marshall Aid, through the European Integration Departments of the 1960s and 1970s, to the European Community Departments (Internal and External) in the 1980s. EPC caused a further change in that the FCO modified its position on integrating the economic and political aspects of policy by establishing a Political Director (a deputy to the Permanent Under-Secretary) and a Political Correspondent linked to ECD but working to the Political Director.[31]

In view of the administrative, mediatory, and representational roles demanded of the Presidency of the Council of Ministers, the FCO rather than the Cabinet Office has been given responsibility for organizing Britain's three Presidencies (its fourth term of office is due in 1992). For its first term, in 1977, a Presidency Unit was established, led by a junior minister at the FCO, John Tomlinson.[32] This, with hindsight, was regarded as an over-insurance and a more low-key role was emphasized on subsequent occasions, when of course there was also greater familiarity with the Community and EPC and its political divisiveness had been ameliorated. The demands of the Presidency on the FCO and the Foreign Secretary were summed up by Lord Carrington in 1981 when he said:

It is very hard work. I didn't fully understand, I think, two and a half years ago when I became Foreign Secretary, that I was going to be expected to understand such abstruse subjects as multi-fibre agreements and cocoa agreements and things of that kind. . . . But it has proved of course that because as President I have to take the chair, I really do have to know about these things and they are inevitably complicated and one does realise

[31] For a fuller description of the structure within the FCO and other Whitehall departments, see Geoffrey Edwards, 'The Presidency, the Case of the United Kingdom', in C. O'Nuallain, *The Presidency*.
[32] Ibid.

the problems, the differences of interest that there are between the various countries. . . .[33]

The statement suggests perhaps the potential costliness of the Presidency in having to check the pursuit of purely national interests. But the emphasis has tended to be on efficiency and good management—in part, at least to begin with, in order to show not just the competence of the British Civil Service but also how it has adjusted and adapted to Community membership.

THE MINISTRY OF AGRICULTURE, FISHERIES, AND FOOD

Peter Walker, a former Minister of Agriculture, declared:

It is quite a tribute to the civil service that a department, which was I suppose the most inward-looking and domestically-oriented department in Whitehall until we joined the Community, now probably has the best negotiating team . . . in Brussels of any member country.[34]

Whether or not the rest of the Community would agree with the last part of the statement (and the evidence suggests that MAFF's reputation is high), Community membership certainly wrought radical changes. Each of the department's constituent parts has been affected, whether the commodity divisions of Agriculture, which now more or less take their decisions in Brussels, the Fisheries Department with its battles over quotas, or Food, which has been heavily involved with the harmonization of EC food laws as part of the 1992 process. As one former Permanent Secretary in MAFF has written:

Involvement with the EC . . . has profoundly altered the lifestyle of the Ministry. There are few corners of the department which are not influenced to a greater or lesser degree by what goes on in Brussels. . . . In Whitehall terms it has moved the Ministry from the periphery to the centre. European negotiations involving Heads of Government rarely take place these days without the need for a MAFF presence . . .[35]

[33] Quoted in O'Nuallain, *The Presidency*, 256.
[34] Young and Sloman, 74.
[35] Sir Michael Franklin, 'Metamorphoses of the MAFF', *Journal of the Royal Agricultural Society of England* (1988), 52–7.

THE TREASURY

If MAFF underwent root and branch change because of Community membership, the position of the Treasury has been very different. For much of the period of Britain's membership, the Treasury and its officials have been far from integrated into the Community 'club', either at ministerial or official levels. The political significance of the Community's Budget and Britain's contributions and receipts from it has always been such as to demand a separate section within the International Finance division of the Treasury[36] even though in terms of British public expenditure, amounts have been relatively small. A European Community Group (of Divisions) emerged as part of the Treasury's Overseas Finance in 1982.

Other parts of the Treasury such as the Banking Division of the Financial Institutions and Markets Group have been obliged to take on policy responsibilities for proposals for Community banking directives. Other parts, too, have taken a keen interest in and a watching brief over other aspects of Community policy; the Industry, Agriculture, and Employment Group for example deals *inter alia* with expenditure aspects of the CAP. Leo Pliatzky, a former Second Permanent Secretary, following Heclo and Wildavsky, has suggested that 'village communities' grow up inside the Treasury on each major subject as well as on areas of public expenditure with their own expertise and responsibilities.[37]

However, the Treasury's adaptation to the Community has been a gradual one, at least in terms of policy. A glance at the department's entries in the *Civil Service Yearbook* suggests also a certain element of reluctance. Division 1 of the EC Group initially dealt with the *reform* of Community policies. This was modified in the 1988 edition to a *review* of budgetary financing, which gave way in the 1990 *Yearbook* to the *co-ordination* of work on financial and economic policies including EMU and the single

---

[36] See O'Nuallain, *The Presidency*.
[37] See Sir Leo Pliatzky, *Getting and Spending* (Oxford, 1982). Pliatzky was referring more specifically to a 'village community' of old hands who had dealt with the Treaty of Rome. See also Hugh Heclo and Aaron Wildavsky, *The Private Government of Public Money* (London, 1981).

market.[38] Division 2 deals with Community Budgetary issues, including, of course, Britain's net payments and the implications of the Budget for UK public expenditure.

DEPARTMENT OF TRADE AND INDUSTRY

The antithesis to the appearance of a smooth, steady, if reluctant adaptation to the demands of Community membership provided by the Treasury has been that of the DTI with its seemingly endless shifts and changes. Few of these changes, however, have had much to do with Community membership as such—changing political ideologies, different organizational theories in the search for efficiency, or the need to provide Cabinet or other ministerial posts for party-political reasons have been very much more significant. Yet since accession, the DTI has been split up into three (Trade, Industry, Prices and Consumer Affairs) and then four (in 1976 when Transport was detached), only to be pulled back together again in 1979 when Prices and Consumer Affairs was reabsorbed into Trade and Industry and Transport was down-graded. It was modified once again in 1983 under Lord Young, whose tenure was marked as much by the extent of his spending, especially on the Enterprise Initiative and 1992, as his internal reorganization of the DTI. To make matters worse, perhaps, few Secretaries of State at the DTI have stayed over-long. European questions were directly involved in two premature departures, those of Leon Brittan and Nicholas Ridley.

Such changes inevitably complicate any assessment of the Department's adaptation to Community membership. To some extent, at the official level, the changes were more illusory than real, a matter as one (anonymous) official put it, of little more than changing the writing-paper. Lord Young's reforms, for example, tended to confuse form with substance in that a central unit had already existed (the old General division) for planning and co-ordination together with a European policy division, which he renamed the Internal European Policy Division, to which he added a 1992 campaign unit, as well as the External Policy Division. In so far as structural changes were largely cosmetic, the impact of

[38] Various editions of the *Civil Service Yearbook*, HMSO.

the Department on policy formulation at the official level was little changed, nor was there any discernable change in the Department's representation at the negotiating table. In both instances, changes in ministers and their ideologies had a much greater impact, whether in terms of reducing the interventionist role of the Department, in trying to square adaptation of the Department to the implementation of Community legislation with reduced expenditure, or in limiting reorganization at the regional as well as the national level in order better to lead on matters relating to the Community's structural funds.

THE CABINET OFFICE

The demands of Community membership, especially in terms of co-ordination, have been considerable. They compounded an already difficult situation created by the growing centralization of authority within the Cabinet and the Cabinet Office. Much has been written about the problems of 'overload' that had begun to afflict central government by the early 1970s.[39] It was not only an issue for the Civil Service, although as Hennessy has pointed out, Sir John (now Lord) Hunt, when in the Cabinet Office, appeared to gather ever more responsibilities to the Cabinet Office; but it was a political problem too. As Hunt himself pointed out, there remained a hole at the centre that 'an overworked Cabinet seemed incapable of filling'. It was against this background that Britain entered the Community.

Those involved in studying the European Community have long held the view that the subject straddled the traditional foreign/ domestic divide.[40] The Community, to use a somewhat later formulation, has:

tended to erode the concept of a discrete category of 'foreign affairs' in which the Prime Minister, Foreign Secretary and the Foreign Office play the predominant roles. The early post-war defence and treaty-based commitments (like NATO) buttressed the insulation of strategic policy from wide ministerial involvement. But trends since the 1970s have worked

[39] See for example A. King (ed.), *Why is Britain Becoming Harder to Govern?* (London, 1976).
[40] See for example Helen Wallace, *National Governments and the European Communities* (London, 1973).

in the opposite direction by involving more and more ministers and departments in direct negotiations with overseas counterparts about sectorally specific policies.[41]

This then has provided the basis for the critical involvement of the Cabinet Office.

The formal position remains very largely that outlined by Stack in 1983.[42] If initially the European Unit was headed by a Second Permanent Secretary reporting to the Chancellor of the Duchy of Lancaster, the return of a Labour Government hostile to the Community led to some reorganization in that the Foreign Secretary became formally responsible for co-ordinating the work of the Unit and the Unit's head was down-graded to that of a Deputy Secretary. In view of the widespread suspicion within the Labour party and Government of the FCO and its pro-membership position—a suspicion at least recognized by Harold Wilson, the Prime Minister[43]—it was politically vital for Wilson to have a minister of Callaghan's standing in charge. Despite occasional rumours, Conservative Governments under Mrs Thatcher did not change the formal structure, though European issues may well have been removed to smaller *ad hoc* committees and groups of ministers along with other issues described by Peter Hennessy, among others.[44] In these more fluid circumstances, the role of the Cabinet Secretary and especially the head of the European Secretariat (as the European Unit became) have been critical.

The formal Committees of the Cabinet and the structure of the official committees that service them have been described extensively by Hennessy and others.[45] The position of the committee of senior officials, EQ(S), is central to the co-ordination process for it acts as a clearing-house for the dossiers that go to ministers as well as providing guidance for departments on others. As a result the position of the head of the European Secretariat who chairs EQ(S) has become pivotal, and the European Secretariat itself, one (in Seldon's words) of the most 'proactive' of the Cabinet Office's

---

[41] Dunleavy and Rhodes, 'Core Executive Studies', p. 15.
[42] Stack, in Gregory, *Dilemmas of Government*.
[43] See his remarks in Harold Wilson, *Final Term* (London, 1979), 54.
[44] See Hennessy, *Cabinet* in his Introduction and elsewhere.
[45] Despite, of course, this being a breach of the Official Secrets Act. See his *Cabinet*. The committees are also analysed in A. Seldon, 'The Cabinet Office', 103–21.

Secretariats.[46] Not only is the head of the Secretariat responsible for briefing the Prime Minister personally before a meeting of the European Council, but he has been given the initiative in co-ordinating all the Government's policies and Community activities rather than waiting on departments to call them in because of potential inter-departmental differences. David Williamson, one of the former Deputy Secretaries who headed the European Secret-ariat, summed up the different roles of FCO and Cabinet Office as follows:

It is the duty of the Foreign Office . . . to present the Foreign Secretary in the first instance and to the government its view of what result should come out of a particular discussion which is a) favourable to the UK, b) negotiable, and c) coherent with specific objectives . . . But in the Cabinet Office . . . our job is simply to say, taking account of the views of the Foreign Office about the negotiability of the particular product, taking account of the views of another department about the effect on British industry directly, taking account of the costs in additional personnel which appears in the government's budget and all these things, what is in our view the best result to recommend to ministers.[47]

It is perhaps not surprising that such individuals are regarded as future permanent secretaries (as has been the case with Sir D. Hancock and Sir M. Franklin, while D. Williamson himself became Secretary General of the European Commission).

ADAPTATION TO COMMUNITY MEMBERSHIP AND REFORM IN CENTRAL GOVERNMENT

In his assessment, Pollitt suggested that little structural change could be traceable to the Community, at least during the five years following Labour's return to power in 1974. 'The matter was handled by the creation of committees, units and individual posts charged with various species of co-ordination, not by altering the pattern of departments.'[48] Nor, according to G. W. Jones, was the Community a factor in the key changes in central government that took place during the 1980s, which included the abolition of the

---

[46] Seldon, 'The Cabinet Office', 108.
[47] Jenkins and Sloman, *With Respect Ambassador*, 88.
[48] Pollitt, 114.

Civil Service Department (CSD), the reamalgamation of the DTI, and the break-up of Health and Social Security. The main factors in these changes were, Jones suggests, primarily political: to punish a department (the CSD); to reward a minister (Cecil Parkinson); and to rescue the Government from political embarrassment (the DHSS).[49] Moreover, in the longer view taken by Nevil Johnson in 1985:

> In short, we can say that in relation to the changes which have taken place in the functions and tasks of administration there was a remarkable time-lag in the adaptation of the administrative world itself to these changes. In thinking about the evolution of the civil service since 1945, it is of cardinal importance to recognise that it survived into the era of the welfare state more or less in the form and with the precepts of its role and functions which it had acquired at the maturing of the developments set in train by the Northcote-Trevelyan reforms.[50]

Against such a backdrop has Community membership had any great impact? Has it been the case that, in terms of functions and processes of decision-making (and perhaps even ethos), Whitehall, while not impervious to the gradual 'encroachment' of European business, has taken it in its stride? Is it therefore not suprising that the traditional machinery-of-government debates over efficiency and management should have ignored the demands of adapting to Community membership? And yet, even if the shift of focus has been gradual in some departments, though not in all, Community membership has had both a quantitative and qualitative impact on Whitehall.

The stress on efficiency in the 1980s focused especially on the organization of departments and the division between advising ministers on policy and delivering services to the public. The emphasis lay increasingly on delegating responsibilities down the line within the Civil Service or to agency managers in the privatized sector. Such divisions do not always fit easily with the demands of Community decision-making. At one level, it is a question of officials ensuring that they have adequate information available on which to advise ministers. At another level it is also a question of

---

[49] G. W. Jones in *West European Politics*, 12 (July 1989), 240. Interestingly it is an article that makes barely a mention of Europe other than to point to continental 'legalism'.

[50] Nevil Johnson, 'Change in the Civil Service: Retrospect and Prospects', *Public Administration*, 63 (1985), 417.

being able to ensure implementation of the policies finally agreed for, as Mrs Thatcher frequently pointed out in her last years in office, implementation can be a highly political issue. It has potentially important implications for both those who tend to implement Community legislation quickly, such as the British, and those who delay, the most quoted defaulters being the Italians. But the question goes beyond the simple passage of Community directives into national law—where British Governments, given their control of the parliamentary timetable, have the advantage—to joint Community/national responsibility for enforcement and control. This lays further stress on co-ordination both within and between departments in order to gain a central overview not only of policy preferences but also of the potential capacity to execute policy decisions. Implementation, in other words, becomes a part of the negotiating process.

There are implications here too for the debate on ministerial and Cabinet responsibility in Britain. The debate in part has been over whether a minister is responsible for all that goes on in his/her department; and there seems a strong feeling that while responsibility as in the Crichel Down case of 1952 may be dead, nothing else has emerged to replace it in terms of ensuring the accountability of administrators.[51] Inevitably Mrs Thatcher's long tenure of office complicates the position and makes it difficult to discern the underlying trends. On the one hand, however, there are those such as George Jones, who hold that:

Each Department under its own minister remains very much an independent unit, responsible for its own running and the way it organises its staff. Central bodies can only exhort; but what makes their urgings more influential now than in the past is the backing of the Prime Minister, who does not favour ministers and top civil servants thought to be slow on reshaping their departments and the processes of the civil servants.[52]

Others have suggested that ministers and officials often attempt to keep cross-departmental issues away from the Cabinet Office and inter-departmental committees with as much as possible resolved by telephone or other bilateral communication.

On the other hand, there are arguments which suggest that the

---

[51] For a good example of the debate see 'Symposium on Ministerial Responsibility' *Public Administration* 65 (spring 1987), 61–91.
[52] Jones, *West European Politics*, 12 (July 1989), 255.

centre does more than simply exhort. The accretion of authority at the centre long pre-dates Mrs Thatcher's term of office, even if, as one former Cabinet Secretary suggested, it created 'a cabinet which has collective responsibility without sufficient information or power to exercise it'.[53] But Lord Hunt was none the less persuaded that all was not necessarily lost:

I accept that Cabinet Government must always be a somewhat cumbrous and complicated affair and that this is a price well worth paying for the advantage of shared discussion and shared decisions provided the system can keep up with the demands put upon it.

What taxed many commentators during Mrs Thatcher's premiership was the extent to which decisions were shared and whether Cabinet government had given way to prime-ministerial government. Certainly the Cabinet was used less in the Hunt sense and the role of the Cabinet Secretary and the Prime Minister's own office were considerably enhanced. Whether this presages a permanent shift in the locus of authority remains to be seen.

Whatever the long-term balance, Britain's Community membership suggests a number of points that need to be taken into account. The divisiveness of the European issue for both the major parties when in power has demanded prime-ministerial attention. Given the known or suspected positions of the departments of state, it is perhaps not surprising that advice has been sought not only from the Cabinet Office but also from elsewhere, especially from the Prime Minister's own Office and the Policy Unit at 10 Downing Street.[54] Mrs Thatcher very clearly sought to define the Government's general attitude towards the Community. In terms of the briefings she and/or her Press Secretary provided on Community decisions, the PM rather than government appeared to be attempting a gatekeeping role. Certainly there were constant battles with her Foreign Secretaries and successive Chancellors of the Exchequer, the results of which contributed significantly to her subsequent defeat.

Increased prime-ministerial involvement in so many if not all aspects of Community business has stemmed, however, not only

[53] Quoted by Hennessy in *Cabinet*, 250.

[54] The Policy Unit included at least one individual responsible for covering Community affairs. See David Willetts, *Public Administration*, 65 (winter 1987), 443–54, 446.

from the demands of the domestic political debate but also from the extent to which and the manner in which Community decisions affect hitherto national policies. If national co-ordination is at a premium, it pushes priority setting towards the centre, to the Cabinet Office and the Prime Minister. To some extent this can be countered, as suggested by Dunleavy and Rhodes on the basis that there is a:

progressive transition to joint UK–EC control of some key policies previously autonomously controlled by Whitehall—such as monopolies and mergers policy or the setting of clear water and environmental standards. Such policy areas have also become more important in wider EC relations because of the transition to a single European market in 1992. These changes have intensively constrained prime ministerial control over external relations policy.[55]

However, apart from an element of inconsistency in the argument in view of the difficulty of placing foreign and domestic affairs in discrete categories, the argument can work in the opposite direction, heightening the role of the Prime Minister, especially given the role of Heads of Government in the decision-making process.[56] The point is perhaps that simply in terms of the scale of Community business no individual or even the Cabinet's European Secretariat can now exercise any effective controls. Nor, given the range of interests involved in policy, whether formal, informal, organized, or diffuse, is it a straightforward task to identify Britain's 'national interest'.

Finally, the role of Heads of Government has become increasingly institutionalized within the Community, in the European Council. The primary functions of the Council are to provide a strategic overview and to bring about a greater sense of cohesion and consistency within the Community. Only Heads of Government (and of state, in the French case) could provide such leadership or impose such control over competing interests and ministers. That they may not always seek or be able to seize the opportunity to fulfil these functions is, of course another matter.

But there are, in other words, a range of pressures acting on any

---

[55] Dunleavy and Rhodes, 'Core Executive Studies'.
[56] It could of course be argued both ways at the same time in that the pressures to co-ordinate may enhance the Prime Minister's role but in practice the role is constrained because of the blurring of domestic/external distinctions.

Prime Minister. Quite how they balance out depends inevitably on circumstances and personalities. While clearly there has been a drift towards more prime-ministerial government under Mrs Thatcher for the reasons suggested above, trends may not continue in quite the same way under her successors. None the less what is clear is that the Community has imposed a raft of new challenges to British Governments. Their responses, whether at prime-ministerial or departmental levels, have tended to be *ad hoc* and piecemeal. The blurring of the internal/external divide has been a slow process. Little account has perhaps as a result yet been taken of the Community dimension in the various plans for reform, whether in the interests of efficiency or of accountability. The changes that are being brought about because of Community membership are profound; it is unlikely that central government and its administration is or will be immune from them.

4

The Legislative Dimension

Stephen George

THIS chapter deals with the way in which EC legislation is handled by the British political and legal system. First, the role of the two Houses of Parliament is considered, with especial attention on the extent to which it has proved possible for the House of Commons to maintain adequate scrutiny of executive actions in the EC. Secondly, attention is given to the implementation of EC decisions within the British system. Finally, the attitude taken by British Courts to EC law is examined.

THE ROLE OF THE HOUSES OF PARLIAMENT

There are several ways in which Parliament can keep itself informed on EC developments and make an input into the decision-making process. The Prime Minister always reports to the House of Commons on meetings of the European Council, and the report is followed by a debate; and questions on European matters can be addressed to the Prime Minister or to Departmental Ministers during normal parliamentary questions. In addition, Select Committees can investigate issues with an EC dimension that fall within their sectoral remit. The Commons Select Committee on Foreign Affairs and the Treasury Select Committee have both made several such reports. However, these Committees obviously have much more far-reaching responsibilities, which limit the amount of time that they can spend on EC matters, and inevitably it falls to the specialized committee with responsibility for scrutiny of EC legislation to act as the main parliamentary watch-dog on such matters.

The two Houses have adopted very different approaches to the scrutiny of proposed EC legislation. The House of Lords has a Committee which prepares detailed reports, whereas the Commons has a Scrutiny Committee which is charged simply to distinguish between significant and less significant proposals for legislation, and to recommend the more significant for debate in the House.

The Lords Committee was set up in 1974 following the report of the Maybray-King Committee. Most of its work is carried out in six subcommittees covering:

(a) Finance, Trade and Industry, and External Relations
(b) Energy, Transport, and Technology
(c) Social and Consumer Affairs
(d) Agriculture and Food
(e) Law and Institutions
(f) Environment.

Occasionally *ad hoc* subcommittees are set up on general issues such as European union, or the question of fraud against the Community which was a matter of particular concern early in 1989.

In all some eighty members of the Lords are involved with the work of the subcommittees, and any member who has an interest in a particular topic may attend the relevant subcommittee. The main Committee has twenty-four members.

EC documents are initially sifted by the Chairperson of the Committee on the basis of information contained in the Government's explanatory memoranda, and those considered most significant are referred to the relevant subcommittee, which may decide either to clear the proposal without further scrutiny, or to conduct an examination, which may be either small-scale or a full-scale investigation for which both written and oral evidence is taken. At the end of a full-scale examination a report is issued. Many of these reports receive coverage in the Press, and they are highly regarded within the institutions of the EC. As a result the House of Lords can be said to have considerable influence on the making of EC policy, even though its formal powers are limited.[1]

Although the Lords' pattern was recommended to the House of Commons Select Committee on Procedure when it took evidence on the scrutiny of EC legislation in 1989, that Committee decided against recommending a similar system for the Commons. Instead

[1] House of Commons Select Committee on Procedure, Fourth Report, Session 1988–9, *The Scrutiny of European Legislation*, vol. ii Minutes of Evidence, HC 622-II, 8 Nov. 1989, app. 21, pp. 145–6.

it proposed some extension of the remit of the Select Committee on European Legislation, which is generally known as the Scrutiny Committee because of its limited function as the committee that scrutinizes EC documents and recommends for debate by the whole House those which it considers raise issues of major importance.

The scrutiny system was instituted in 1974, following the report of the Foster Committee, which had been especially created to consider the issue. Initially the main problem of the Scrutiny Committee was simply catching up with the considerable backlog of EC documentation, some 271 unsorted documents, which had accumulated between Britain's accession on 1 January 1973 and the Committee starting work in May 1974.[2] This backlog of work meant that the Committee struggled to keep abreast of new proposals, and debates on matters of EC legislation which the Committee chose for further consideration were held very late in the decision-making process of the Community. This resulted in some decisions on items selected for debate being taken in the Council of Ministers before the debate was held.

On 30 October 1980 a Resolution of the House expressed the opinion that no Minister of the Crown should normally give agreement in the Council of Ministers to any proposal which had been recommended for debate by the House before the debate had been held.[3] In August 1984, in its reply to the 1983–4 Special Report of the Committee, the Government made a statement of policy that it would consider the Resolution of October 1980 to apply also to proposals not yet scrutinized by the Committee.[4] Generally these principles have been observed in practice, but other difficulties have arisen concerning the terms of reference of the Scrutiny Committee and the time available for debating proposed EC legislation.

In its Second Special Report for 1985–6,[5] the Committee expressed its concern that the House was not being adequately informed on Community matters because the Committee's terms of reference allowed it only to report on proposals for EC legislation, whereas important developments of considerable constitutional

---

[2] Martin Kolinsky, 'Parliamentary Scrutiny of European Legislation', *Government and Opposition*, 10 (1975), 55.
[3] The Resolution is reproduced in HC 622-II, p. 17.
[4] The Government's statement is reproduced in HC 622-II, pp. 26–7.
[5] HC 400, 14 May 1986.

significance were in fact negotiated through different mechanisms. The example quoted by the Committee was the Single European Act (SEA). Although Parliament had to ratify the SEA, the Scrutiny Committee was debarred by its terms of reference from reporting to the House on its content and implications, or indeed from reporting on the intergovernmental conference that preceded it. Similarly, intergovernmental agreements to increase the resources of the Community fell outside of the Committee's remit.

In its reply to this report,[6] the Government indicated that it was not prepared to concede the extension of the Committee's terms of reference, because it did not believe that the time was ripe for such an extension. No explanation was given for this judgement, which might be seen as simply an attempt by the Government to preserve its role as gatekeeper between the EC and the domestic political system. However, the reaction from the Chairmen of other Commons' Committees and from back-benchers on both sides of the House was such that in July 1989 the Leader of the House indicated that he would provide the Committee with a wider range of documents than just those specified in its terms of reference, and would take steps to remove the procedural impediments to such documents being further considered by the House as though they were EC Documents as defined in the standing orders.[7] He thereby conceded a *de facto* extension of the Committee's competences.

Another problem in ensuring adequate parliamentary scrutiny of EC legislation is the lack of time available for debate, and this has worsened as the range of issues covered by the EC has extended into new areas such as the environment and security. Debates have been held late at night, and have been sparsely attended. The Select Committee on Procedure in its 1989 Report proposed tackling this problem by transferring more debates upstairs to the Standing Committees. However, it did not favour a Grand Committee on European Affairs, preferring to see the establishment of five Special Standing Committees, each concentrating on a particular area of EC Documents. The five areas were: agriculture; trade and industry; Treasury matters; transport and the environment; and a general committee.[8]

[6] Cmnd. 123, 1986–7; reproduced in HC 622-II, pp. 20–2.

[7] HC 533, 19 July 1989.

[8] House of Commons Select Committee on Procedure, Fourth Report, Session 1988–9, *The Scrutiny of European Legislation*, vol. i, HC 622-II, 8 Nov. 1989, para. 127, pp. xxxix–xli.

In its response,[9] the Government accepted this recommendation, with the reservation that it might be difficult to find enough Members with sufficient expertise and interest to operate five such committees, so the Government proposed that initially there should be three committees with ten members each plus a Chairman. This compromise was accepted, although there was some discontent that the Government reserved to itself the right to decide which items would be debated in the Committees and which items would be debated in the full House.[10] Since debates in Standing Committees are much less likely to be reported in the media than plenary debates, this was seen as a procedural device that could be used to bury away from the public gaze matters that might prove embarrassing to the Government.

Taken together, the pressure on the Government to extend the terms of reference of the Scrutiny Committee and the recommendations of the Procedure Committee indicate a heightened awareness on the part of the Commons of the importance of EC matters. This has been a slow process of adjustment, slower than that of the executive branch, which has been given a significant boost by the 1992 project and by the SEA. The campaign around the slogan '1992' has raised awareness of the importance of the EC generally within the country, including amongst MPs. The SEA was presented to Parliament as a technical measure which would enable the 1992 legislation to be passed against the opposition of vested interests in the various member states.[11] It was only after its acceptance that the full implications of the additional erosion of sovereignty that it involved became fully clear (perhaps even to the Government). The consequence has been a new determination on the part of many MPs to prevent further leakage of sovereignty by default, and a drive to regain as much control as possible over a widening range of legislative matters that are being determined at EC level.

THE IMPLEMENTATION OF EC LEGISLATION

Britain's reputation as a semi-detached member of the EC is largely based on the record of the Government in resisting developments

---

[9] Cmnd. 1081, 1989–90.
[10] *Hansard* (Commons), 24 Oct. 1990, cols. 393–5.
[11] *Hansard* (Commons), 1985–6, Vol. 96, cols. 317–21 and Col. 326.

that the other member states have felt to be desirable. In particular, the British have tended to oppose any commitments to grand-sounding concepts such as 'political union'; and they have also been very tough negotiators on other more minor matters. But by the end of the 1980s the Government was putting a great deal of stress on its record of implementation of those measures to which it had agreed, especially in comparison with the record of other member states which claimed, on the basis of their declaratory statements, to be better 'Europeans'.

Two studies of implementation tended to support the claims of the British Government. A ten-nation study which appeared in 1988[12] examined the implementation of seventeen directives covering a wide range of topics—from life insurance to plant diseases, from electrical equipment to freshwater fish—and followed them through from the negotiation phase to implementation. This was followed up by a more detailed examination of the implementation of two regulations in the field of road transport, relating to lorry drivers' hours and tachographs. The conclusion of the study was that wide variation existed between member states in the degree to which EC rules were enforced. The United Kingdom emerged with a good record from this survey in comparison with several of the other member states. As Alan Butt Philip and Christina Baron, the authors of the British study, put it: 'The government must be seen to stand up strongly for the interests of the UK at the pre-decision stages, but it will loyally try to implement any decision that the Community eventually agrees.'[13]

Much the same results came out of a survey by the Commission in 1989 of the extent to which measures agreed in pursuit of the 1992 objective of freeing the internal market had been implemented by the member states.[14] Again wide variation was found between states; again the United Kingdom had one of the best records on implementation.

The picture which emerges from these studies is not of Britain as a semi-detached member of the EC, but of Britain as an exemplary

[12] Heinrick Siedentopf and Jacques Ziller (eds.), *Making European Policies Work: The Implementation of Community Legislation in the Member States*, vol. i: *Comparative Syntheses* (London, 1988); vol. ii: *National Reports* (London and Brussels, 1988).

[13] Siedentopf and Ziller, *European Policies*, ii, 666.

[14] *Independent*, 7 Sept. 1989.

member in the forefront of Community developments, a theme that was adopted in the course of 1989 by spokespersons for the British Government. Although Britain is a tough negotiating partner, the awkwardness expressed at the negotiation stage is a reflection of the fact that if Britain agrees to something, it does it. Some of the other member states, it might be concluded from the surveys cited above, are quite prepared to agree to all sorts of things because they have little intention of honouring the agreement anyway.

On the other hand, it should also be noted that it is much easier for the British Government to embody EC directives in national statutes than it is for the Governments of some other member states, because of the control that the British Government exercises over the parliamentary timetable, and the control that it can exercise over the vote in the Commons through the existence of a clear majority of members supporting the single party of Government. In contrast other Governments are coalitions, which often have to construct a majority in the legislature on each issue, and do not have complete control over the legislative programme. Such institutional factors could go some way to excusing the difficulties that Italian Governments, apparently the worst offenders on implementation, have in fulfilling their commitments.

It would also be wrong to conclude that the positive record of the British on the implementation of EC legislation was an indication of a rapid adjustment by the Civil Service to membership of the EC. Alan Butt Philip and Christina Baron, the British research team on the ten-nation implementation study, noted that the civil servants who were charged with implementation often did not know that a particular measure was of EC origin.

The British civil servant's insistence on conforming to the law serves to ensure the smooth passage of most EC directives into the law and administrative practice of this country, without most people being aware of the Community source of many of the changes that are being made. This leads to integration by stealth, often without the development of supporting communautaire attitudes in the political class, the administration itself, or among the public at large.[15]

The very positive record of Britain as indicated by the implementation studies influenced the approach of the British Government

---

[15] Siedentopf and Ziller, *European Policies*, ii, 666.

to the discussion of political union in the course of 1990. Whereas the French and Germans, who initiated the discussion in April 1990, were talking in terms of improving the decision-making system, the British Government tabled proposals to give increased powers to the Council and European Parliament to scrutinize the compliance of member states with EC law, and stronger powers of enforcement to the European Court of Justice (ECJ) and the Commission.[16]

THE RELATIONSHIP BETWEEN EC LAW AND DOMESTIC LAW

There is a conflict between the traditional constitutional principles of the United Kingdom and those of the EC as enunciated and elaborated by the ECJ. Under the British constitution, the fundamental principle is the sovereignty of Parliament, whereas under EC law the fundamental principle is the supremacy of EC law over national law.

The sovereignty of Parliament means two things. First it means that statute law (i.e. a law enacted by Parliament) overrides any other source of law, such as the common law. Appeal can be made to other sources of law in the Courts where the issue in question is not covered by statute; but if a statute exists there can be no question but that it has primacy. Secondly, it means that no Parliament can bind its successor. If Parliament passed a law which conflicted with a law enacted earlier, the Courts would be obliged to apply the principle *lex posterior derogat priori* (the later law overrides the earlier). This is seen as a fundamental safeguard of democratic government. Clearly if a Government with a majority in Parliament were to pass legislation that came into conflict with legislation passed by a previous Government, it would be a breach of the principle of democracy were the Courts to rule the later law invalid because of the existence of a law that had been passed by a majority in an earlier Parliament against which the electorate had voted in a subsequent election.

Both these principles were called into question when Britain

[16] Isabel Hilton and David Usborne, 'Europe's Guiding Stars', *Independent*, 27 Apr. 1990.

joined the EC. There already existed a number of significant statements by the ECJ of the principle that Community law must always take precedence over national law, most clearly in its judgement on the 1964 case, *Costa* v. *ENEL*.[17] The logic behind these statements was that if Community law were to be subject to different interpretations, and even derogations, in different member states in the light of particular national laws, it would lose its character as Community law applying equally throughout the EC. For British Courts the implication was revolutionary. They were being asked to give precedence to Community law where it came into conflict with national statute law, even where the national law had been passed later in time.

It took a little time for the implications of this position to sink in. Although the ECJ had already made its position abundantly clear in earlier rulings, the first occasion after British membership when it reiterated its position, in its judgement on the *Simmenthal* case in March 1979,[18] led to a series of letters to *The Times* from senior members of the legal profession, some expressing surprise at the implications of this 'new' doctrine.[19] For a time the Courts made contradictory rulings; possibly most of these were made in ignorance of the conflict of principles involved, but there was a debate among senior figures. Although some eminent lawyers maintained that there was no conflict of constitutional principles, on the grounds that in entering the EC the United Kingdom had entered into a new legal order, the rules of which had to be observed,[20] there was obviously some unease.

Eventually the dilemma was resolved by adopting as a 'rule of construction' the principle that Community law should take precedence where it came into conflict with a later statute, on the grounds that Parliament could not really have meant to breach Britain's obligations as a member of the EC, and that the conflict must therefore be the result of parliamentary error unless there was

---

[17] Case 6/64, *Flaminio Costa* v. *ENEL*, *European Court Reports*, 1964, 565; *Common Market Law Reports*, 1964, 425.

[18] Case 106/77, *Amministrazione delle Finanze dello Stato* v. *Simmenthal SpA*, *European Court Reports*, 1978, 629; *Common Market Law Reports*, 1978, 263.

[19] *The Times*, 19–21 Apr. and 27–9 Apr. 1977.

[20] J. D. B. Mitchell, 'The Sovereignty of Parliament and European Community Law: The Stumbling Block That Isn't There', *International Affairs*, 55 (1979), 36–46.

some clear indication to the contrary.[21] This device allows the Courts to operate under two apparently contradictory legal regimes, but the situation is still not entirely satisfactory and would place the Courts in a difficult position were Parliament to pass an Act that conflicted with EC legislation, and to state categorically that the statute should take precedence.

In June 1990 a new dimension was given to the whole issue of loss of parliamentary sovereignty through the application of the ECJ's doctrine that EC law takes precedence over national law. The Court decided that the British 1988 Merchant Shipping Act might be in breach of EC law because it banned Spanish fishermen with boats registered in Britain from fishing in British waters. Pending the hearing of a case brought by the Spanish fishermen, the Court instructed the British Courts to suspend the Act. This led to noisy scenes in the House of Commons, in protest at the constitutional implications of allowing the Courts to set aside an Act of Parliament, something that had previously been considered impossible in the United Kingdom. However, on 11 July the House of Lords did issue an injunction to the Courts to refrain from applying the Act until judgement had been reached in the ECJ.

CONCLUSION

What light does the discussion in this chapter of the legislative dimension throw on the three themes that structure the analysis in this book of Britain's relationship with the EC? The themes, to reiterate, are Britain as an allegedly semi-detached member of the EC; the existence of different rates of adaptation to membership in different parts of the British political system; and the attempt of central government to play a gatekeeper role, controlling all contacts between the British system and the EC system, and thereby restricting the emergence of the phenomena of transnationalism and transgovernmentalism as identified by Keohane and Nye.[22]

First, what of Britain's role as a semi-detached member of the EC? This chapter does not give much support to that idea. It is true

[21] Josephine Steiner, *Textbook on EEC Law* (London, 1990).
[22] Robert O. Keohane and Joseph S. Nye, *Power and Interdependence*, (Boston, Mass. 1977).

that only recently has EC business been integrated into the normal business of the House of Commons; but the reports of the House of Lords Select Committee on the EC have long been required reading in Brussels and other national capitals as well as in Whitehall. Also, British scrutiny procedures, whatever their inadequacies, have generally been seen as superior to those of the Parliaments of most other member states. In a famous speech to the EP in 1988, Jacques Delors singled out Britain and the Federal Republic of Germany as the only two member states whose Parliaments had fully woken up to the implications for national sovereignty of the 1992 project.[23] This tribute does not indicate a semi-detached attitude on the part of the British legislature, but on the contrary one of greater vigilance than exercised by the legislatures of other member states.[24]

Nor can Britain be considered to be semi-detached in respect to the implementation of EC legislation. On the contrary, the British record in this respect gives weight to Mrs Thatcher's 1986 claim, also to the EP, that Britain is 'fully *communautaire*' and is in many cases 'leading the pack'.

Constitutionally Britain has perhaps had a greater adjustment to make to EC membership than have most other states, because of the different historical basis for the British constitution and legal system. Nevertheless, Britain is no more out of line than other member states which have constitutional traditions more in harmony with that of the EC as a whole. Both the Italian Constitutional Court and the German Federal Constitutional Court have unresolved differences with the ECJ over the relationship between national and European law.

Turning to the differential rate of adaptation of various parts of the British political system to membership, it is probably true to suggest that Parliament has adapted more slowly than the Civil Service or the Courts. This reflects a difference between the role of overviewer of the system, which is played by Parliament, and the

---

[23] *Official Journal of the European Communities, Annex. Debates of the European Parliament*, 1988–9, No. 2–367/140.

[24] This view is not universal, however. Evidence submitted to the House of Commons Procedure Committee's investigation of parliamentary scrutiny included a memorandum from Dr Juliet Lodge of the University of Hull which affirmed that 'Since the UK's accession to the EC, the House of Commons' scrutiny of EC legislation has been seriously deficient and weaker than that of its counterparts in other EC states' (HC 622-II, p. 154).

practical role in daily business played by the Civil Service and the Courts. The latter institutions have adapted 'on the job' as it were, because they have had to deal with the practical consequences for their daily business of EC membership. This adaptation has, however, been pragmatic to the extent that Butt Philip and Baron even suggest that British civil servants may often not realize that they are involved in implementing EC decisions. Whether this can be seen as adaptation to membership at all must be open to question. It is adaptation to the consequences of membership, but there is no sense in which a learning process about the EC can be said to be in train for civil servants who are adapting only to changes in their working environment without apparently being aware of the source of those changes.

It also seems that Parliament is now catching up with the level of adaptation of the Civil Service and the Courts, and this may be a sign of the weakening of the gatekeeper role of the Government. EC membership considerably increased the scope for executive action, with only weak parliamentary control. The changes which have recently been made in parliamentary procedure for scrutinizing EC affairs reflects a growing resistance from back-benchers to the inadequacy of the previous system. Evidence to the Procedure Committee came from a number of eminent back-bench figures, including the former Leader of the House, John Biffen. But added to that pressure, the Government may also have been responding to a growing pressure to increase the powers of the EP, on the grounds that a democratic deficit had opened up in the EC. Defenders of this view argued that national Parliaments were not an effective check on the actions of Governments in the Council of Ministers, and therefore democratic control could only be ensured through a stronger European Parliament. For the British Government the alternative of stronger control at national level was much preferable to giving more power to a supranational institution, and so there was an incentive to ensure that legitimate criticism of national parliamentary control was met so far as possible.

One other aspect of the Government's attempt to play a gatekeeper role is relevant to the legislative dimension, and that is with respect to the Courts. Where a question of EC law is raised in a national Court, even a low-level Court such as a Social Security Commission, Article 177 of the Treaty of Rome (EEC) allows the national Court to refer the question to the ECJ for a preliminary ruling. This step has become common practice for British Courts, and in keeping with the principle of judicial independence no attempt has been made by the Government to interfere with this example of direct national-EC contact.

Overall, then, the legislative dimension gives little support to the idea that Britain is a semi-detached member of the EC; it does lend some support to the idea of differential rates of adaptation to membership in different parts of the political system, although it also raises the interesting question of whether adaptation is the same as learning to think in European terms; and it suggests that the efforts of the Government to act as gatekeeper for contacts between the national and EC levels has begun to break down in the case of Parliament and has never existed in the case of the Courts.

5

Local Government and the European Community[1]

Jill Preston

INTRODUCTION

Over the last decade an increasing number of EC policies have had a direct impact on local authorities in the UK. For example, many local authorities have been able to take advantage of the resources provided by the EC structural funds and other Community financial instruments.[2]

Local authorities are one element in a complex system of government. In structural terms the UK is a unitary state, in the sense that Parliament is omnipotent. The formal constitutional position is reflected in the traditional doctrine of 'ultra vires'. Parliament has the authority to allocate functions to local authorities or take those functions away. In general terms local authorities may only lawfully engage in activities for which they have statutory authority. The political subordination of local government to central government is illustrated by the range of controls exercised by central government departments over local authorities. Yet in many policy sectors, in spite of the increasing degree of centralization imposed by central government departments since 1979, the

[1] The author would like to acknowledge the assistance given in the research for this chapter by the following organizations: the Association of County Councils, the Association of District Councils, Belfast City Council, Cambridgeshire County Council, Clwyd County Council, the Convention of Scottish Local Authorities, the Department of the Environment, the Department of Trade and Industry, Directorates General V and XVI of the European Commission, Essex County Council, Hull City Council, Humberside County Council, the Northern Ireland Office, the Institute of Environmental Health Officers, the Institute of Trading Standards Administration, the Local Government International Bureau, the Scottish Office, Strathclyde Regional Council, and the Welsh Office.
[2] The EC structural guidance funds are the European Regional Development Fund (ERDF), the European Social Fund (ESF), and the European Agricultural Guidance and Guarantee Fund (EAGGF).

localities, outside Northern Ireland, have a significant degree of autonomy.

In the UK there is not one relationship existing between central and local government but a series of relationships, for as Gerry Stoker notes, 'interdepartmental conflict and inter section disputes, means that local authorities are often faced by a complex and shifting group of allies and enemies at the centre.'[3] In addition, the structure of local government has become increasingly fragmented, for services are provided not only by the principal multi-purpose elected authorities but also by an increasing array of statutory joint authorities and non-statutory committees which are not directly elected. This chapter is concerned with the principal multi-purpose elected local authorities in England, Scotland, Wales, and Northern Ireland.

Local authorities in the UK are involved in the implementation of a range of services that have been influenced by our membership of the European Community. In a number of respects each local authority is a unique political and administrative unit and therefore the manner in which individual authorities have responded to Community membership has been different. In addition, this local response has been crucially influenced by the relationships existing between central and local government. Having made this caveat a number of general points can be made about the impact of Community membership on local government.

This chapter examines the impact of Community membership on local authorities by first looking at the effects in the context of central/local government relations. The second section examines the organizational response within the localities resulting from membership. The third section identifies methods by which the national local government system as well as individual local authorities have attempted to influence the EC policy-making process. The impact on the provision of local services is examined in the fourth section and some of the major themes of the chapter are drawn together in the conclusion.

---

[3] G. Stoker, *The Politics of Local Government* (London, 1988), 131.

COMMUNITY MEMBERSHIP: THE IMPACT ON CENTRAL/
LOCAL GOVERNMENT RELATIONS

During the 1980s the relations existing between central and local
government were characterized by much tension and at times open
conflict.[4] The Conservative Government increased the intensity and
strength of its interventions at the local level and it attempted to
pursue strategies based on control and direction rather than on
consultation and negotiation. In turn this resulted in some resistance and resentment within the localities. In addition, many local
authorities were able to evade certain policies that they disliked
and a wide range of councils, in the context of greater central
control and changing economic circumstances, responded with
policies that were unwelcome to the centre. It is a truism to state
that the style of these relations affected the manner in which local
authorities responded to EC membership.

It is impossible to determine with any accuracy the specific
impact that EC membership has had on central/local government
relations, for one faces the problem of attempting to separate
'European' issues from other factors. But there are certain issues
which may be relevant when viewing these relations. For example,
membership of the EC has given local authorities additional
resources to enable them to pursue objectives that have not always
been well received by national government departments.[5]

In the area of vocational education and general economic
development, the financial resources obtained by local authorities
from the European Regional Development Fund (ERDF) and the
European Social Fund (ESF), have enabled them to pursue policies
in the area of economic intervention, including job creation policies, in spite of tight central government controls. These policies
have not always been popular in central government departments.
In addition, the programme approach to funding in effect commits
central government to provide resources for a period of up to five

---

[4] See P. Dunleavy and R. A. W. Rhodes, 'Government Beyond Whitehall', in H.
Drucker (ed.), *Developments in British Politics 2* (London, 1986); R. A. W. Rhodes,
Beyond Westminster and Whitehall: The Sub-Central Government of Britain
(London, 1988); Stoker, *The Politics of Local Government*.

[5] For example, a number of job creation schemes introduced by left-wing local
authorities were not welcomed by the centre.

years, whereas normally central government prefers to make this type of commitment for a period of one year at a time.[6]

EC legislation has provided local authorities with additional legal powers to pursue their policy objectives. In a number of instances these objectives have not always been consistent with those of central government. For example, in the area of environmental health, various EC directives defining water quality standards, have gone far beyond the wishes of central government. A similar comment can be made about the various EC directives concerned with air quality.

In a number of policy sectors it is clear that sections within the Commission have tried to develop closer links with sub-national units of government. This is particularly true of DG V (Employment, Industrial Relations and Social Affairs), DG XVI (Regional Policy), and DG XXII (Co-ordination of Structural Policies). Since 1989 the implementation of the reformed structural funds has necessitated the establishment of various formal partnerships between local, central, and EC agencies. But within local government circles there has been much disappointment with the way in which central government departments have actually implemented these reforms. There is a general feeling that local authorities have only been approached by central government departments once the key decisions have been made, and then they have been given insufficient time to formulate a considered response, thus reinforcing the belief that central government departments are pursuing a gatekeeping function. It is the responsibility of central government departments to exercise a controlling role in the implementation of the Funds and consequently to exercise significant influence over the structure of the programmes. The criticism from local authority circles is that there has been a lack of genuine consultation in this process. To quote Stephen Barber, the Deputy Director of the Local Government International Bureau, 'partnership is not working as it should, it remains difficult to point to a single major decision that the Department (of Employment) has taken reflecting genuine consultations with the partners.'[7] In spite of pronouncements from

---

[6] The EC introduced a programme approach to funding as opposed to supporting *ad hoc* projects as a way of increasing the impact of Community interventions on specific problems.

[7] Stephen Barber, Deputy Director of the Local Government International Bureau, speaking at a Conference on the European Social Fund, Bristol University,

various officials from the Commission, fears that the partnership approach would result in greater central control have yet to be disproved by experience.

Local authorities both individually and via their various associations can influence policy development. In many areas local authority officers have been involved in European work for a number of years, thus developing extensive knowledge and practical experience. UK civil servants, especially in the regional offices, move around far too frequently to obtain this level of expertise. It is not unusual for civil servants in the regional offices to rely on local authority officials to give guidance on policy interpretation, a situation that clearly gives the local authorities concerned some additional resources in the central/local relationship.

In some policy areas the centre's responsibility for implementing EC legislation has in effect reduced the autonomy of local authorities to deliver a service. For example, the EC's policy of allowing vehicles to have increased axle weights has obvious implications for the highways authorities. Central government has promised financial support via a Transport Supplementary Grant, but in effect this approach has reduced the degree of discretion that local authorities have in determining their own transport priorities.

ORGANIZATIONAL RESPONSE AND RESOURCE IMPLICATIONS

By the mid-1980s most local authorities had developed some type of organizational response to EC membership. A number of authorities established specific EC committees but the majority appeared to deal with EC items within the existing committee system. By the end of the decade a few councils were thinking strategically about the consequences of membership, while others relied on the individual departments most affected to keep themselves updated technically. For example, by the end of the 1980s

---

May 1990. The Local Government International Bureau was established by the Association of County Councils, the Association of District Councils, the Association of Metropolitan Authorities, the Convention of Scottish Local Authorities, and the Association of Local Authorities of Northern Ireland to act as their European and international affairs unit.

Essex, Kent, and Strathclyde Councils had established committees to look specifically at the strategic implications of membership.

The extent of the organizational response has in part depended on the perceived financial opportunity presented by the EC for a particular local authority. For example, all local authorities in the regionally assisted areas have established some type of EC liaison post. In the main these officers tend to deal with the financial implications of membership, leaving individual departments to develop appropriate EC links and information channels. In the area of economic development the EC liaison person tends to have a more direct involvement, for in many local authorities the EC post is found in the department for economic development. With the movement towards 1992 many local authorities have established some type of 1992 officers' working party to look at the corporate issues arising from the completion of the single market. For example, Humberside County Council has developed a 1992 Group centred on its Economic Development Services Department.

Membership of the EC has brought with it important resource implications for individual local authorities. One of the most significant costs of membership is that associated with information-gathering. This activity is particularly expensive if either the Commission or central government is slow to clarify policy guide-lines. For example, in the area of both the ERDF and the ESF many local authorities have had to use extensive resources to try to clarify policy objectives and interpret policy guide-lines. This type of information-gathering from both national and EC agencies is expensive whether an authority is relying on its own local authority association and the Local Government International Bureau, making trips to Brussels, hiring external consultants, or developing its own in-house expertise. Yet by developing alternative channels of communication the constraining influence of government departments acting as gatekeepers of information is somewhat lessened. Thus in some instances local authorities have been able to ease the problems resulting from central departments giving inadequate information and advice.[8]

Information-gathering is a major cost facing the environmental health service, EC legislation and draft legislation as well as

---

[8] Comment made in an interview by a senior officer of Strathclyde Regional Council.

decisions of the European Court being particularly important. The main sources of information are the Institute of Environmental Health Officers, the local authority associations, and other local authorities. Community membership has major resource implications for the trading and consumer-protection services in the area of information-gathering. Before the UK joined the Community, the Institute of Trading Standards Administration (ITSA) put together a training package to assist staff to obtain information on EC items. From 1984 the Institute set up an information service which covers both national and EC law. It is perhaps significant that in a number of policy areas, such as environmental health and trading standards, national government departments are not normally regarded as a major source of information and guidance.

The monitoring procedures required by the Commission when a local authority is in receipt of EC finance are comprehensive in the extreme. In addition, there are resource implications in the disseminating of information to the local community, for example, the business opportunities and threats resulting from the completion of the single market.

LOCAL GOVERNMENT IMPACT ON EC POLICY-MAKING

Local authorities have attempted at times individually and more frequently via their associations and professional institutes to influence the EC policy formulation and implementation processes. This activity has to be viewed within the context of central/local government relationships existing within the UK. For the local authority community attempts to influence EC policy via national government as well as by the more direct lobbying of EC institutions.

Influencing EC Policy-Making via National Government

There is a wide range of national government advisory committees and working parties dealing with European topics which include representation from the local authorities. For example, the Department of the Environment's European Joint Group is composed of members of the Department plus representatives from the local authority associations. This Group meets twice a year to discuss items within the field of regional policy.

In addition, local government interests lobby national government departments centrally and in the regions, in an attempt either to alter a national stand on a proposed policy or to make alteration during the process of implementation. For example, in the area of environmental health, individual local authorities as well as the IEHO, and the local authority associations have lobbied national agencies to keep certain frontier controls in place until the disease of rabies has been eradicated on mainland Europe.

Direct Contacts with the European Institutions

A number of sections within the Commission have a declared intention of developing closer links with regional and local authorities. Local authority interests are represented on a wide range of advisory committees and working groups within the various DGs. For example, the local authority associations are represented in Brussels by the Local Government International Bureau, and in 1989 the consultative Council of Regional and Local Authorities with the European Commission was established. The Council, which is composed of elected members from regional and local councils, serves as a major means of direct dialogue between the Commission and European regional and local government. A wide range of professional bodies representing local authority interests, for example, the ITSA, are involved in the EC policy-making process. In addition, local authorities across Europe with similar interests are coming together to prepare joint advocacy for presentation to the Commission and other relevant bodies; for example, in 1990 the association of North Sea local authorities was established for this purpose.

With the development of a programme approach in the EC structural funds, which requires co-operation across a range of organizations, partnerships in the form of local co-ordinating committees have encouraged closer links between European, national, regional, and local authorities. EC officials as well as national and regional civil servants attend these meetings on a fairly regular basis.

Over the years elected representatives as well as officers from individual local authorities have made trips to Brussels, either on fact-finding missions or to forward their particular interests. Informal relationships between officials in Brussels and those in UK local authorities have always been important, especially in the area of the implementation of the structural funds. By the end of the 1970s a number of authorities in the UK had close informal relationships with sections within the Commission; a small minority of larger authorities having an office in Brussels. This type of informal relationship is particularly useful in determining 'the Commission's thinking' on items such as the interpretation of Fund guide-lines.

Individual local authority groupings as well as individual local authorities at times lobby the European Parliament. In addition, some MEPs have close links with the local authorities in their areas and meet both elected members and officers on a regular basis; the UK's single-member constituencies obviously assist this process. UK local authorities are represented on the European Economic and Social Committee, but it is the Secretary of State for the Environment who in effect decides the UK representatives on this Committee.

THE IMPACT ON LOCAL AUTHORITY SERVICES

In the main, local authorities are concerned with the implementation of nationally determined policies, although as stated earlier in this chapter in many areas there is scope for local initiatives. To examine the impact of EC legislation on local authorities, four policy areas will be reviewed: vocational training, economic development, environmental health, and trading standards and consumer protection. These areas have been chosen because in each case local authorities have been required to make some sort of response to EC policies.

Vocational Education

In England and Wales non-metropolitan counties and metropolitan districts have responsibilities in the area of vocational education, whereas in Scotland the regional councils are the main providers of this service. In Northern Ireland the local authorities do not have any direct responsibilities in this area. In addition to course provision within their colleges, many local authorities are involved in other schemes, for example those run by the Training Agency.

In the provision of mainstream vocational courses many local authorities are using monies under Section 137 of the Local Government Act 1972 to provide various forms of training, especially for the young and long-term unemployed.

Education *per se* is not covered by the Treaty of Rome, although vocational education has always formed part of Community policy. This policy has been slow to develop, but by the end of the 1980s it was beginning to have an increasing impact on local provision. Its major priorities are: easing youth and long-term unemployment, encouraging equality of opportunities, preparing for technological change, supporting the mobility of young people, and encouraging a European dimension within the curriculum.

The European Social Fund (ESF) is one of the main financial instruments supporting vocational education. This Fund provides grant aid for schemes of training, retraining, and resettlement, as well as job creation. In terms of the local provision of services there are clear monetary gains to be had for some local authorities from this Fund. Money obtained from the ESF is genuinely additional and it does not count against total spending. However, it is clear that in some authorities ESF schemes would go ahead even without Community support; but the acquisition of this aid does allow the local authority money to be released and used elsewhere. It is equally clear that some local authorities are able with the benefit of Fund support to extend what they would be doing without this assistance.[9] The application for EC funds, especially from the ESF, has also resulted in less tangible benefits; for example, in developing training schemes many authorities have started to think in a more innovatory way in an attempt to be successful.[10] In recent years greater emphasis has been given by ESF managers to a programme approach to funding. This in turn requires greater team-building within the localities, not only across departments but also across organizations. In a number of instances collaboration developed for an ESF programme has been used for other local activities.[11]

---

[9] Comment made in an interview by a senior officer of Humberside County Council.

[10] Comment made in an interview by a former senior officer of Humberside County Council.

[11] Comment made in an interview by a senior officer of Clwyd County Council.

General Economic Development

Non-metropolitan counties and metropolitan districts in England and Wales and the regional councils in Scotland have responsibilities for the development of infrastructure. All types of local authority outside Northern Ireland have the right to pursue economic development activities.

The EC is particularly concerned with encouraging economic development in the poorer regions, thus improving 'the social and economic cohesion' within the Community.[12] A number of EC policies have important implications for local authority economic development activities, for example, regional policy, the common agricultural policy, and competition policy.

The European Regional Development Fund (ERDF), is the main policy instrument concerned with correcting regional imbalances. In general terms local authorities located in the UK regionally assisted areas can benefit from this source of funding. The ERDF can provide opportunities for appropriate local authorities to develop infrastructure projects and although there is no additionality in resource terms, it has helped to maintain regional aid in the UK above levels it would have been if it were not for the ERDF. Local authorities which are in receipt of grant aid benefit to the extent of not having to pay interest charges. In addition, the programme approach has provided local authorities with the substantial benefit of a predictable five-year package of support which commits other organizations to provide multi-annual investment. Evidence would suggest that in spite of rigorous central government control of local authority capital expenditure, receipts from the Fund do enable some schemes to be tried which would not be possible without this source of finance.[13]

Environmental Health

In England and Wales significant environmental functions are the responsibility of the district authorities, whereas in Northern Ireland some, but not all, of these functions are the responsibility

---

[12] See Article 130A of the Single European Act, 1987.
[13] Comment made in an interview by a senior officer of Humberside County Council.

of the localities. Environmental issues were not mentioned in the original Treaty of Rome, but this situation was rectified in 1986 by the signing of the Single European Act.[14] However, in 1972 the Paris Summit of Heads of Government decided that the Community should develop an environmental policy and between 1973 and 1987 four action programmes were presented.

The development of EC environmental policy has been slow, and frequently intent has not been followed by action. Legislation in the area of environmental policy normally takes the form of directives, and in many areas the interval between a statement of intent and practical compliance has been substantial. In addition, there are a number of instances where the content has been altered during the process of policy implementation.

In some areas of environmental policy EC legislation has provided local authorities with additional and more specific powers to achieve their overall professional objectives and thus provide a better service. For example, in the area of water for domestic and industrial use, the standards required for compliance with EC legislation are far higher than previous national legislation. And prior to the EC's Bathing Water Quality Directive 1975, UK legislation in this area did not exist.

Prior to the implementation of various EC directives on air quality, there were no specific standards in the UK, only general statements referring to air 'that may be prejudicial to health'. In terms of the control of atmospheric pollution, successive British Governments only stated that 'firms should do as much as they can afford'. The EC Commission has developed a wide range of parameters; these parameters can be tested and where necessary legal action can be taken.

In some policy sectors local authority environmental health officers have attempted to ensure that European standards are as high as those in operation in the UK, for example, the status of their own professional qualification. The profession of environmental health officer (EHO) is unique in the UK and Ireland. On mainland Europe veterinarians are responsible for some environmental services, but most of the areas covered by EHOs in the UK are the responsibility of veterinary surgeons. As a result of EC

[14] See Article 130R of the Single European Act 1987. The Act was signed in 1986, but came into effect in 1987.

legislation veterinary surgeons as well as EHOs have to be present during the cutting of meat in slaughter houses. The EHOs are concerned that their status could be reduced to that of a veterinarian.

Trading Standards and Consumer Protection

In the UK the trading standards function covers a comprehensive range of services, including weights and measures, fair trading, trade descriptions, consumer credit, and consumer protection. In England and Wales this group of services is provided by the non-metropolitan counties and the metropolitan districts. In Scotland most of these services are provided by the regional councils, whereas in Northern Ireland consumer protection is a district council responsibility.

The EC has legislated in a number of areas which directly affect the trading standards and consumer protection departments. For example, product safety, product liability, consumer credit, and trade descriptions. It has been estimated that in 1987 25 per cent of legislation enforced by local government in this area emanated from Brussels, and there is a generally held belief that by 1992 nearly 80 per cent of trading standards legislation will be amended to assist harmonization.

In some areas of consumer legislation, EC law tends to be more consumer orientated than previous national legislation. For example, much of the legislation under the Consumer Protection Act 1987 would not have become law without appropriate EC directives. This Act makes it possible for the consumer to claim directly from the manufacturer; previously a claim could only be made to the retailer and then it was for the consumer to show that there had been some negligence.

Quality assurance is becoming an increasingly important issue as organizations seek accreditation. With the mutual recognition of national standards and technical regulations, an EC mark will provide a basic passport or presumption that a product conforms with the safety requirements in question. For example, in most cases what is acceptable in Germany will automatically be acceptable in the UK. This situation is already resulting in extra work for trading standards departments, as they must check to see if a product has in fact satisfied its own national standards. UK officials are beginning to check national standards with colleagues in other member states. A major source of assistance is the local authority co-ordinating body on trading standards, LACOTS.

The trading standards profession tries to ensure that EC law does not result in lower standards than those found in the UK. In the area of consumer credit, UK standards are in advance of practice in other member states; for example, UK national legislation defines what can be advertised. The Institute of Trading Standards Administration is concerned that if a European compromise is reached, then consumers in the UK could lose some protection.

CONCLUSIONS

With the movement towards the completion of the single European market, it is clear that the Community will have an increasing impact on UK local authorities. To take one example, it was stated earlier in the chapter that in the area of Trading Standards it has been estimated that by 1992 80 per cent of legislation will be amended to assist harmonization. In addition, most local authorities have set up some type of 1992 machinery.

Existing EC legislation which attempts to open up public procurement contracts to greater competition within the EC has not been very successful in the UK. For a number of reasons firms in other member states have not submitted tenders for these contracts. So although the local authorities have the expense of advertising their larger works and supply contracts, as yet very little benefit has accrued to them. With the move to the single market, the Community is tightening up the existing directives with the aim of improving the transparency of tendering and award procedures and opening contracts to greater competition. It seems likely that local authorities will benefit from these changes.

Evidence would suggest that the EC has had only a limited impact on local authority employment policies. The social dimensions of the single market are likely to be felt in areas such as health and safety at work, equal opportunities, and the increasing harmonization of conditions of employment, such as maternity/paternity leave, and dismissal procedures. Obviously these developments will have resource implications for local authorities.

What general themes emerge from this overview of the impact of

Jill Preston

EC membership on local government? Clearly membership has provided some authorities with a significant funding opportunity. In a number of respects Community membership has had an impact on central/local government relations. For example, in some functional areas EC legislation has given local authorities additional powers to provide better services, but in other areas the requirements of Community legislation have in effect reduced the level of local autonomy. The Commission has attempted to develop closer formal and informal links with regional and local authorities, but in the UK national government is able to dominate much local activity. In terms of information-gathering, national government departments are frequently 'the gatekeepers' of information, although it is significant that in a number of functional areas the localities have other sources of information, notably their professional institutes and local authority associations. These sources help to ease any reliance on national government.

In an earlier chapter, the UK national government was described as a semi-detached Community partner. This attitude has had an impact on local government. Firstly, during the early days of membership local authorities in general were slow to respond to the opportunities and demands posed by Community membership. In part this slow, and at times apathetic reaction can be viewed as a response to the Centre's 'neutral stance' *vis-à-vis* membership. Secondly, the UK bureaucracy has not viewed European affairs as a prestigious career path. Therefore at both national and regional levels civil servants have tended not to specialize in European matters. So in a number of functional areas there is as much expertise and experience in the localities as in regional or central administration.

6

The Political Parties[1]

Nigel Ashford

THE role of the political parties in determining Britain's approach to membership, policies, and future of the EC has been great. They contributed to the slow adjustment of British politics by the failure to present clear and consistent views of Britain's relations with Europe; undermined the role of government as gatekeeper by domesticating membership of the EC as an issue but failing to develop views on European issues; and reinforced the semi-detached image of Britain in the rest of the Community by their failure to co-operate effectively with their fellow parties in the EC. Europe could have been integrated more effectively into British politics if either there had been a party consensus that membership of the EC was in the national interest, or there had been a sharp distinction between the parties on their attitudes to Europe, which would have encouraged a clearer appreciation of the issues involved. The British parties failed to pursue either of these options.

Three factors explain the response of the parties to Europe: the adversarial nature of British politics; the considerable intra-party divisions on this issue; and the threat posed by integration to the parties' ideological self-image. Firstly, the convention of adversarial politics is for the opposition parties to oppose the policies of the government, even while behaviour in government may reflect a high degree of continuity. This was seen in Labour's opposition to Europe in 1962, 1971, and 1980. It can be contrasted with more consensual styles of politics such as that in Germany. Parties in government have been reluctant to lead public opinion into acceptance of the constraints imposed upon the UK as a result of our interdependency, so that any movement towards integration is used as a weapon by the opposition to attack the incumbent Government. Evidence of a lack of enthusiasm for Europe amongst the

---

[1] I am grateful for their comments to other members of the study group, especially Neill Nugent, and also to Scott Hamilton.

electorate has reinforced this tendency. So even when a high degree of consensus has emerged among the party élites, such as on the virtues of membership of the EC or of entry into the Exchange Rate Mechanism of the EMS, this has not been clearly articulated to the public. This has also made it difficult for them to co-operate with continental parties who have experience of coalition governments.

Secondly, intra-party divisions have hindered the articulation of clear positions with regard to the EC. The Conservative party had a vocal but distinct minority against British membership, but has been more seriously split on the future direction of integration. Labour has suffered from serious divisions on membership, and will continue to be divided on the degree of willingness to surrender sovereignty. In the UK political issues are structured in the media through inter-party conflicts, reflecting the adversarial style. When differences between the parties are obscure, those issues are largely ignored, and when issues divide the parties internally, they are discussed primarily as evidence of a divided party, with predicted negative electoral consequences. The result has been that the EC has been a major topic for intra-party management.

A third factor is the threat posed to the ideological self-images of the two main parties by European integration. The Conservative party has presented itself as the embodiment of the national interest, and has claimed that Conservative Governments have helped to maintain Britain as a significant power in the world, a position which would be threatened by Labour. The advocacy of integration undermines these claims, as it would require acceptance that some short-term national interests may have to be sacrificed for broader and more long-term interests, and that even under Conservative Governments the capacity of Britain to maintain sovereignty in global affairs has been severely diminished. The Conservatives are also the party of free markets, but have been reluctant to acknowledge that the creation of a single European market requires the surrender of some economic sovereignty. The basic theme of Labour party ideology has been the parliamentary road to socialism. The EC is perceived to threaten both the goal, socialism, and the means, parliamentary sovereignty. Full acceptance of the EC therefore required a re-examination of the ideological principles of both main parties.

By the beginning of the 1990s, there did appear to be a consensus on Britain's membership, and the emergence of sharper ideological differences between the parties on the future of Europe, most notably on their approach to 1992 and the internal market; whether it should be based on free deregulated markets or have a substantial element of social regulation. However the degree of acceptance of loss of sovereignty to supranational institutions still divided the parties internally more than it divided them from each other.

In the rest of this chapter we shall examine the development of party policies towards Europe, policy-making within the parties on Europe, and the relations of the British parties with other EC parties.

DEVELOPMENT OF POLICIES ON EUROPEAN INTEGRATION

Conservatives

Under the inspiration of Winston Churchill, the Conservatives emerged as the more European of the two main parties in the immediate post-war period. However, despite the existence within the party of a number of Europeans, after Churchill came to power in 1951, his Government and that of his successor Anthony Eden felt unable to join any European organization with federalist goals and a commitment to political integration.

The first application to join the EC, by the Conservative Government in 1961, reflected a whole series of considerations such as the decline of Britain as a world power, the growing economic and political independence of the Commonwealth, Britain's relative economic weakness, the unexpected economic success of the EC, and the shift of élite opinion in favour of membership. The conversion of the Conservative party to Europe has been described as 'one of the more remarkable of Macmillan's political achievements, for the whole enterprise stood in flat contradiction to all the traditional instincts of the party, which were for national sovereignty at any price'.[2] Macmillan himself feared that it would

[2] T. Lindsay and M. Harrington, *The Conservative Party 1918–79* (London, 1979), 214.

be a repeat of the 1846 repeal of the Corn Laws which split the Tory party and excluded it from power for much of the nineteenth century. However, this view neglected the substantial support within the party for Europe: amongst ministers and prominent back-benchers, in the business community, in the pro-Conservative Press, and in the constituencies among the more politically minded activisits.[3]

The case for entry based upon the contribution to Britain's prosperity through increased trade, and to peace by strengthening Western Europe against the Soviet Union, had a powerful appeal to Conservatives once it was clearly articulated. The obstacles to membership—EFTA, the Commonwealth, agriculture, and sovereignty—failed to mobilize substantial opposition within the party. Special arrangements were made for Britain's EFTA partners; the Commonwealth had lost much of its traditional appeal in its transition from the Empire; agricultural interests were divided on the issue; and the EC had failed to develop into a supranational institution and therefore was not the threat to sovereignty that had been feared at its creation.

De Gaulle's veto in 1963 shook Macmillan and the Conservatives and contributed to the crisis of confidence within the party in the early 1960s. However, by 1965 the party had renewed its commitment to Europe, noticeably by the election as leader in 1965 of Edward Heath, the chief negotiator on the membership talks, and by the strength of Tory Gaullism which argued for a strategy of Franco-British co-operation to obtain British entry, followed by a close partnership based on a shared vision of a 'Europe of Nations'. The Conservatives supported the Labour Government's applications in 1967 and 1969, while being critical of their approach.

Heath as Prime Minister, after his election victory of 1970, quickly established British membership as his major priority. There was concern about the size of Conservative parliamentary support, with the sense that Europe was not an electoral asset, the emergence of Enoch Powell as leader of the anti-market Conservatives, and a feeling of a lack of knowledge and consultation within the party. The party conducted a massive education campaign, to provide

---

[3] N. Ashford, 'The European Community', in Z. Layton-Henry, *Conservative Party Politics* (London, 1980), 99.

factual information, to counter specific concerns, such as over horticulture, and to reassure party activists, members, and voters of the wisdom of membership. The 1971 Conference voted over-whelmingly for entry, by 2,474 votes to 324 against, and the parliamentary party voted on the principle on 28 October 1971 by 282 in favour and 39 against with only two abstentions.

The dominance of the Europeans within the party can be attributed to a number of factors: the appeal to loyalty to the leader and the party; the whipping of the parliamentary party; the consensus among the business, financial, agricultural, and press supporters of the party; the hardening of support among party activists; the shift in pubic opinion; the opposition of Labour; and the weakness of the anti-marketeers.[4]

By the 1975 referendum the internal opposition was so weak that there was no doubt that the party would strongly endorse a 'Yes' vote, and it submerged its organization fully into the all-party Britain-in-Europe campaign. This was done to strengthen the support of Labour pro-marketeers, to maximize the pro-market Labour vote, to avoid splits within the party, and to limit the damage amongst anti-market Tory voters.

The election of Mrs Thatcher as leader in 1975 did not alter the party's commitment to membership, but led to less enthusiasm and a lower priority for the EC. Mrs Thatcher was a convinced, rather than an enthusiastic European. In her major statement on Europe as Opposition Leader she declared, 'We are the European Party in the British Parliament and among the British people and we want to venture wholeheartedly with our partners in this joint venture.'[5] She articulated the main goals of Conservative European policy as a stronger foreign policy role for the Community, opposition to bureaucratization, and reform of the Common Agricultural Policy. As someone with little foreign policy experience, she was very active in visiting fellow centre-right parties in West Germany, Italy, and the Netherlands. *The Right Approach*, the interim manifesto of 1976, stated with regard to Europe: 'The European Community provides the framework not only for many of our domestic policies but also increasingly for the development of our foreign policies . . . Our view is that those who want it to succeed would do well

---

[4] Ibid. 106.
[5] M. Thatcher, *Europe As I See It* (London, 1977).

to concentrate on what is practicable and what is attainable. But, while it is not sensible to set Utopian and unreal targets, we do need to recognize that there are many problems, beyond the range of national governments, which can best be dealt with on a European level.'[6]

The Thatcher approach to Europe is summed up in the 1983 manifesto: whole-hearted commitment to membership and the promotion of British interests within the EC. From the Dublin summit of 1979, when Mrs Thatcher first demanded 'our money back', to the Fontainebleau Summit of 1984, when the budgetary problem was at least temporarily resolved, the issue of the budgetary contribution dominated Britain's relations with the Community. The second issue which the early Thatcher Government pursued was 'budgetary discipline', that the EC should exercise severe restraint on its expenditure, most notably in agriculture. This reflected the application of the Thatcherite approach to the EC.

The Conservatives were sensitive to the accusation, both internally and externally, that they were unenthusiastic Europeans. This was partly a question of style. Mrs Thatcher was unimpressed with great rhetorical flourishes in favour of European unity, especially when she felt they were frequently a mask to hide national interests, such as over the budgetary contributions or the CAP. The Conservatives wished to present a positive set of proposals for the EC, while avoiding movement towards federalism as implied in the EP's Draft Treaty on European Union. This approach was presented in *Europe: The Future*,[7] which was largely the work of the Foreign Secretary, Sir Geoffrey Howe. The first theme was to strengthen the EC's role in foreign policy. The Government recognized that Britain was a middle-ranking power, which was unable to exercise significant influence in the world alone, but could take a leading role in a common foreign policy for Europe. The system of European Political Co-operation (EPC) also had the advantage that it was conducted on intergovernmental lines. The second theme of the paper was the creation of an internal market. This reflected the belief that deregulation and open competition would improve

---

[6] Conservative Central Office, *The Right Approach* (London, 1976), 67–8.
[7] Her Majesty's Government, 'Europe: The Future' *Journal of Common Market Studies*, 23 (1984), 74–81.

employment and the standard of living, without substantial increased expenditure, and demonstrated a positive commitment to the goals of the Treaty of Rome. The paper resisted institutional reforms which would move the EC in a federalist direction.

In response to what she saw as growing federalist pressure from the European Commission, Mrs Thatcher presented her alternative vision of Europe in her Bruges speech to the College of Europe in September 1988.[8] The six principles outlined there were intergovernmentalism, practical reform of the CAP and the budget, policies to promote enterprise and to deregulate the European economy, free trade with the rest of the world rather than a 'Fortress Europe', and a growing role in defence. The speech was an attempt to present a positive approach to Europe, but it was interpreted as negative in tone on the continent and in the UK. It stimulated a debate within the Conservative party in which Edward Heath, Michael Heseltine, Lord Cockfield (the former Commissioner), and Lord Plumb (the President of the EP), criticized her attitude to Europe as being too negative and combative rather than co-operative and constructive, a criticism which gained support after the poor results in the 1989 European elections. This debate came to focus around the issue of European monetary union, which led to the resignations of the Chancellor, Nigel Lawson, and the Deputy Prime Minister, Sir Geoffrey Howe, and eventually contributed to that of Mrs Thatcher herself.

Labour

From the beginning of the debate on integration the themes were established of the protection of socialism and sovereignty from European infringements. The immediate post-war Labour Government was hostile towards any attempts to create a United Europe which would have threatened their own plans for the nationalization of British industry, state economic planning, and the creation of a national welfare state. They persisted in the belief that Britain could play a major role in the world, particularly as the head of an emerging Commonwealth. Labour supported British participation in intergovernmental organizations, such as the Western European Union, the North Atlantic Treaty Organization, and the Council of

---

[8] M. Thatcher, *Britain and Europe: The Bruges Speech* (London, 1988).

Europe, but it firmly rejected supranationalism as represented by the ECSC, Euratom, and the EEC.

In opposition during the 1950s, Labour gave little attention to Europe. When Macmillan made the application in 1961, Labour was initially unsure of its response, marked by its decision to abstain on the issue of principle in the Commons vote. There was a group of fervent Europeans, who also supported the leader Hugh Gaitskell in his attempt to move Labour in the direction of social democracy, along the lines of the 1959 Bad Godesberg programme of the German Social Democrats. Membership was bitterly opposed by the left, and more significantly by the trade unions, which envisaged a reduction in their industrial muscle and limitations on the introduction of socialist economic policies in a Europe devoted to the free movement of factors of production. Gaitskell was personally uncertain on the issue. What finally turned him against entry was his deep commitment to a multi-racial Commonwealth and lobbying by Commonwealth Prime Ministers from many developing countries. Much to the disappointment of some of his closest supporters, he rejected membership in a passionate speech to the 1962 Labour Conference, with a reference to the betrayal of 'a thousand years of history'.

Labour came to power in 1964 on a platform of stringent conditions of entry, which effectively excluded membership, but the Wilson Government became convinced of the benefits of entry. A number of factors were involved in this shift: Britain's continuing economic crisis; the recognition that the technological transformation at the heart of Labour's programme required substantial research and development that Britain could not afford alone; the growing rift between Labour and the United States over the Vietnam War; and the existence of a group of articulate supporters of Europe in the parliamentary party, including a strong advocate in the Foreign Secretary, George Brown. In 1967 a second application was made, with the support of the Conservatives, with 36 Labour rebels and 40 to 50 abstentions in the Commons. This application met the same fate as the first, a French veto, but with the resignation of de Gaulle the application was revived in December 1969.

Under pressure from the left, which had been sharply critical of the Wilson Government, Labour in opposition reversed its support for membership. The claim that this was due to the unacceptable

Tory terms was undermined by the statement of George Thomson, who had been Labour's negotiator with the Six, that the terms would have been acceptable to the Labour Cabinet. The 1970 Conference only narrowly defeated a motion calling for opposition to entry under any Tory terms. In July 1971 a special conference rejected the negotiated terms, and the National Executive Committee (NEC) recommended all-out opposition, which was endorsed by the October Conference. On 28 October 1971 Labour voted against entry in the Commons, but 69 Labour MPs led by Roy Jenkins supported entry and 20 abstained, defying a three-line whip. Under considerable pressure within the party, the Labour pro-Europeans were willing to abstain or if necessary support the Government to enable the Bill to pass. This led to a state of civil war within the party.

This reversal of position, which reflected the fact that Labour had never been enthusiastic, led to severe criticism in the Press condemning the party for irresponsibility, inconsistency, and opportunism. Earlier support was largely due to Labour being in power, and there was much talk of insisting on conditions incompatible with membership. The emphasis on the importance of the terms during the Labour negotiations made it easy for Labour MPs to support the negotiations and later to oppose the Tory terms. There was a natural tendency to oppose the Conservative Government, especially one that was deeply unpopular in Labour and trade union circles. The party itself had also moved to the left, partly in response of the sense of failure at the lack of achievements of the 1960s Labour Government.

King has carefully explained how Wilson's attempt to reconcile the various factions within the Labour party and to retain EC membership without a deep split in the party led Labour to endorse the idea of renegotiation followed by an opportunity for the electorate to endorse the final decision, which eventually led the Labour Government to hold a referendum on Britain's membership in 1975.[9] The terms of entry were renegotiated, but it was widely felt that the changes introduced were marginal. However, the renegotiation did provide an excuse for Wilson and others to endorse continued membership under the revised terms. The Cabi-

---

[9] A. King, *Britain Says Yes: The 1975 Referendum on the Common Market* (Washington, DC, 1977).

inet voted by 16 to 7 in favour of Europe and agreed that the principle of collective responsibility should not apply during the campaign. A majority of the parliamentary party voted against membership by 137 in favour, 145 against, and 33 abstentions. The NEC recommended opposition to membership and a special conference voted overwhelmingly against the recommendation of its own Cabinet. The basis for the anti-European campaign in the country was Constituency Labour parties and trade unions. However, the referendum result appeared to be accepted by anti-marketeers as decisive; Tony Benn declared, 'It is clear that by an overwhelming majority the British people have voted to stay in, and I am sure everybody would want to accept that. That has been the principle of all of us who have advocated the referendum.'[10]

In opposition after the 1979 election defeat, the left again reasserted its power, most notably by the election of Michael Foot as leader, and through three fundamental constitutional reforms designed to strengthen the grip of the left: the election of the leader by an electoral college, the introduction of the reselection process for MPs, and the control of the election manifesto by the NEC. One major symbol of this change was the 1980 Conference decision to call for withdrawal from the EC, endorsed in 1981, which contributed to the creation of the Social Democratic Party (SDP). The 1983 election manifesto stated that Labour would 'open immediate negotiations with our EEC partners, and introduce the necessary legislation, to prepare for Britain's withdrawal from the EEC, to be completed well within the lifetime of the Labour Government'.[11] Withdrawal was an essential element in the Alternative Economic Strategy of the left, which would involve strict import controls, renationalization, and reflation.

Hostility to Europe was one of the factors that contributed to the image of a left-wing party which many commentators believed contributed to Labour's massive defeat in 1983. Soon after the election the process began of extricating the party from that commitment. In Neil Kinnock's manifesto for the leadership, he stated, 'By 1988 Britain will have been a member of the Common Market for 15 years. That does not make withdrawal impossible . . . After that length of time however, withdrawal should be

[10] Ibid. 133.
[11] Labour party, *A New Hope for Britain* (London, 1983).

regarded as a last resort that is considered only if and when the best interests of the British people can be feasibly safeguarded by other means.'[12] By the 1987 election the policy of withdrawal had been dropped. By the 1989 European elections, Labour was presenting itself as the more European party. In the 1989 Policy Review, mention of withdrawal was dropped and a more positive tone adopted: 'We believe that Europe must be a Community as well as a Market. We want a community that modernises industry, protects the environment, generates jobs, advances women's rights and helps the regions.'[13] The Review also endorsed further enlargement, developing EPC, and strengthening Westminster's scrutiny of EC affairs.

The abandonment of its policy of withdrawal can be attributed to several factors.[14] First, there was the belief that it was an obstacle to the return to power. Labour's rival for the anti-Conservative vote was the Liberal-SDP Alliance, which was strongly European. Even many strong opponents came to realize that acceptance of membership was a price that had to be paid to form a credible opposition. Second, there was a change of attitude among trade unions, who began to feel that their exclusion from power by the Thatcher Government meant that they would have to look elsewhere for political influence, and that the European Community, in the form of a Social Europe as articulated by the President of the Commission, Jacques Delors, provided a more sympathetic environment. Particularly important was the experience of working within the European Trade Union Confederation (ETUC) and the Economic and Social Committee. Thirdly, the experience of the Mitterrand Government in France between 1981 and 1986 suggested that socialist reflation in one country was not feasible. Fourthly, many intellectuals on the left came to take the view that the internationalization of capital made impossible a policy of domestic expansionism combined with controls on imports, foreign exchange, credit, and foreign investment. Expansionism and interventionism could only be achieved through international institutions, and the EC, for all its faults, was the most

[12] N. Kinnock, *A Summary of Views* (London, 1983).

[13] Labour party, *Meet the Challenge, Make the Change: Labour's Policy Review for the 1990s* (London, 1989), 79.

[14] J. Grahl and P. Teague, 'The British Labour Party and the European Community', *Political Quarterly*, 59 (1988), 72–85.

plausible instrument. *New Socialist* magazine encouraged a dialogue with socialists in the rest of the Community who had long come to a similar conclusion. A fourth factor was the increased influence of the Scots in the party leadership, led by John Smith. The Scots had always been more sympathetic to European co-operation, going back to 'the Auld Alliance' with France, and were less sensitive to concerns about sovereignty since Scotland already shared it within the UK. The Labour party in Scotland was also eager to counter the Scottish National Party (SNP) appeal of an independent Scotland in Europe. A fifth factor was the transformation of Kinnock's own views, arising partly from electoral considerations, but also from his contacts with fellow socialist leaders which forced him to re-examine his previously anti-European views. Labour fought the successful 1989 European Elections on the platform of the creation of a Social Europe, EC regional and environmental policies, equal rights for women and ethnic minorities, and a European peace policy. Divisions within Labour still ran deep but were hidden by being in opposition and by the desire to present a united front to the electorate.

Centre Parties

The Liberal party was an early advocate of a federal Europe,[15] which was consistent with Liberal ideas of internationalism, peace through international co-operation, free trade, and the dispersal of the power of the nation state up to international institutions and down to the regions. This position met opposition only from a minority of free traders. Thus the party urged membership of the ECSC in 1951, and of the EEC and Euratom in 1957. A major concern was the development of common European defence and foreign policies. 'Although Liberals have all along supported European economic integration, they have always laid the greatest stress on the need for a political union.'[16] The replacement of national sovereign states was felt necessary for the achievement of world peace and the creation of a Europe of the Regions. The Liberals supported all the applications for EC membership by both Conserv-

[15] A. Butt Philip, 'The Liberals and Europe', in V. Bogdanor, *Liberal Party Politics* (Oxford, 1983), 217–40.
[16] Liberal party, *The Liberal Programme for Europe* (London, 1975).

ative and Labour Governments, and campaigned actively for a Yes vote in the 1975 referendum; but they had little influence over European policy, except for the pressure that they placed upon the minority Labour Government during the Lib-Lab pact of March 1977 to support direct elections to the European Parliament.

The leaders of the Social Democratic party (SDP) formed in March 1981 (Roy Jenkins, David Owen, Shirley Williams, William Rodgers) had led the pro-European faction in the Labour party during the passage of the European Communities Bill. That experience had created a sense of cohesion and emphasized their fundamental differences with the left. Jenkins was President of the European Commission in 1977–81, and his return to British politics provided one of the sparks for the creation of the SDP; but the Labour Conference decision to vote for withdrawal was one of the major factors which led this group to decide to depart from the Labour party. Ian Bradley stated, 'Of all the SDP's policies, commitment to Britain's continued membership of the EEC is the most widely and strongly held by the leadership and its activists.'[17]

The Labour Europeans had experienced close co-operation with Liberals during the Britain-in-Europe campaign in the referendum. The SDP's Europeanism made co-operation with the Liberals in this area at least fairly simple. However they did not all share the Liberal commitment to federalism. This caused some difficulties in agreeing the joint manifesto for the 1984 European elections, *United for a Democratic Europe*, when references to the EP's Draft Treaty of European Union had to be dropped and there was a rewording of references to the exercise of the veto. The other problem was defence, over whether the emphasis should be on the value of European arms co-operation, as Owen desired, or on Europe's contribution to world peace. In the 1989 European elections, after the split with Owen, the Liberal Democrats were able explicitly to support a federal European Union.

Other Parties

The SNP was consistently against membership of the European Community until 1983. It argued that the EC took power even further away from the Scottish people. Its manifesto for October

---

[17] I. Bradley, *Breaking the Mould* (London, 1981), 124.

1974 declared, 'The SNP opposed British entry basically on political grounds of opposition to the centralist thinking inherent in the
Treaty of Rome, and in the belief that, within the Common Market,
not only Scotland, but the United Kingdom, would find its quality
and standards of life deteriorating.'[18]

After its unsuccessful campaign against Europe in the referendum, with Scotland voting 58.4 per cent Yes, SNP policy was that
it would participate actively in EC institutions in order to further
Scottish interests, but that when a Scottish Government was formed
a referendum of the Scottish people would be held on the question
of withdrawal. An attempt to oppose participation in the elections
to the European Parliament was defeated at the 1977 Conference
by 384 votes to 315. The initial implication was that the SNP
would campaign in any such referendum for withdrawal, but over
time, notably in the 1983 manifesto, the tone became much more
friendly towards the EC. In 1988 the SNP launched a new slogan
of 'Scotland within Europe', which would involve an independent
Scotland negotiating for full membership of the EC.

The factors leading to this change were: the success of Winifred
Ewing, 'Madame Ecosse', as the MEP for the Highlands and
Islands in obtaining publicity both within Scotland and the rest of
Europe for the SNP and Scottish interests; the recognition that the
fear of isolation was a factor in the lack of support for independence; the belief that the SNP required a credible foreign policy; the
establishment of co-operation with other regionalist parties
throughout Europe, and the adoption of the idea of a Europe of
the regions; and finally the awareness of the considerable economic
advantages for Scotland of membership of the EC, most notably in
regional aid.

Plaid Cymru, the Welsh Nationalists, opposed British membership on similar grounds to those of the SNP up to the 1975
referendum, when 64.8 per cent of Wales voted Yes. It then
changed its policy to one of reform of the EC to turn it into a much
looser organization, including the rejection of any defence role, the
end of the CAP, and the abandonment of the free movement of
capital and labour. This would require wholesale revision of both

---

[18] Scottish National party, *Election Manifesto for October 1974* (Edinburgh,
1974).

the Treaty of Rome and the subsequent Single European Act, and would clearly be unacceptable to the EC.

In Northern Ireland, the Official Unionists remain totally opposed to British membership, but recognizing that withdrawal is unlikely send member to the European Parliament seeking to protect Northern Ireland's interest in agriculture and fishing. The Democratic Unionist party, under Ian Paisley MEP, remains totally opposed to membership and he has used the EP as a platform to denounce Popish influences in the EC. The moderate Catholic SDLP, under the leadership of MEP John Hume, supports membership and a positive approach to Europe as a means to reduce the divide in Ireland, while the pro-IRA Sinn Fein are against a capitalist EC.

The Green party is sharply critical of the EC on the grounds that it is developing into another superpower perhaps with its own nuclear weapons, that 1992 would place economic growth before environmental protection, and that the EC is centralizing power, contrary to their demands for a more decentralized society. They successfully used the 1989 European elections to promote themselves as a party, attracting 15 per cent of the vote, but failed to win any seats.

Both the neo-Fascist National Front and the Communist parties have always advocated immediate withdrawal.

INTER-PARTY RELATIONS

Neither the Conservative party nor the Labour party has been able successfully to establish close relationships with similar parties in the EC, illustrating the semi-detached nature of Britain's relationship with the rest of the EC. Inter-party relations have been conducted in three forums: the party groups in the EP, transnational party federations, and at the national level.

Conservatives

The Conservatives have no natural allies in the EC, outside the Danish Conservatives, due to the different nature of social and political cleavages in most of the rest of Europe. On the continent the centre-right has mainly developed either as Christian Democrat parties with a strongly Christian and usually Catholic orientation, or, as secular and professional middle-class Liberal parties. The Conservatives have sought to alleviate this problem at three levels: by co-operation with other party groups in the EP, the creation of the transnational European Democrat Union, and the encouragement of bilateral and multilateral links with other parties.

When Britain joined the EC, there was considerable discussion about whether the Conservative MEPs should join the already existing Christian Democrat group, which was strongly urged by the German Christian Democrat Union (CDU). Eventually it was decided to form their own group, first called the European Conservative Group and then, in an attempt to improve inter-party relations, the European Democrat Group (EDG). However approaches to the Christian Democrats, led by Edward Heath, were rebuffed by the Italian, Benelux, and French parties, who felt that the Conservatives were too secular, too right-wing, and too class-based. The Conservatives reluctantly created their own group, in order to gain the financial and organizational advantages that it provided.

The EDG is dominated by British Conservatives, with a few Danish Conservatives and Centre Democrats, and until 1989, the Spanish Allianza Popular. They have developed a close working relationship with the Christian Democrats, co-operating on committees, having representation at each other's meetings, engaging in extensive consultation before voting, and sometimes having joint spokesmen and joint group meetings. Central to this co-operation is the close relationship with the CDU. The EDG is part of the centre-right coalition which dominated the EP until 1989, and was able to elect a succession of centre-right Presidents, including Lord Plumb. However the centre-right is heterogeneous, including: the Christian Democratic European People's party (EPP), who have a substantial left wing; the Liberals, who include the Gaullists and Ireland's Fianna Fáil; as well as the EDG. The EDG has had considerable influence within the coalition because of its size and strong degree of cohesion, assisted by an efficient whipping system, and a high level of attendance at plenaries and committees. However the history of Britain's lack of commitment to European unity, the British experience of coalition-style politics, hostility towards Mrs Thatcher, the lack of appreciation of the political situation in other countries, and the perception of the EDG as a national interest group made them a source of suspicion among the other groups. Their position was further undermined by the loss of 13 seats in the 1989 European elections.

The EDG is faced with the problem that while it has substantial advantages in terms of finance, staff, and opportunities to speak, it is increasingly isolated from other nationalities. With the movement of their Spanish allies to the EPP and the loss of seats in the 1989 election, the EDG, under the leadership of Sir Christopher Prout, made an application to join the EPP in July 1989, but the question of membership was deferred for two years because of Italian and Dutch opposition. Soon after becoming Prime Minister, John Major used his good relationship with Chancellor Kohl to promote British entry into the EPP.

The Conservatives are very conscious of their relative isolation from other parties. They were therefore the main instigator, with the CDU, of the creation of the European Democrat Union (EDU), which emerged out of a series of informal gatherings known as the Inter-Party Meeting. The necessity to demonstrate co-operation with other parties led them to seek the creation of a transnational party organization which would bring together the centre-right non-socialist parties. The EDU was launched in 1978 with a declaration of principles, the creation of a small secretariat and officers and a programme of regular meetings between party chairmen and working groups of politicians and party organizers. The problem with the EDU for Conservative purposes within the EC is that its membership is much broader than the EC, with only 14 out of the 25 member parties being in the EC. The EDU Chairman is the Leader of the Austrian People's party. The second problem is that the member parties within the EC belong to three different party groups in the EP: the EDG, the EPP, and EPD. The EDU European Institutions committee has been a channel for inter-group co-operation. The EDU publishes a declaration of principles for the European Elections, but it cannot achieve the degree of significance of the party federations such as the EPP.

The third area of inter-party co-operation is at bilateral and multilateral level. There is an International Office which arranges visits and contacts with other parties who are invited to the Annual Party Conference. Many bilateral exchanges with the CDU have been conducted involving MPs, party organizers and researchers, and activists. Some attempt has also been made to achieve twinning of constituency parties. MEPs sometimes ask colleagues from other parties to speak in their constituencies, particularly during elections. Outside the CDU/CSU, however, bilateral contacts are very limited.

The party auxiliaries all belong to transnational groups. The Women's Advisory Committee participates through the British branch of the European Union of Women, which brings together 14 affiliates from 14 countries. The Young Conservatives are members of DEMYC, the Democratic Youth Community of Europe, with 15 affiliates in 14 countries, and the Conservative Students belong to European Democrat Students with 18 affiliates in 14 countries. These groups have been at the forefront of promoting inter-party contacts and were behind the motion carried at the 1975 Party Conference calling for a centre-right alliance to be called the European Democrat party. However all these international bodies include parties from outside the EC.

While there is a great deal of contact between the Conservatives and other parties, mainly multilaterally, it is almost exclusively at the level of the élites and has failed to influence the consciousness of most party activists, members, or voters.

Labour

After entry, Labour boycotted the EC institutions, and did not nominate members to the EP until after the 1975 referendum. Unlike the Conservatives, they had a natural home within the Socialist Group. There was some discussion of whether to form their own group, as the Group was too federalist for many Labour MEPs. The left-wing Campaign Group initiated an unsuccessful campaign to withdraw from the Socialist Group in 1985. The British Labour Group (BLG) of MEPs, renamed in 1990 the British Socialist Group in the EP, are internally divided over Europe with clear pro- and anti-market factions, with factional voting for their leaders. Barbara Castle, who became more sympathetic to Europe after a history of fervent opposition, was removed as leader and replaced by Tribunite Alf Thomas in 1985, and the same occurred in 1988 to David Martin who was replaced by committed anti-marketeer Barry Seale. Martin had been influential in convincing Kinnock of the merits of the EC. Seale in turn was replaced by Glyn Ford, a loyal Kinnockite. Yet while Kinnock was attempting to change Labour policy, a majority of MEPs, by 18 to 13, called for a renewed commitment to withdraw. The BLG has been an obstacle to the new policy of a more positive attitude to the EC.

Within the Socialist Group the MEPs tend to act as individuals seeking friends and allies on the basis of shared political views. While the leader always holds office within the Group, the BLG has tended to wield little influence. Their record of hostility to membership has led to great suspicion by the rest, reinforced by their emphasis on national issues, such as the miners' strike, rather than European issues. However, the strong and influential German SPD group has moved to the left, the BLG emerged after the 1989 elections as the biggest national group within the Socialist Group, and since Labour has accepted membership the BLG has developed more congenial relationships within the Group.

At the EC level, in 1974 there was formed the Confederation of Socialist parties of the European Community (CSP) which Labour refused to join until 1976, following its boycott of the EC. The CSP organizes regular congresses, finances and organizes common election meetings, writes a common manifesto for the European elections and liaises with the Socialist Group in the EP. In 1977 the NEC refused to participate in the working parties to draw up a common programme or to fight the European elections on the CSP manifesto. It signed the 1984 CSP manifesto, with a series of reservations and proceeded to ignore it during the campaign. The 1989 manifesto was easier to endorse, and Kinnock participated in election activities on the continent, but the CSP manifesto still received little attention in the Labour campaign which was primarily focused on national issues. Labour sought to turn the European elections into a vote of no-confidence in the Thatcher administration, and specifically European issues were downplayed.

While Labour has been active in the Socialist International, which provides some opportunity to meet with fellow EC socialists, bilateral contacts are minimal. However, of significance are the contacts between British trade unions and their fellow unions in the EC, through participation in the Economic and Social Committee and the European Trade Union Confederation. Discussions with continental trade-unionists have tended to spread a more positive attitude towards Europe among union leaders and this was a significant factor in the abandonment of the policy of withdrawal.

Other Parties

The Liberals have not been represented in the EP since the introduction of direct elections. They are however members of the Federation of European Liberals and Democrats (ELD). They have little difficulty in supporting ELD's calls for a federal Europe, and the ELD has been a consistent champion of the introduction of proportional representation in the UK for the European elections. The Liberal Group has given funds to the British party to assist in its Euro-election campaigns and David Steel was on the list of the Italian Liberal party in the 1989 elections. However, the British do not always feel comfortable with their continental allies, who tend to be more in favour of the free market and strong defence. The 1980 Liberal Assembly unsuccessfully urged the expulsion from the ELD of the French Giscardiens although they were members of the Liberal Group in the EP. During election campaigns the British actively promote the election programme, publicity material, and symbol of the ELD, and seek to associate themselves with governing Liberal parties in EC countries.

The SDP were in the ironic situation of feeling the closest to continental politics yet being unaffiliated with any European organization. They were not welcome in the Socialist Group, and they felt that the ELD was too right-wing. Michael Gallagher, the MEP who defected from Labour to the SDP in 1981, sat as an independent.

Winifred Ewing is a member of the Rainbow Group in the EP, but this reflects, as did her previous association with the French Gaullists and Fianna Fáil, the advantages of being in a group more than ideological affinity, and the SNP does not have active contact with other parties in the group. Plaid Cymru belongs to the European Freedom Alliance of nationalist or regionalist parties. The Official Unionists did belong to the EDG, but broke away after the Anglo-Irish agreement to join the European right. The SDLP belongs to the Socialist Group; and Paisley is an independent. The Greens have no MEPs, but see themselves as represented by the Rainbow Group.

POLICY-MAKING WITHIN THE PARTIES

Conservatives

Opinion on Europe can be divided into six groups, which mostly support membership, but are divided on what sort of Europe they wish to see. First there are the Tory Gaullists, who see no contradiction between strong commitment to the EC and firm advocacy of British interests within a 'Europe des patries' as enunciated by de Gaulle. This was clearly expressed by Mrs Thatcher in her Bruges speech in September 1988: 'My first guiding principle is this: willing and active co-operation between independent sovereign states is the best way to build a successful European Community.'[19] This is not the same as simple nationalism, which implies the belief that Britain could act alone. This is recognized by confederalists as no longer possible. As Thatcher continued in her Bruges speech: 'I am the first to say that on many great issues the countries of Europe should try to speak with a single voice. I want to see us work more closely on the things that we can do better together than alone. Europe is stronger when we do so, whether it be in trade, in defence, or in relations with the rest of the world.' Duncan Sandys and Julian Amery were early advocates of British membership who belonged to this group. Confederalists were often active in the Conservative Group for Europe when the issue was membership. The Bruges speech led to the creation of the Bruges Group, which describes itself as 'the Campaign for a Europe of Sovereign States' and supports a Europe of economic but not political unity.[20]

Secondly, there are 'the Tory modernizers' who, while generally sharing a confederalist view of European co-operation, believe that British interests are best protected by Britain playing a more active leading role within the EC, which may sometimes involve the sacrifice of short-term interests for wider goals. There is a fear of Franco-German domination, with Britain left behind. Geoffrey Howe represented this tendency within the Government until his resignation. Edward Heath belongs to this group, but is isolated.

[19] Thatcher, *Britain and Europe*, 2.
[20] Bruges Group, *The Bruges Group: Statement of Aims* (Oxford, 1989).

Michael Heseltine is an advocate of this approach, most notably in his book *The Challenge of Europe: Can Britain Win?*[21] He has emphasized the necessity of the development of a single market, particularly for technological industries to compete internationally, and of common defence and foreign policies. They are often associated with the more interventionist or 'wet' wing.

Thirdly, there are free-market neo-liberals who are enthusiastic about the free-market principles of the Treaty of Rome and are willing to accept a loss of national sovereignty in order to obtain the benefits of a larger and freer market. They are less nationalist and more pragmatic about the appropriate level of decision-making. John Major belongs to this group and they are well represented in the *Sunday Times* and *The Economist*. The opposition to the social Europe by the Bruges Group has attracted some of these economic liberals, but they have come into conflict with those primarily concerned with sovereignty.

The fourth group are the federalists, influential within the EDG but a distinct minority within the parliamentary and extra-parliamentary party. They believe that Britain must surrender a considerable degree of national sovereignty in order to benefit to the full from membership. William Newton Dunn and Derek Prag are the most prominent federalists among the MEPs, and there are some in the Conservative Parliamentary Committee on Europe, led by Ian Taylor, Hugh Dykes, and Sir Anthony Meyer, and many within the Conservative Group for Europe, which is affiliated to the explicitly federalist European Movement. They are largely but not exclusively found on the left of the party.

The fifth group are the anti-marketeers, who opposed membership both before and after the referendum, and now seek to minimize further integration. They are found almost exclusively on the right. Enoch Powell was the most famous spokesman until he left the party in 1974 over the issue of Europe. The most consistent anti-market MP is Teddy Taylor, who frequently uses parliamentary questions and debates on the EC to launch critical attacks, and he is supported by Jonathan Aitken and Rhodes Boyson. There have been many short-lived anti-market groups in the party, from the Anti-Common Market League to the Anti-Common Market

---

[21] London, 1989. See also M. Heseltine, *Where There's A Will* (London, 1987), ch. 12.

Information Service to Conservatives Against the Treaty of Rome. As the prospect of withdrawal has receded, they formed the Conservative European Reform Group. As this group has little influence, some have seen the Bruges Group as a useful instrument to oppose further integration.

The final, and largest group, is the passive supporters of Europe. The bulk of the party share what is called 'common sense Euro-peanism', that the benefits of membership are clear in terms of the contribution to peace and prosperity and there is no obvious alternative. However they cannot share either the enthusiasms or the hostilities of the various groups. Provided they feel that British interests are satisfactorily protected they fail to be engaged in the debate.

With regard to the making of European policy, a major role is played by the leader. This is established both constitutionally and in practice. The leader has the final decision on the party manifesto for the general and European elections, and particularly when Prime Minister is the chief foreign spokesman for the party. However, the leader must show some appreciation of the balance of political forces within the party. While the tone of Mrs Thatch-er's campaign for the budget rebates was strong, no threat was made to withdraw Britain's payments to the EC, which had been advised by some close to the Prime Minister. Despite Mrs Thatch-er's doubts, the Conservative Government adopted a policy of Britain's membership of the EMS 'when the time is right' or when certain conditions are met, and entered in October 1990 under pressure from significant elements within the party. The Thatcher Cabinet was dominated by the second and third of the above groups, who are less concerned about loss of sovereignty than the confederalists.

The parliamentary party does not give European issues a high priority, as evidenced by the low attendance at European debates. Both pro- and anti-Europeans tend to be active in the Commons. The National Union has usually chosen a debate on Europe every year at the party conference which has tended to demonstrate further support for European co-operation. The fringe meeting of the Conservative Group for Europe has consistently been the largest unofficial meeting at the Party Conference. Central Office has an International Office which is primarily involved in European issues. The informal groups within the party, such as the Tory

Reform Group and the Selsdon Group, all support EC membership, although the left tend to be more sympathetic to federalism and the right more confederalist.

Conservative MEPs have a high degree of independence from the government line in their voting behaviour. There are not the same factors to encourage party discipline (e.g. appointment to ministerial office) as there are in Westminster. Thus MEPs have not always followed appeals from government ministers. Most MEPs favoured an increase in the regional and social funds as a way of compensating for Britain's budget contributions rather than a cash refund. Twenty-two MEPs voted for the federalist Draft Treaty of European Union in 1984. There was a division between the federalists, led by Newton Dunn and Prag, and the 'blue circle' of more Thatcherite MEPs, led by John Marshall and Dame Sheilagh Roberts, who lost their seats in the 1989 election. Most MEPs are critical of Mrs Thatcher for failing to understand the positions and the political style of the other member states, and for ignoring the MEPs.

The creation of the large Euro-constituencies of usually eight Westminster constituencies led to the formation of Euro-Constituency Councils (ECC) made up of representatives of the constituency parties, who elect officers to run the ECC. The functions of the ECCs are the selection of candidates, the appointment of a Euro-Agent (usually a Westminster agent with additional pay) and the organization and financing of the campaign. The ECCs meet around four times a year, but attendance may be low betweeen elections except for the AGM.

Candidate selection is vigorously conducted at the national level by the Standing Advisory Committee on European Candidates (Euro-SAC), which has sought candidates with knowledge and experience of Europe, the ability to speak other languages, and some record of political activity within the party. Candidates selected have been diverse: mainly businessmen, farmers, Eurocrats, and local government councillors. While some candidates clearly saw the EP as a means to enter Westminster, most Conservative MEPs have a particular interest in European affairs.

Policy-making on Europe for the Conservatives has reflected the existence of different perceptions of Britain's role in Europe and the balance of power within the party. While Europe does not claim the overwhelming loyalty of most Conservatives, there is an active element for whom Europe is a highly salient issue, and the party has to seek to satisfy this group while not alienating those more passive on Europe. The debate on membership did not divide the party as much as the issue of the direction of Europe, as support for membership was broad-based within the party, while the debate on direction has been complicated by the association with the conflict between Thatcherites and 'wets'. The separate issues of federalism and interventionism have become confused in the debate within the party, summed up in the phrase 'socialist superstate'. Thus federalists and confederalists, interventionists and free marketeers, can be found in the Conservative Group for Europe, while the Bruges Group includes confederalists, free marketeers, and anti-marketeers.

Labour

The issue of membership of the EC has been highly divisive within the Labour party, marked by the existence of five groups.[22] There has been a group of strongly committed Europeans for whom Europe was associated with a mixed economy, economic growth to fund the welfare state, Western strength against the Soviet Union, a recognition of the decline of Britain, internationalism, and the strength of social democratic ideas. They were mostly on the social democratic wing of the party. While strong within the Parliamentary Labour Party between 1964 and 1979, with up to 25 per cent of MPs, they had little support among party members and the unions. They were active in the Labour Committee for Europe (LCE), an important actor in the votes on British membership in 1973. When the SDP was formed, the LCE virtually collapsed. The pro-Europeans who remained, such as Denis Healey and Roy Hattersley, believed that Europe should not be promoted at the expense of party unity, and they recognized that their position was that of a distinct minority.

The left, who formed a second group, was virtually united in its opposition to Europe, believing in socialism through the British state. For them Europe represented a capitalist and militaristic

[22] K. Featherstone, *Socialist Parties and European Integration*, (London, 1988), ch. 2; M. Newman, *Socialism and European Unity: The Dilemma of the Left in Britain and France* (London, 1983); and L. Robins, *The Reluctant Party: Labour and the EEC, 1961–75* (Ormskirk, 1979).

bloc, 'the economic arm of NATO', an ally of the United States and multinational corporations, and a repressive and alien society. The EC was perceived as a major obstacle to the achievement of socialism in Britain and thus concerns over ideology and sovereignty were combined in opposition to an EC created by and for business interests. The left's economic policy, the Alternative Economic Strategy, was incompatible with membership of the EC. Michael Foot and Tony Benn were leaders of this group. All the left-wing organizations such as the Tribune Group and the Campaign Group shared this view, and were supported by most of the trade unions, notably the powerful Transport and General Workers Union. Recently some elements of the left have begun to re-evaluate this position.

The primary concern of the third group, the nationalist right such as Douglas Jay and Peter Shore, was the loss of sovereignty involved in the European enterprise. Sovereignty weighed more heavily than socialism as the primary source of opposition for most of the Labour party. Veteran anti-marketeer Ron Leighton MP expressed this in opposition to the Single European Act. 'Sovereignty is the right of people to run their own country in their own way. It is the right to democratic parliamentary government.'[23] They rejected the EC as being an obstacle to the achievement of their ideas, notably economic planning.

The fourth group consists of those on the left who have come to the conclusion that the achievement of their socialist goals can only be achieved at the European level. Early proponents of this view were Tom Nairn and the *Guardian*'s European correspondent John Palmer.[24] Barbara Castle, through her experiences as Leader of the British Labour Group in the EP, became converted to this position. They were later joined by Frances Morrell and the *New Socialist* magazine, which organized an international conference in 1986 with prominent socialist speakers from the continent on the theme of 'Alternatives to Trade Wars'.[25]

A fifth group, the pragmatic centre, recognized political realities

---

[23] Quoted in D. Judge, 'Incomplete Sovereignty: The British House of Commons and the Completion of the Internal Market of the European Communities', *Parliamentary Affairs*, 41 (1988), 441–55.

[24] T. Nairn, *The Left Against Europe?* (Harmondsworth, 1973); and J. Palmer, *Trading Places* (London, 1988).

[25] F. Morrell, 'An Alternative to Trade Wars', *New Socialist*, 1986.

which led them to accept membership without enthusiasm, but for them party unity and electoral prospects were more significant than the issue itself. This group included most of the leadership and the centre-left of the parliamentary party.

The debate on Europe was more about the control and direction of the party between the factions than the issue of Europe itself. Europe therefore became an issue of party management for the leader. Party opinion was a significant factor in the decision of Gaitskell to oppose the application in 1962. The evidence of strong support for Europe in the Parliamentary Labour Party was a major factor in Wilson's decision to apply in 1967 and 1969, and his subsequent recognition of the degree of opposition led him to renegotiate the terms and hold the referendum. Foot's hostility to the EC was a factor in his election to the leadership, and Kinnock had to carry out a series of careful manœuvres in order gradually to abandon the commitment to withdraw, supported by a 'soft left' eager to win power.

The Parliamentary Labour Party (PLP) has had a majority against the EC in virtually every Commons vote on British membership. For example in the 1975 debate 38 ministers and 107 back-benchers voted against the Labour Cabinet's recommendations to support Britain's continued membership. The exception was the vote on the exploratory talks of 1967, with 36 against and 51 abstentions which reflected the fact that Labour was the Government, and also the more favourable balance of opinion within the PLP. The PLP has come reluctantly to accept continued membership. However a Gallup poll of Labour MPs commissioned by a consultancy associated with the Conservatives found 39 per cent believed that Britain's membership had been for the worse and only 33 per cent for the better, with 38 per cent opposed to a single currency and 45 per cent in favour.[26]

The National Executive Committee (NEC) and the Party Conference have been in the forefront of hostility to Europe. From the first NEC statement on Europe in 1950 it has been hostile to integration. An exception was in 1967 when it endorsed the Labour application, but repeated the five conditions it had made in 1962 when it had opposed membership. It moved to the left in 1970,

---

[26] Policy Research Associates, 'Poll Shows Labour MPs Deeply Split on Europe', press release, 7 Dec. 1989.

and in 1972 called for a referendum. The 1983 manifesto that it drew up stated, 'British withdrawal is the right policy for Britain' and it would be 'completed well within the lifetime of the Parliament'.[27] But Kinnock managed to capture control of the NEC, which subsequently endorsed his positions on the EC.

The Party Conference long opposed British entry. In 1972 it voted against by 3.72 million to 1.97 million. The special conference on the referendum in 1975 voted 3.74 million to 1.986 million in support of the NEC's stance in favour of a No vote and against the recommendation of a majority of the Cabinet. The Conference voted against direct elections to the European Parliament in 1976, against the Labour Government, by 4 million to 2.2 million, and in the selection of candidates for the European Parliament constituencies have chosen a majority of anti-marketeers. In 1980 the Conference voted for withdrawal by 5.04 million to 2.09 million. But in 1989 the Conference indirectly reversed its policy on withdrawal by endorsing the party's Policy Review.

The trade unions have viewed the issue on Europe almost exclusively in terms of wages and working conditions, in economic rather than political terms. Most unions, led by the TGWU and the AUEW, were anti-European, with the GMWU the only major union with a consistently pro-European position. At Party Conferences the union votes have been predominantly against Europe, reinforced by the TUC votes for withdrawal. However, the exclusion from power under Mrs Thatcher and the experience of co-operation with other European unions has led to a more sympathetic attitude to Europe, marked by the invitation to Commission President Jacques Delors to address the 1988 TUC Congress.

The Labour MEPs in the British Labour Group (BLG) have been deeply divided between pro- and anti-marketeers, with a clear majority for the latter. Their position in Europe has made them peripheral to the Labour party in Britain, while their opposition to direct elections, increasing the powers of the EP and further integration have caused them to lack influence within the EP. Newman stated that Labour 'MEPs therefore played a subordinate role in determining "European" policy, and no role at all in general policy-making', while Featherstone described them as 'more likely

---

[27] Labour party, *A New Hope for Britain*.

to be seen as unco-operative and controversial than any other group in the Chamber'.[28]

In the early post-war period Europe was predominantly a 'foreign policy' issue for Labour and a responsibility of the leadership. However by 1961 it was addressed in terms of sovereignty, socialism, and working conditions, and the party as a whole participated in the debate. While the leadership and the PLP was more supportive of Europe than the rest of the party, there was always significant opposition within the elected leadership of the party which could mobilize the party membership against Europe. Therefore the party has acted as a considerable constraint on the actions of Labour leaders over Europe. Newman concluded in his study of Labour and Europe that 'It is clear that the "European" policy of the Labour leadership has been influenced by opinion within the party both in 1962, and, more particularly, in 1971–72 and 1979–81.'[29]

CONCLUSION

Europe has fitted neither the consensual nor adversarial styles of British party politics. First, Europe has been a controversial issue in British politics for most of the post-war era, but it has not followed the normal pattern of conflict between the parties' adversarial politics. While the Conservatives have been more European than Labour, in opposition they have not usually attacked Labour on this difference. While Labour in opposition has usually been anti-European, Labour Governments since 1967 sought membership. Thus there has emerged neither a consensus nor a clear choice between the parties on the merits of membership. That consensus on membership may now be created.

Secondly, the issue of Europe gained such saliency within the parties due to its relationship to broader factional disputes. For Labour it was the fight between the social democrats and the left, the victory of the left in 1980, and its reversal by Kinnock in his search for power by the end of the 1980s. For Conservatives it has

[28] Newman, *Socialism and European Unity*, 278; and Featherstone, *Socialist Parties and European Integration*, 104.
[29] Newman, *Socialism and European Unity*, 273.

recently come to reflect the struggle between the Thatcherite and interventionist wings of the party. Thus the debate on party ideology becomes tied to attitudes to Europe. This intra-party conflict has prevented the presentation of clear policies towards Europe by the parties, which would encourage an informed debate. This is still likely to continue as there is no intra-party consensus.

A third factor is that Europe has been an important area of party management for leaders and reveals the limits placed upon them by the party. Macmillan, Wilson, Heath, Callaghan, and Thatcher have all been inhibited in their policy towards Europe by party considerations.

Fourthly, the lack of clear party cues on Europe has confused the voters and led to a low level of saliency and consistency amongst the public, voters, and party members, whilst it is of high saliency to party élites and activists.

Fifthly, the intra-party divisions have made co-operation with sister parties in the rest of the EC difficult. Only a minority of Conservatives have shared the federalist vision of their 'natural' partners in the Christian Democrats. Labour has not shared the whole-hearted commitment to European integration of their social-ist colleagues, and a significant minority have not even accepted membership. Even the Liberals have had difficulties co-operating with the more free-market and defence-oriented continental Liberals.

Finally, Governments still try to treat European issues as 'foreign policy', which is felt to lie within the prerogative of government to determine the national interest. However Governments cannot remain effective gatekeepers on European issues, when both sub-stantial principles and substantive interests are affected. While Europe still lacks saliency amongst the general public, it is per-ceived by opinion-formers as having such a profound impact on Britain, for conceptions of the role of government, and for sectional interests such as farmers, businessmen, and trade-unionists, that it is now a 'domesticated' issue, which the parties can avoid only at their peril. In the 1990s Europe may be emerging as an issue arena in which the parties will present alternative visions of Europe's future and address the merits and costs of particular European policies, and thus help the United Kingdom finally to adjust to the realities of membership.

7

British Pressure Groups and the European Community

Alan Butt Philip

MEMBERSHIP of the European Community has not only led to significant constitutional and organizational changes for British government, it also introduced a major new area of work for non-governmental bodies representing British interests. This brought about big organizational changes for many UK pressure groups and caused them to rethink their lobbying strategies to include a European dimension. This process of integration into Community decision-making attracted only limited attention in the early years of British membership, although it has in fact been continuing slowly from the 1970s onwards. Such changes did not all occur in the immediate aftermath of UK accession.[1]

LOBBYING EC INSTITUTIONS

Policy-making and policy development in the European Community had already spawned a complex system of lobbying by the time of British entry. The focus of this lobbying was primarily the permanent officials of the European Commission in Brussels, whose sole right of initiative enshrined in the EEC Treaty made this a much more powerful agenda-setting body than the British Civil Service.[2] Within five years of the establishment of the EEC some three hundred Community-wide interest groups were in evidence and by the mid-1970s this number had grown to nearly four

[1] Hansard Society, *The British People: Their Voice in Europe* (Farnborough, 1977), 88–137.
[2] A. Butt Philip, *Pressure Groups in the European Community* (London, 1985). See also E. Kirchner and K. Schwaiger, *The Role of Interest Groups in the European Community* (Farnborough, 1981).

hundred.[3] By 1990 the number of such Eurogroups was estimated to be between 500 and 700. But the coverage of interests by such groups proved to be patchy, reflecting particularly the over-development of policies related to agriculture and the food industry compared with most other sectors.[4] In a few cases UK accession to the Community caused new Community-wide pressure groups to be formed, for example to represent consumer and environmental interests in Brussels, because national British groups representing these interests found themselves otherwise unrepresented in Brussels and relatively well developed at home in comparison with their continental counterparts.

One major difference between the situation in Britain and in the European Community was immediately clear. The range of pressure groups in and around the EC institutions was greatly skewed towards sectional groups with closed memberships and specific economic interests at stake, while very few open-membership promotional or 'cause' groups were on the scene.[5] British interest groups did not follow this pattern to the same marked extent—hence the appearance of new Eurogroups in the mid-1970s for which British membership of the Community provided the catalyst.

ADAPTING TO THE EC DIMENSION

British-based pressure groups of all kinds have had to adapt to new issues and new decision-making processes, following UK accession to the European Community in 1973. They have also found that it is not always easy to persuade their own members to devote the necessary effort and resources to representing their interests at the European level. Indeed there is a potential conflict of interest between Eurogroups and their own national member organizations over who should be responsible for which activities, especially as multilevel lobbying is often required to be undertaken simul-taneously, in the EC decision-making process.

[3] D. Sidjanski, 'Pressure Groups and the European Economic Community', in M. Hodges (ed.), *European Integration* (London, 1972), and A. Butt Philip, *Pressure Groups*, 27–36.
[4] A. Butt Philip, *Pressure Groups*, 28–9 and Hansard Society *British People*, 104–8 and 125 *et seq.*
[5] A. Butt Philip, *Pressure Groups*, 2–7. For further definition of these terms see G. Wootton, *Pressure Groups in Contemporary Britain* (Lexington, KY, 1978).

In order to slot into the policy-making system of the European Community British pressure groups have had to undergo considerable changes of orientation and organization, and indeed working methods. The obvious first step has been for each British pressure group to identify an analogous Eurogroup at the EC level which it could join and through which to gain access and influence in the Community's institutions. This is particularly important as the European Commission enjoys the sole right of initiative under the EC treaties, and the Commission is always keen to encourage EC-wide interests to organize themselves into a single organization with a single point of view. The Commission has on several occasions helped to establish Eurogroups as suitable interlocutors and can often assist such groups at a practical level in carrying out their functions. The EC is also unusual as a system of government in offering a wide range and diversity of channels of influence and points of access.

While many UK pressure groups have found no difficulty in linking up with appropriate Eurogroups, from animal feed merchants and the makers of chocolate biscuits to trade unions and lawyers, others have encountered problems. Banking interests in Britain for example had to be reorganized into a single, all-embracing organization, the British Banking Association, in order to be eligible to join their appropriate Eurogroup, the Fédération Bancaire.[6] Other interests found there was very poor representation at the Brussels level available to them and set about creating more appropriate EC-wide bodies that they then became active in. The most notable examples here are the strengthening of BEUC in the 1970s, under pressure from the British Consumers' Association, to represent European consumers more effectively, and the setting up of the European Environmental Bureau in 1975 at the behest principally of UK environmental interests, such as the Conservation Society, Friends of the Earth, the CPRE, and the Civic Trust. British building societies were surprised to find how few genuinely analogous organizations existed in other EC member states with which to team up.

All pressure groups, especially trade associations and 'peak' associations such as the CBI and TUC, have had to improve their

---

[6] A. Butt Philip, 'Pressure Groups and Policy Formation in the European Communities', *Policy and Politics*, 10/4 (Oct. 1982), 461–6. See also J. Sargent, 'Pressure Group Development in the EC: The Role of the British Bankers' Association', *Journal of Common Market Studies*, 20/3 (Mar. 1982).

own understanding of the Community dimension, their monitoring of policy development at the EC level, and their methods of communication to their members—since EC decision-making can be both speedy and commercially sensitive, especially at the policy management stage. But it is clear that many UK interest groups were disinclined to give this matter much attention in the early years after UK accession because they did not see the importance of the EC institutions and did not have resources to spare.[7] Some British groups still have not made this leap of imagination, and may have been encouraged in their inaction by the fact of the crucial role played by national governments in the Council of Ministers.[8] Community decision-making was thus seen by many interest groups still to reside in the last resort with the British Government, so long as the idea of a national veto remained operational. The governmental role as 'gatekeeper' was reassuringly still intact, with British pressure groups remaining 'semi-detached' in regard to the EC.

Some pressure groups clearly found the new demands being placed upon them by EC membership beyond their capacity. Restructuring of their role was the eventual outcome, for this and other reasons, the clearest example coming from the thirty-six British food and drink trade associations that have been grouped in the Food and Drink Federation as '*serviced*' members since 1985.[9] The FDF services these groups on all EEC business, and acts as their representative when lobbying in Brussels.

Those organizations in Britain that have taken the EC dimensions fully on board have found and often exploited many additional opportunities for bringing pressure to bear on government, both at national and EC levels. New working groups on particular items of EC legislation or to cover whole policy areas have been established. Representatives from national pressure groups have been found to serve on Eurogroup specialist committees covering policy and institutional matters. Representatives from national pressure groups have also been chosen to represent Eurogroup interests on the Commission's advisory committees or to represent

[7] O. Gray, 'Pressure Groups and their Influence on Agricultural Policy and its Reform in the European Community' (unpublished Ph.D thesis, University of Bath, 1989), 49–51 and 300–9.

[8] O. Gray, 'Pressure Groups', 343–51.

[9] O. Gray, 'Pressure Groups', 312–17.

national socio-economic interests on bodies such as the EC's Economic and Social Committee (ECOSOC), to which the UK Government nominates twenty-four individuals. Small business interests, consumers, bankers, farmers, industrialists, trade-unionists, and academics have all found a home in ECOSOC. Basil de Ferranti, an industrialist and British politician, was Chairman of ECOSOC from 1977 to 1979; Jack Jones, General-Secretary of the TGWU, was also an early ECOSOC member, and Larry Smith, Assistant General-Secretary of the TGWU and a TUC General Council member, was a member of ECOSOC at the time of writing.

British organized interests have also had to reorganize themselves in response to the changes in structure within the UK Civil Service to accommodate the new work-load emanating from the European Community. The Whitehall departments covering trade and industry matters and agriculture have set up separate new divisions concentrating on EC business and these have needed to be matched by pressure groups. The permanent diplomatic representation of the UK Government in Brussels (UKREP) is also open to briefing from those interests that understand the new system. At the highest level even the Prime Minister can be involved through membership of the European Council and by virtue of the responsibility of the Cabinet Office European secretariat for co-ordinating UK government responses to EC initiatives.

Another area of work that has mushroomed alongside UK membership of the EC has come from the demands of parliamentary select committees sitting at Westminster. House of Commons select committees specializing in subjects such as trade and industry, treasury or foreign affairs, or agriculture frequently solicit evidence from UK pressure groups on EC matters. So on occasion does the House of Commons EC Scrutiny Committee on EC Legislation. The House of Lords Select Committee on the European Communities with its six subcommittees consisting of up to eighty peers is a constant source of requests for oral and written evidence from British pressure groups. The Lords Select Committee produces up to forty reports every parliamentary session, filled with interest group memoranda and evidence that in all run to thousands of pages annually.[10]

[10] For further discussion of the work of the House of Lords Select Committee on the European Communities see St J. N. Bates, 'Select Committees in the House of Lords', in G. Drewry (ed.), *The New Select Committees* (Oxford, 1985).

British interests have also to be represented directly to European Community institutions where avenues can be found. This can be done indirectly through perhaps daily contact with UK civil servants representing the UK Government during detailed negotiations within the Council of Ministers or within EC management committees. But this influences only part of the decision-making process. The most adept British interest groups will also try to develop as many lines of contact as they can to the European Commission, planting ideas wherever the ground is fertile, and they will ensure that at least British MEPs and members of ECOSOC are fully briefed on matters of concern. This will involve regular visits to Brussels and some visits to Strasburg.

MEPs are now subject to lobbying from a variety of interest groups from all over the world, but British MEPs with individual constituency interests to represent are often very keen to take up casework fed to them by socio-economic interests from their own area. All such pressure group activities have to be paid for out of members' subscriptions and have to be achieved without cutting across the work of the Eurogroups, on which most British interest groups are also represented. A few of the best-resourced interests now have their own representative offices in Brussels, such as the CBI and the National Farmers' Union, as well as several individual local authorities and a few large companies such as British Coal or IBM Europe.

There may occasionally be opportunities for pressure groups based in the United Kingdom to reopen at Brussels level political issues that appear closed or settled at UK government level. These are exceptional cases which point to the inability of Whitehall to exercise the role of 'gatekeeper' to the EC policy process on all fronts. Some would argue that the British trade unions' interest since 1987 in the capacity of the EC to impose legislation on the UK, especially in social and employment policy, is just such a case. The British savings bank, women's organizations, and environmentalist groups in Britain, as well as representatives of local government can also show that lobbying Brussels has forced the hand of the British Government, over equal pay, lorry weights, the scope of banking law, and the administration of the Regional Fund.

RELATIONS WITH WHITEHALL AND WESTMINSTER

It would be a mistake to think that on many EC issues British interest groups frequently find themselves at loggerheads with their own national government. In the vast majority of cases the British Government and a small group of representatives of interested parties usually find themselves working hand in hand to secure the best deal for British interests. The policy network involved is very small and the subject-matter is highly specific and low profile (rarely discussed in Press or Parliament)—such as the harmonized definition of instant coffee or the system for levying VAT on cigarettes.[11] The UK Government, alongside others in the Council of Ministers, may thus find itself enmeshed in negotiations where few if any of its direct interests are involved and where it is put in the position of making the best case it can for private commercial interests located within its territory. It is in circumstances such as these that allegations of neo-corporatist behaviour can be made with some justice, even if the policy-making circle is not completely closed because of the involvement of several EC institutions in the decision-making process.

In many cases, especially where more controversial subjects are concerned, the UK Government will be forced to arbitrate between competing national socio-economic interests as well as trying to assert its own views. The key to successful lobbying in Whitehall is the right of access to civil servants directly handling the subject in question, which is at the discretion of the Civil Service, and the ability to maintain a dialogue with the government department throughout the often lengthy period in which EC proposals are discussed. It is not uncommon for interest groups to complain that they have been consulted too late by the UK Government, for example after an EC directive has been adopted at EC level but before it is implemented by national government. The scope for influencing the UK Government is thus confined within parameters set in Brussels. This complaint is raised not just by smaller interest groups but by other parts of government, particularly enforcement

---

[11] A. Butt Philip and C. Baron, 'United Kingdom: The Application of the Social Regulations in the Transport Sector', in H. Siedentopf and J. Ziller (eds.), *Making European Policies Work* (London and Brussels, 1988), ii. 675–715.

agencies—such as the police or health and safety inspectors—not directly linked to government departments handling UK government negotiations in the Council of Ministers and perhaps suffering from lack of regular exposure to EC issues.

Interest groups can also find that they have uneven access to the different parts of the governmental machine in Whitehall, a feature which is mirrored at the level of the European Commission. Thus food industry groups complain that while they have good access to the Ministry of Agriculture, Fisheries, and Food (MAFF), they find it difficult to interest the Department of Trade and Industry in their concerns.[12] Access to the very small European Secretariat of the Cabinet Office is necessarily very restricted, and may not be particularly useful since 'lead' departments on much detailed EC legislation do not necessarily involve the Cabinet Office in relatively low-profile negotiations, or issues involving policy administration.[13]

British pressure groups do not simply stick to direct approaches to UK Government when EC policy affects them, although this is likely to be the most productive method of influencing government. They also lobby individual MPs and peers at Westminster, and sometimes the political parties, in the hope that parliamentarians and political leaders will be interested in taking up their concerns. Several campaigns were mounted in the late 1980s to stop the extension of VAT to cover books, children's shoes, and building work for village halls. Since much of the time spent by the House of Commons on EC business is either calling ministers to account on immediate or recent issues, the most effective ways of getting a hearing for EC concerns may be through parliamentary questions, or private approaches to ministers, or by raising issues through the select committees or by proposing amendments to legislation going through the House. The most effective strategy is to raise issues before the Government or the political parties have adopted fixed positions, and thus to try to influence the framework in which the merits of proposals are judged in Whitehall. Again, the House of Lords Select Committee on the European Communities can exercise considerable influence, if it is well briefed and well prepared with its own reports, for issues rising on the EC agenda. This influence

[12] O. Gray, 'Pressure Groups', 272–82.
[13] A. Butt Philip and C. Baron, 'United Kingdom', 645–9.

is sometimes exercised privately through correspondence between subcommittee chairmen and senior ministers, or it can be felt more publicly in the debates on the floor of the House and in examination by subcommittee. The pressure of the peers, on a fairly apolitical, technocratic but *communautaire* basis, can be both politically persistent and yet unthreatening—hence its effectiveness, an indication that alternatives to adversary politics already exist in the British political system.

PEAK ASSOCIATIONS

A peak association may be defined as an organization at a cross-sectoral level that brings together a number of other organizations with more specific interests and clienteles.[14] The typical peak associations in the United Kingdom are those representing the general interests of employers and trade-unionists, the Confederation of British Industry (CBI) and the Trades Union Congress (TUC).

The CBI and its antecedents have taken a consistently pro-Community stance since the 1960s. Unsurprisingly, therefore, the CBI has from before Britain's eventual accession to the Communities in 1973 built up an infrastructure of contacts in the EC institutions, mobilized its members behind the main goals of European economic integration (including support for EC regional development institutions), and has provided in-house resources to promulgate the importance of the EC and the critical role the CBI can play in shaping EC decision-making. By the end of the 1980s the CBI had spawned several posts within its own organization and specific committees on which its members are represented whose sole remit was and remains EC business.

The CBI has long had its own representative office in Brussels, housed in the same building as its analogue at EC level, UNICE, the Union of Industries of the EC. The CBI has played a critical role in UNICE in hardening its response to Commission initiatives on worker participation and social policy development, but UNICE's remit does not extend to cover the financial services industries which are, however, well represented in the CBI. The

---

[14] G. Wootton, *Pressure Groups*, 156.

CBI has also worked hard to brief Commission officials, UKREP, British ECOSOC members, and MEPs on a very wide range of subjects. At home, the CBI has also played a most active role in helping to shape government opinion on EC policy issues, and appears to have gained a much more attentive hearing on most points from the Thatcher administration on European matters than on issues connected with the running of the British economy. The main point on which the CBI and the Government continued to be at loggerheads in the 1980s was over UK membership of the Exchange Rate Mechanism of the European Monetary System. On the moves to complete the Single European Market by 1992, the CBI worked very closely with the Department of Trade and Industry, under Lord Young of Graffham, to promote company awareness and interest in the programme. It published its own special briefings for companies on '1992' matters under the title '*Europe sans frontières*' and hosted in 1989/90 a circus of corporate seminars on detailed aspects of EC policy, travelling all over the country.

The main areas for criticism of the EC, in CBI terms, have been in the fields of harmonization and social policy. The CBI has since the mid-1970s been very wary of Commission attempts to 'over-regulate' business through EC legislation and was clearly pleased with the shift towards a mutual recognition rather than a uniform regulatory approach to harmonization inaugurated in 1985. Yet there is a paradox in this approach since mutual recognition of different standards in effect licenses the continuation of an unlevel playing-field, which in so many other ways the CBI is dedicated to eliminate, as the trade barriers come down. This deregulatory anti-bureaucratic policy stance has however helped the CBI to fend off competition from the rival Institute of Directors which has taken an increasing interest in detailed EC policies, establishing a policy unit, working parties, and a radical and critical image encapsulated by the assertions of its Director-General, Sir John Hoskyns, that '1992 was bound to fail'.[15]

The CBI has avoided taking very critical public stances of the Community, perhaps for fear of weakening company support for the EC in general. It has certainly never taken a high-profile stand on the need to reform and to cut back spending on the common

---

[15] See the *Financial Times, The Times*, and the *Guardian*, 1 Mar. 1989.

agricultural policy, as its German counterpart, the BDI, has done, much to the annoyance of German agricultural interests. The CBI, in contrast, counts the National Farmers' Union as one of its largest members.

Yet on social and employment issues, the CBI has not hesitated to criticize EC intervention, even appearing at times to deny the EEC Treaty's clear invitation to member states to develop an EC-wide social policy. The announcement in 1988 by Jacques Delors, as President of the European Commission, of a 'social dimension' to complement the completion of the single European market was scarcely received with enthusiasm by the CBI, but then CBI strictures subsequently have fallen on fertile ground in Whitehall. The Thatcher Government and the CBI were as one in resisting the extension of Brussels' jurisdiction to the relatively less regulated UK labour market, although the CBI, like the UK Government, was curiously acquiescent in regard to the Single European Act's application of qualified majority voting to EC health and safety legislation.

The CBI's resistance to the social dimensions of '1992' placed it in clear opposition to the position adopted by the TUC, for whom the promised social dimension, backed up by the EC social charter and social action programme of 1989, proved something of a lifeboat, rescuing British trade-unionism from the political cul-de-sac of hostility to the Community and all it stands for, while opening up the prospect of a warm reception in Brussels for its ideas long after the doors of Whitehall and Downing Street had seemed permanently closed. The TUC, like the Labour party, spent most of the 1970s and 1980s in opposition to British membership of the EC and, between 1972 and 1975, it refused, like Labour, to take part in the work of EC institutions, such as ECOSOC or the joint employer–union committees monitoring particular sectors, or the European Social Fund. This position was reversed once the decisive pro-EC referendum result was known, but it was not replaced by positive espousal of the virtues of European integration. The TUC is a loose confederation of individual trade unions, each of which has had to build its own links with related trade unions and Eurogroups throughout the twelve EC states. The TUC's role has been one of information-gathering and dissemination within the Labour movement and of filling in as a general representative of trade-unionism in Britain while individual trade unions preferred to concentrate on more domestic activities. This task has been given to the TUC's small International Department and has been supplemented with advice from the EC-wide European Trades Union Confederation which was only founded in 1973. This link to mainstream European labour representatives has never been entirely comfortable for the TUC owing to the difference in structure, affiliation, and style of most of their European counterparts. The leadership of the TUC has preferred to lead from behind where possible on EC issues, given the prevailing antagonism towards the Community throughout the union movement.

The small 'realist' wing among the TUC general council attracted growing support after the catastrophic defeat in the 1983 general election of the Labour party, which had been committed to withdrawal from the Community. The TUC, as the founder and principal subscriber to the Labour party, was to a considerable extent constrained by Labour's own programme commitments. But leaders, such as David Basnett of the General and Municipal Workers and Bill Jordan of the AUEW, had long argued that it was time for trade-unionists to make the EC work for them, implying a more permanent commitment to integration through the EC. Growing support for this approach emerged in debates at the autumn conferences of the TUC each year from 1986, and after Labour's third successive electoral defeat in 1987 the tide of revisionism in regard to the stance adopted towards the EC proved to be unexpectedly rapid and powerful. The lead from the TUC helped the Labour leadership in the autumn of 1987 to move their party away from the EC withdrawal option, and the TUC itself was swept by a wave of Europhilia at its annual conference in Bournemouth in September 1988 when Jacques Delors, the President of the European Commission, and himself a socialist, spoke to delegates about the opportunities available to them through the EC framework of improving the social and employment conditions of workers and their families.[16] This new interest in European affairs was accompanied by a detailed exposition of the workings of the Community and of the policy areas on the EC agenda where trade unions had interests they could press, prepared by the TUC's

---

[16] *Financial Times, Guardian*, 9 Sept. 1988.

international department.[17] The pro-EC stance of trade unionists was undoubtedly coloured by the EC's commitment in the Single European Act to promote 'economic and social cohesion', the agreement to double the EC's structural funds for regional, employment, and rural development made at the Brussels summit in 1988, and the launching of the EC social charter in May 1989, even though this was only adopted by eleven member states in a diluted form at the Strasburg summit in December 1989, despite Mrs Thatcher's public opposition. The completion of the single European market was also supported by the TUC, but with some caution—especially in regard to the company rationalizations and employment losses this might trigger. The Labour party, however, chose to adopt its new European clothes with some panache, no doubt sensing rising Tory discomfiture over the speed and direction of European integration in the 1990s. Labour's conversion to pro-EC orthodoxy has overtaken the TUC's caution on the direction of EC policy and appears to have forced the TUC to suppress any reservations it may have on the implications of British entry into the ERM, let alone of economic and monetary union under the Delors plan, at least in public.

The overall impression given by the behaviour of the CBI and the TUC is one of great contrast. The CBI has never allowed itself to approach EC business in a 'semi-detached' fashion. Rather it has displayed a full commitment to a somewhat narrow vision of European integration, minus most of its social policy implications. Nor has it really been constrained by the UK Government's role as 'gatekeeper', given its extensive links into EC institutions at Brussels level. The TUC did however conform to the 'semi-detached' stereotype of British attitudes towards the EC, at least until 1986. Since that date the TUC has evolved a much more positive approach to European integration and, unlike the CBI, its new position balances carefully the economic and the social dimensions. Whereas in the late 1970s, with a minority Labour Government in power, trade union influence on UK government policy—including EC policy—could be very important,[18] the arrival of the Conserv-

---

[17] Trades Union Congress, 'Report on Europe 1992. Maximising the Benefits. Minimising the Costs' (1988).

[18] One instance is the importance of TGWU opposition to the installation of the tachograph in commercial road vehicles (also known as 'the spy in the cab') leading to the then Labour Government's decision not to implement the relevant EC social regulations in 1978. See A. Butt Philip and C. Baron, 'United Kingdom', 699–701.

atives in power from 1979 heralded a more arms-length relationship with the Labour movement and the opening of an almost
unbridgeable ideological gulf separating the two political actors. In
these circumstances, while low-level contacts between trade unions
and civil servants remained in tact in conformity with the Government's 'gatekeeper' role, at the level of high politics the notion of
the UK Government as 'gatekeeper' became irrelevant. The TUC
and the Labour movement slowly came to realize that they had
little to lose by becoming more positive about the European
Community and that the prospects of influence at EC level were
distinctly brighter than those at national level.

SECTORAL INTEREST GROUPS

The extent of the involvement in EC decision-making of British
sectional and promotional interest groups very much exemplifies
the imbalance in Eurogroup activities in Brussels. It is the commercial interests that have displayed the greatest awareness of and
commitment to the EC dimension.

Some sectors very quickly became fully versed and occupied with
developments in the EC institutions. In agriculture, with the shift
of decision-making to Brussels, the National Farmers' Union found
substantial resources to devote to influencing the Community, to
working within COPA—the farmers' Eurogroup—and taking leading positions in COPA. Sir Henry Plumb moved from the Presidency of the NFU, through election as a Conservative MEP, to
become the President of the European Parliament from 1986 to
1989. Food industry interests in the UK have found it more difficult
to operate at the EC level with such ease, partly because they are
organized in such a fragmented fashion in Britain, and partly
because this fragmentation is continued at the EC level with a
multiplicity of sub-sectoral Eurogroups competing for attention in
Brussels, with no single group emerging to assume a leadership
role. The efforts of the newly created Food and Drink Federation
from the mid-1980s to strengthen its EC-wide counterpart, the
CIAA, appear not to have borne fruit. The result is that food-
processing interests, which in the UK are substantial, have all too
often been submerged by the more deeply entrenched interests of
agricultural producers. This outcome repeats a pattern already

evident at the UK government level where food industry interests have long complained of lack of support from the agriculture, trade, and industry departments.[19]

Banking interests moved rapidly to secure recognition of their needs in the European Community. In the early 1970s the European Commission was proposing that the laws on banking practice should be harmonized along highly regulated German lines. The prospect was anathema to the City. The British commercial banks reorganized themselves in order to comply with membership requirements of their Eurogroup. They led the opposition within the EC Banking Federation. They lobbied the European Parliament and they successfully persuaded the UK Government to press for a person with an appropriate City background to be appointed to head up the relevant directorate in the Commission handling the legislation. By the end of 1974 the Commission had completely changed its policy approach.[20] Building societies and savings banks have not found operating at the EC level so smooth. In part this is because the building societies do not have such powerful counterparts elsewhere in the EC, while the British savings banks suffer from being so much smaller than their European allies on the continent.

Road transport organizations have inevitably taken a close interest in developments in Europe generally, since international regulation in this sector has its origins in the 1930s. The hauliers' organizations have, for example, been much exercised by EC limits on the working hours of lorry- and bus-drivers and the rules on the installation and use of the tachograph (sometimes known as the 'spy in the cab'). Obliged to implement EC legislation that had been adopted before UK accession, British commercial road transport interests then found that they were faced with trade union refusal to work to these EC rules. The Road Haulage Association and the Freight Transport Association were unable to persuade their EC counterparts to take up their position, and they relied on their close links with Whitehall to shield them (albeit only for a few extra years) from the established law of the Community.[21] In the longer term British resistance among hauliers to EC 'over-

---

[19] O. Gray, 'Pressure Groups', 277–81, 300–9, 501–7.
[20] Butt Philip, 'Pressure Groups', 461–6.
[21] A. Butt Philip and C. Baron, 'United Kingdom', 675–713.

regulation' did find support on the continent and led to a relaxation of these regulations in 1985.

Manufacturing interests have a rather thinner record of achievement in the EC policy-making field, although most of their general concerns have been voiced by peak associations representing all employers. British textile interests, for example, do not seem to have been able to persuade the UK Government of the need for a more protectionist trade policy at EC level, nor have they been prominent on the Eurogroup circuit. The British chemical industry has fared better in both regards, perhaps because it has worked with the grain of UK government policy and because its share of the EC-wide industry is more significant. Two key issues emerging from the single European market programme have been the concerns of EC industries about direct EC investment by non-EC companies; and the worry shared by EC and non-EC industrialists that a 'fortress Europe' might be in the making that would shut off market access to 'outsiders'. Non-EC commercial interests have already found a base within the EC, not least in the United Kingdom, and this will usually entitle non-EC-owned manufacturing companies to membership of appropriate industry associations and representation within analogous Eurogroups. Such has been the transformation of Britain's industrial base since the early 1970s that by 1990 the British Radio and Electronic Equipment Manufacturers' Association (BREMA) comprised fifteen members, no less than eleven of whom were controlled by Japanese or Korean parent companies.[22] BREMA is itself a member of the European Association of Consumer Electronics Manufacturers (EACEM), but its views at the EC level could well appear to other EACEM members to be rather more global than British or European.

Local government has acquired a major interest in the EC dimension as a result *inter alia* of the Community's regional and social funds, its environmental legislation, and its rules on trading standards, employment conditions and practices, and public purchasing. British local authorities have a long history of involvement in international local authority representative bodies (such as IULA and CEMR) and have developed their own centre of expertise, the Local Government International Bureau, to help brief local councils

---

[22] Annual Report, The British Radio and Electronic Equipment Manufacturers' Association, 1989.

and represent their interests on Community business both to Whitehall and Westminster, and to the EC institutions. Their constant refrain that there was too little local government input into the pattern of spending from the EC's regional and social funds has certainly helped to persuade the EC institutions to overhaul the administration of the structural funds in a way that now requires local authority involvement.

Consumer interests across the European community have been thinly organized throughout the EC's existence. The accession of the UK brought into the EC consumer lobby (BEUC) some relatively strong national consumer organizations such as the Consumers Association and the National Consumer Council. Most unusually, the UK Government has since the 1970s provided a large annual grant to an umbrella organization, Consumers in the European Community Group (CECG), which represents the interests of over twenty different UK organizations with consumer concerns (including the women's institutes) to the EC institutions. Not only has the European Commission publicly recognized in the 1980s that it must take more account of the consumer point of view and devised some mechanisms for this, but within BEUC the British consumer interests have supplied a more than proportionate share of initiatives and resources in carrying out their role. Although the policy climate is now more favourable to the consumer both in Whitehall and in the Berlaymont, British consumer interests still express considerable frustration at the imbalance between the representation of producer interests in Brussels compared with the under-resourced consumer lobby, and at the implications for consumers of some of the details of the single market programme.

As with the consumer lobby, so with many of the 'cause' groups that are now organizing at EC level, it is often British organizations that have taken the lead. This is true in the environmental field, in animal welfare, in regard to pensioners, and the rights of migrants and refugees. Late in the day, groups such as the National Council for Civil Liberties, the Family Law Solicitors Association, and the Minority Rights Group have recognized that there are important implications for individual freedoms as a frontier-free Europe develops. Equally 'cause' groups are learning how to play Whitehall off against Brussels, by alerting the Commission to possible breaches of EC law on the part of UK authorities—a recent example being the allegation by conservationist groups that planning permission for the extension of a motorway in the Winchester area was not valid as an environmental impact assessment on the proposals had not been made in accordance with EC law.

POLITICAL PARTIES AND PRESSURE GROUPS

British political parties are frequently targets for pressure from special interest groups, and this phenomenon remains true for EC issues, even if trying to change the policy of a party is often a second-best strategy that interest groups embark on when they have failed to change the policy of the Government. Clearly industrial and City interests are likely to be most happy to lobby the Conservatives while trade union interests will naturally try to influence Labour's position above all others.

The resistance on the part of Mrs Thatcher's Government to employer and City demands for the United Kingdom to become part of the Exchange Rate Mechanism of the European Monetary System throughout the 1980s is one of the clearest examples of how political ideology can still override the economic interests of a party's own natural constituency of support. City and industrial interests, among whom Sir Michael Butler of Hambros Bank was the most conspicuous spokesman, pursued a long behind-the-scenes campaign early in 1989 directed at Conservative ministers and back-bench MPs in the hope of persuading the Government to adopt a more constructive approach towards economic and monetary union in the Community. On the Labour side, trade unions such as the engineering workers also lobbied steadily within Labour ranks to achieve a more positive policy stance towards UK membership of the Community.

Within party ranks there were also more formal organizations set up to campaign for more European integration or to resist it. The European Movement initially set up subsections of its own membership to form the core membership of a Conservative Group for Europe, a Liberal European Action Group, an Association of Social Democrats for Europe, and a Labour Committee for Europe. After 1987 the commitment of the business community to the European Movement fell away once it became clear that UK membership of the EC was irreversible and that Labour was becoming reconciled to EC membership. This connection had endured since the early 1970s and had been cemented by the 1975 referendum when business contributions largely financed the 'Yes to Europe' campaign.[23] The scaling-down of the European Movement's operations in the late 1980s meant that the party sections within it had to become largely self-financing; yet they remained in existence as an active nucleus of some hundreds of committed and informed partisans for European integration inside each party. The total membership of the European Movement, however, remained small, at around 5,000 by 1990.

Those party activists opposed to European integration through the EC appeared to have suffered even more from a reduction of activity and support for most of the 1980s. The Conservative European Reform Group never led more than a shadowy existence, anchored around a few well-known anti-Community ultras such as MPs Teddy Taylor, Jonathan Aitken, and Tony Marlow. The Labour Common Market Safeguards Campaign also went into decline in the 1980s, although some leading figures in the party, such as Peter Shore and Tony Benn, refused to adopt the emollient European line embraced by Labour's front bench after 1987. No attempt was even made in Liberal or Social Democratic party ranks to oppose European integration or the commitment to the EC, these being unshakeable articles of faith in both parties.

When Mrs Thatcher made her staunch defence of national sovereignty in a speech at the College of Europe in Bruges in September 1988, this spawned the creation of an anti-federalist group on the right of the British political spectrum dedicated to a conception of European co-operation which would leave national sovereignty undisturbed. William Cash, a Midlands Tory MP, and Lord Harris of High Cross, a cross-bench peer associated with the Institute of Economic Affairs, were the most prominent spokesmen for the 'Bruges Group' which published a number of pamphlets by academics and others from a wide variety of disciplines and political backgrounds. By the end of 1990 there were signs that critics of the new wave of European integration in Labour and Conservative circles were beginning to make common cause, and the 'Bruges Group' was evidently happy to offer a platform for all who shared its unease about the direction of change in the

[23] D. E. Butler and U. Kitzinger, *The 1975 Referendum* (London, 1976).

Community. This could be interpreted, however, as a sign of weakness rather than of strength.

One of the interesting innovations in the 1980s was the willingness of British political activists to seek allies elsewhere in the EC for their viewpoints. The 'Bruges Group' did succeed in finding intellectual support for its defence of national sovereignty in France, Belgium, and Germany. Mr Norman Tebbit, former Chairman of the Conservative party, was reported to be setting up an alliance of politicians in EC member states committed to retaining power in national Parliaments.[24] Less surprisingly, pro-integrationists also found friends on the continent of Europe through the European Movement, and more strikingly through the Kangaroo Group which was founded by a British Conservative politician, Basil de Ferranti, in 1982 to campaign for genuine free movement of people as well as goods, capital, and services throughout the Community. The Kangaroo Group became genuinely multinational and cross-party, and also attracted business support, including the National Westminster Bank in whose offices the Group is now based.

INFLUENCING THE DIFFERENT LEVELS OF GOVERNMENT

The multilevel decision-making process that characterizes the EC policy system requires of national pressure groups a considerable suppleness in attempting to influence government. A clear lobbying strategy, willingness to work in partnership with and through EC-wide groups and with other interests at the national level, and persistence are all essential elements for success. Eurogroups, at least on individual issues, can be captured by a determined and vociferous national group, as British banking interests demonstrated on the first banking law co-ordination directive between 1972 and 1977. But Eurogroups may also prove to be feeble, divided, and ill-resourced and not therefore effective, in which case they can be bypassed by those with a case to present. As they frequently have the right to nominate representatives to serve on the EC's numerous advisory committees, Eurogroups are not usually ignored, however weak they may be. But EC-level lobbying

---

[24] 'Tebbit Joins New European Club', *Guardian*, 19 Oct. 1990.

is increasingly necessary at the policy formulation, the legislative, and the implementation stages, so national pressure groups must seek alternative routes to EC decision-making, by employing consultants or by direct approaches, if Eurogroups do not adequately fulfil their needs. The most important function of the Eurogroups is that of information exchange, both with the Commission and with their own national members.

National pressure groups, if they have established links with and access to Whitehall, can expect to be consulted by civil servants on all EC proposals relevant to them as the UK Government works out its negotiating positions as the Council of Ministers works through the legislation. But many interests may have to take a pro-active rather than a reactive line. In the revision during 1983–6 of the EC social regulations for commercial road transport (drivers' hours) the sixty-one organizations on the Department of Transport's consultative list were only all invited to submit their views on the implementation aspects of a legislative instrument already agreed in Brussels. This is particularly true in the case of directives, where the Community decides the ends but leaves many of the means to be decided at national level. It is also more likely to be the case for smaller or marginal interests. It is up to civil servants in their role as 'gatekeepers' to decide when and to whom the gates are opened. For many organizations the national 'gatekeeper' only offers access on EC matters when all the major issues have already been settled.

An important role played by national pressure groups is to alert the Community authorities to possible breaches of EC rules: this is a task that individuals and companies can assume but it often looks more impressive if a national organization, especially in trade disputes, is fronting for a particular interest. The European Commission has considerable watch-dog powers to see that EC rules are enforced but it has few resources at its disposal and has never claimed to be omniscient as far as the view from the grass-roots of each member state is concerned. The Commission relies upon interest groups to raise cases of possible rule-breaking with it, so that it may investigate them, take court action or even impose fines or levies. This is especially useful, from the Commission's point of view, when it is a Government that is at fault for not correctly implementing a directive. Some pressure groups such as Greenpeace and Friends of the Earth have used this tactic very effectively, for example in regard to water quality and bathing water directives. Trade unions in Britain have backed several actions in the European Court of Justice (ECJ) which have extended the interpretation of equal pay for equal work as between men and women. The Civic Trust complained to the Commission about the non-implementation in the UK of the 1969 and 1970 social regulations on drivers' hours and tachographs. That led to the commission taking the UK Government to the ECJ and forcing the Government to comply. Sometimes it is an interest group that finds itself in the dock rather than in the role of accuser. The Publishers' Association in 1989 defended itself successfully from Commission attack in the ECJ over the net book agreement, a system of resale price maintenance operated by publishers and booksellers, which the Court found on balance to be in the public interest. Another case spanning 1989 and 1990 involved the opening of shops on Sundays. The British do-it-yourself store group, B & Q, used as a defence for breaking UK Sunday closing rules the EEC Treaty's requirement that no measures should be adopted at national level which have the effect of frustrating trade with other member states in a discriminatory fashion. Nor is it just the Commission or the ECJ to whom pressure groups turn; they can also bring suspected abuses to the attention of MEPs or to a sympathetic Government.

CONCLUSIONS

Pressure groups may have been mistaken initially in thinking that only those committed to full European integration would get a hearing in Brussels. British banking interests never made this error, seeing their role as being to keep the Commission out of their hair as much as to encourage it. Trade union interests were much slower in learning this lesson. The EC decision-making system is open to any group that is prepared to make use of it. But at first it was almost entirely commercial interests which took advantage of this new opportunity for exercising influence. More recently British initiatives from groups concerned with animal welfare and the interests of the elderly have begun to add weight to the relatively small number of Eurogroups that exist to press the interests of large sections of society or to promote particular causes. Nevertheless the real weight of British pressure group interests active in the

EC domain is commercial, even if some of the non-commercial groups, such as the National Council for Voluntary Organizations and the local authority associations, command considerable respect among policy-makers.

The serious players in the EC policy system know that they have to invest time and money in tracking and monitoring EC policies, and in building and maintaining networks of contacts at the national and Community levels, in Whitehall, in the Commission, among public representatives, journalists, and among other lobbyists. Relatively few British pressure groups can afford this, but they will exert disproportionate influence along the corridors of power—money and human resources also being 'gatekeepers' to the EC dimension of policy-making.

Both serious and more spasmodic British pressure groups with interests in the EC level of government can encounter problems in trying to find recognized Eurogroups to which they should affiliate. Eurogroups have difficulty in reflecting fully all the different concerns of each national member, especially as the common label linking, for example, mortgage institutions may prove to be more nominal than real. The lack of fit between national interest groups and Eurogroups, and the importance of EC decisions to individual firms and public authorities at the national level has prompted many to employ consultants in Brussels and a few to open offices there. This marked trend in the last three years does tend not only to undermine the Eurogroups, but also to affect adversely national pressure groups, if companies and consultants appear to be telling a different story from the official compromises that interest groups have collectively agreed. The expansion of so many consultancy firms to serve this market suggests that British pressure groups will encounter mounting problems both in Whitehall and in Brussels in managing the content of representations to policy-makers on EC matters. Just as national government itself has to some extent been bypassed by the arrival of the EC dimension in policy-making, so national pressure groups risk being bypassed by direct action taken by their own members.

8

British Public Opinion and the
European Community

Neill Nugent

A MAJOR initial difficulty in attempting to deal with British opinion—be it opinion on the European Community or on any other matter—is that the very term 'British opinion' is often used and applied in different ways. At its broadest and, it may be thought, its most correct, the term is taken to refer to the opinion of the British people as a whole This is commonly referred to as public opinion. A second, and frequent, use of the term is as a sort of shorthand for 'the opinion of the British Government'. In this context the assumption is frequently made—not always with much evidence—that governmental opinion is the same as public opinion. A third use of the term is when it refers to what is sometimes called 'informed opinion', that is, the opinion of élites in influential spheres of activity such as politics, administration, business, trade unions, and the media.

It is with public opinion that this chapter is primarily concerned. Governmental and non-governmental élite opinions will be considered only in so far as they touch on, and have implications for, the nature and role of public opinion.

MEASURING PUBLIC OPINION

A variety of methodological difficulties arise when attempting to measure public opinion. The main reason for this is, quite simply, because public opinion, by its very nature, is complex: some people have a clear view on an issue, others are uncertain as to what they think; some hold an opinion with great intensity and passion, others lean only marginally in a particular direction; the opinion of some is based on knowledge and expertise, that of others on uninformed prejudice.

Public opinion polls—the mechanism by which public opinion is customarily gauged—cannot always deal satisfactorily with such complexities. Amongst the problems that are associated with public opinion polls the following are particularly worth noting:

1. Polls invite people to express opinions on issues to which little or no thought may have been given. This is a key reason why opinion poll findings on issues can vary considerably depending on the way in which questions are phrased, and the extent to which issues have or have not recently been in the news.

2. Polls have to assume that responses to questions on opinions have meaning whereas, in fact, responses may be given only because they are perceived as being expected.

3. Polls place opinions into categories—'in favour', 'against', 'don't know', etc. Frequently such categories are far too limited and narrow in scope to capture the variety of opinion that really exists on a matter.

4. Polls often fail to bring out the fact that people may have different opinions on different aspects of an issue. Further to this, even when differences are detected it is not always easy to evaluate their relative significance. For example, at least three viewpoints can be argued in connection with the relationship between public opinion and Britain's relations with the European Community: that affective sentiment is the most important because it provides the underlying foundation for all developments; that more specific attitudes—on Community membership and particular issues and policies—matter most because the Community is being built via a creeping gradualism rather than by grand visionary strides; that neither affective sentiment nor specific attitudes matter very much because decision-making is in the hands of governmental and non-governmental élites.

Before proceeding to examine just what pollsters have, and have had, to say about British public opinion and the European Community it is worth concluding these cautionary comments about the many problems involved in measuring and describing public opinion with a specific example.

In June 1989 Gallup looked at British public opinion on Europe from a number of different angles. Amongst these angles was concern about future developments. Opinion on this was explored through the questions that are set out in Tables 8.1 and 8.2.

TABLE 8.1   *British worries about European integration, June 1989 (1)*

The European Community is gradually going to become more integrated. Is there anything you fear may come out of that process?

	%*
Loss of sovereignty/identity	12
Too much control from abroad/Brussels	10
Rabies	3
Rise in prices	2
Channel Tunnel	2
Too much bureaucracy	2
Other	17
No, nothing	56

* All replies given on an unprompted basis.
Source: Gallup Political Index, Report No. 346, June 1989.

TABLE 8.2   *British worries about European integration, June 1989 (2)*

Here are some of the things that worry people when they think about the future of Britain in Europe. Could you tell me in each case whether you do, or do not, share this worry? (%)

	Share	Do not	Don't know
Rabies and other animal and plant diseases spreading from the continent to Britain	77	21	3
The transfer of power from the British Parliament to Brussels	54	39	7
That terrorists and terrorist weapons may be able to move more easily from one country to another	67	29	4
That drug smuggling in Europe may become easier	70	27	3
That standardized taxes across Europe may increase the British cost of living	55	36	9
An increase in illegal immigration	52	42	6

Source: Gallup Political Index, Report No. 346, June 1989.

Clearly, as even just the most cursory glance at the tables reveals, the responses to the questions produced significant variations and inconsistencies. To take the issue of the extent to which Europe poses a 'threat' to British sovereignty, Table 8.1 indicates that this concerns just over one-fifth of the population, whilst Table 8.2 indicates that it worries over one-half. What explains the disparity between the tables? Three factors appear to have been particularly important:

(*a*) In Table 8.1 respondents were not prompted or helped with a list of potential worries to work from. Ignorance of Community matters was unquestionably a major reason why 56 per cent were not able/willing to name any issue.

(*b*) In Table 8.2 respondents were not only given specific issue cues, but they were obliged to express a view on each one.

(*c*) The issues listed in Table 8.2 are all potentially highly charged politically—and thus probably weighted the scales in favour of strongly negative views being found.

Which of the two tables is the more useful and the more accurate in indicating the true state of British public opinion is a matter for debate. Suffice it to note here that, taken together, they serve to emphasize the importance of interpreting all public opinion poll findings with caution and care.

PUBLIC OPINION AND THE COMMUNITY: THE EVIDENCE
OF THE POLLS

Over the years hundreds of surveys have been conducted in Britain which have contained questions about aspects of European unity and Britain's relations with the European Community. Obviously only a small fraction of this mass of material can be touched on here. So as to enable the treatment to be manageable, but also so as to be able to bring out some of the differing dimensions of British public opinion on Europe and the Community, attention will be focused on four areas:

1. Opinion on the general idea of Western European unification.
2. Opinion on the United Kingdom's membership of the European Community.

3. Opinion on whether the United Kingdom has or has not benefited from being a member of the European Community.
4. Attitudes towards becoming 'a European' and opinion on the importance of Europe for Britain.

The information that is presented below comes from two main sources. First, from data collected over the years by Gallup. Particular use is made of a major survey, entitled *The Image of Europe*, which Gallup conducted for the Commission in May 1989.[1] Second, from the Commission-sponsored surveys of public opinion which, since 1973, have been regularly conducted throughout the Community on a twice-yearly basis and which are published in the bi-annual publication *Eurobarometer*. These surveys are based on a representative sample of the population of the member states over 15 years of age and are carried out in the spring and the autumn. To facilitate the presentation of the *Eurobarometer* data only the results of the spring surveys are reported in the tables and figures that are to be found on the following pages. For the most part omission of the autumn poll findings does not significantly affect the picture that emerges, but where something about the autumn data does merit comment it is given.[2]

1. *Opinion on the General Idea of Western European Unification*

Public opinion data on British attitudes towards the general idea of unification in Western Europe (what is often described as affective support for West European integration) first began to be collected in the early 1950s. Table 8.3 and Figure 8.1 indicate the principal findings of the data. Four points are particularly worth emphasizing.

First, opinion on integration has not been as negative as is commonly supposed. Even when attitudes towards British membership of the Community have been at their most unfavourable, with

---

[1] The report was produced in two volumes: *Summary Report of General Public Survey*; and *Tabulated Results of General Public Survey*. The author wishes to thank Social Surveys Ltd. for permission to use Gallup material.

[2] Until the spring of 1989 the UK end of the *Eurobarometer* surveys was conducted by Gallup; since the autumn of 1989 it has been conducted by NOP. The author wishes to thank the Commission for permission to use *Eurobarometer* material.

TABLE 8.3 *British attitudes to Western European unification, 1952–1990*

In general, are you for or against efforts being made to unify Western Europe? (%)

	1952	1957	1962	1964	1967	1973	1975	1979	1981	1983	1985	1987	1988	1989	1990
For very much	58	64	47	59	63	14	28	21	17	20	30	29	20	21	27
For to some extent	(58)	(64)	(47)	(59)	(63)	23	22	40	35	40	38	42	40	49	44
(combined For)	58	64	47	59	63	37	50	61	52	60	68	71	60	70	71
Against to some extent	15	12	22	18	15	15	11	14	14	15	11	10	18	13	11
Against very much	(15)	(12)	(22)	(18)	(15)	15	11	6	15	5	4	6	7	5	6
(combined Against)	15	12	22	18	15	30	22	20	29	20	15	16	25	18	17
No opinion/No reply	27	24	31	23	22	33	28	19	19	20	17	13	15	12	12

Source: compiled from *Eurobarometer* surveys.

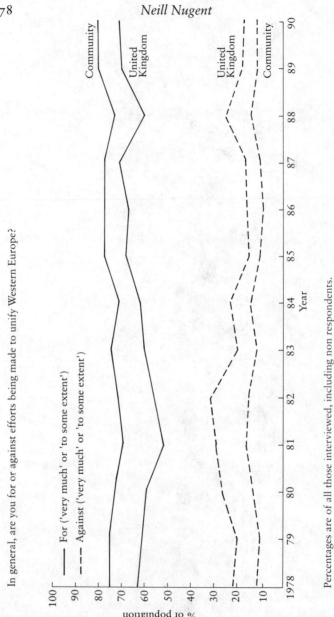

FIG. 8.1.   Results of surveys on British attitudes to Western European unification, 1952–1990
Source: compiled from *Eurobarometer* surveys.

large majorities against membership, there have always been far more British people in favour of the idea of integration than there have been against. Amongst those expressing an opinion there has constantly been majority support, whilst the figure when those not expressing an opinion are included has fallen below 50 per cent on only two occasions: in the early 1960s, when membership was being actively pursued for the first time, and in the period immediately after the 1973 accession.

Secondly, since accession the trend of support has been upwards. From the low point of 1973, when only 37 per cent of the population expressed some support for integration, the figures have climbed, albeit not completely steadily and with some temporary downturns. By the late 1980s figures in the region of 70 per cent were being recorded, if not constantly at least regularly.

Thirdly, British opinion has been significantly out of line with the average Community opinion. The proportion of the British population supporting unification has usually been 10–15 per cent lower than the Community average, and the proportion opposing unification has usually been 5–10 per cent higher. The gap has been even greater, at both the supporting and opposing ends of the spectrum, when compared not with the Community average (which, of course, includes a weighting for the UK) but with the average of the founding six members. Of the now twelve member states only Denmark has shown less support for unification than Britain: not until 1988 did a majority of Danes first express support.

Fourthly, it is important to recognize that the issue under scrutiny here is very loose and open-ended in nature. An expression of support for Western European unity may indicate a general sentiment, but it can hardly be said to call for much commitment on the part of the public. If not quite in the 'are you in favour of the abolition of wife-beating?' category, the question covered by Table 8.3 and Figure 8.1 does not raise sensitive issues in any direct way, or encourage respondents to think of problems and difficulties that might be associated with unification. Indeed, there is not even the implication that the UK should be part of the unification process— a point that is, perhaps, particularly significant when interpreting the pre-1973 figures. It is not, therefore, perhaps altogether surprising to find that something like a third of those who regard Britain's Community membership in a negative light—37 per cent according to *The Image of Europe* survey of May 1989—are prepared to support the idea of the unification of Western Europe.

2. *Opinion on Britain's Membership of the European Community*

In turning to British membership of the European Community the question of British attitudes to West European unification takes on a much more specific form. As such, more negativism is to be anticipated, it long having been established that whilst people are usually willing to express their support for broad and fine-sounding principles, they become more reluctant when these principles are given operational meaning and application. Such indeed has been the case with regard to Britain and Western Europe: a significant, and sometimes a very large, gap has existed between attitudes to the general idea of Western European unification on the one hand and attitudes to Britain's membership of the Community on the other.

Following Britain's first application to join the Community in 1961, which gave the issue of membership a greater saliency than it had had hitherto, opinion in the years up to the 1973 accession was somewhat fickle and volatile.[3] An important reason for this was that few people felt strongly about the Community—Butler and Stokes described it as a matter on which, in the mid-1960s, 'the mass public had formed attitudes to only a very limited degree'[4]—and therefore opinion was always subject to ebbs and flows according to circumstances and the political climate.

Since accession, opinion, though still subject to a certain amount of fluctuation, has tended, for the most part, to be rather more stable. As Table 8.4 shows, until the mid-1980s, apart from a relatively brief period around the time of the 1975 referendum, only between one-quarter and one-third of the population regarded membership in a positive light; a slightly higher proportion

[3] In very general terms, until mid-1967 most polls showed the supporters of British entry to the Community to outnumber the opponents. From mid-1967 opponents were in a majority, apart from a brief period in early 1972. On British public opinion prior to accession see: U. W. Kitzinger, *Diplomacy and Persuasion* (London, 1973); R. J. Shepherd, *Public Opinion and European Integration* (Farnborough, 1975); Social Surveys (Gallup Poll) Ltd., *British Attitudes Towards the Common Market 1957–1972* (1972).

[4] D. Butler and D. Stokes, *Political Change in Britain* (2nd edn. London, 1974), 279.

TABLE 8.4 *British attitudes to membership of the European Community, 1973–1990*

Generally speaking, do you think that the United Kingdom's membership of the Common Market is a good thing, a bad thing, or neither good nor bad? (%)

	1973	1975	1977	1979	1981	1983	1985	1987	1988	1989	1990
Good thing	31	47	35	33	24	28	37	43	37	48	52
Bad thing	34	21	40	34	48	36	30	26	29	21	19
Neither good nor bad	22	19	22	26	24	29	28	25	29	26	24
No opinion/ no reply	13	13	3	7	4	7	5	6	5	5	5

Source: compiled from *Eurobarometer* surveys.

regarded it in a negative light; and a similar higher proportion regarded it as neither good nor bad or were not willing to express an opinion. From the mid-1980s, however, there was a clear increase in the amount of favourable opinion, to such an extent that in May 1989 Gallup, for the first time, found an overall majority—55 per cent—who evaluated Britain's membership of the Community as being a 'good thing'.[5]

The increase in support for Community membership around the time of the 1975 referendum does, of course, raise questions about how deep and how serious much of the opposition of the 1970s and early 1980s really was. For the fact is that on the only occasion when the British people were asked for their opinion in circumstances which really mattered, 67 per cent voted in favour of Britain staying in the Community, 33 per cent voted against, and 35 per cent did not vote. At a minimum, these figures reveal that the proportion of the population which, in the mid-1970s at least, unconditionally wanted British withdrawal was relatively small. When they were doing something more significant than replying to a pollster, many doubters and waverers were wooed into the pro-Community camp—partly because most of the political leaders whom they held in esteem urged them to do so, and partly because there was no satisfactory answer to the question: 'What's the

[5] Social Surveys Ltd., *The Image of Europe: Summary Report*, 21.

Neill Nugent

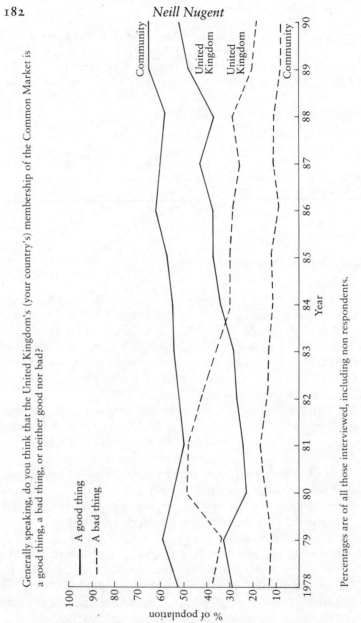

Generally speaking, do you think that the United Kingdom's (your country's) membership of the Common Market is a good thing, a bad thing, or neither good nor bad?

A good thing

A bad thing

Community

United Kingdom

United Kingdom

Community

% of population

Year

Percentages are of all those interviewed, including non respondents.

FIG. 8.2. Results of surveys on merits/demerits of membership of the Common Market, 1973–1990

Source: compiled from *Eurobarometer* surveys.

alternative?' As Butler and Kitzinger observed on the referendum result, the support given was unequivocal, but unenthusiastic; wide but not deep; a vote essentially for the status quo.[6]

Regarding comparisons with opinion in the other member states of the Community, it can be seen from Figure 8.2 that the pattern is similar, though more pronounced, to opinion on efforts being made to unify Western Europe. Whereas on the unification issue the 'positive' gap between UK opinion and the average Community opinion has usually been 10–15 per cent and the 'negative' gap 5–10 per cent, on the membership issue the gaps have commonly been 20–25 per cent and 15–20 per cent. Again, the only country to display a comparable 'European reluctance' has been Denmark: in 1990, 49 per cent of Danes stated Denmark's membership of the Community was a good thing whilst 25 per cent stated that it was a bad thing.

3. Opinion on Whether Britain Has or Has Not Benefited from Being a Member of the European Community

Data on this issue only started to appear on a systematic basis in *Eurobarometer* surveys in 1983. As Table 8.5 shows there has never been a majority which has expressed the view that the UK has benefited from membership of the Community. However the proportion which has perceived an overall benefit has been gradually rising: from 32 per cent in 1983 to 46 per cent in 1990.

It will be noted from the accompanying tables and figures that UK opinion on the question of benefits from Community membership largely parallels opinion on the question of membership itself: on the 'pro-Community' side both sets of figures have kept to within 6 per cent of one another, and both have shown a gradual increase. It should be stressed, however, that there is nothing inevitable about such a relationship, as evidence from other member states demonstrates. In Denmark, for example, which, as has been noted, is the only country whose people have been as

---

[6] D. Butler and U. W. Kitzinger, *The 1975 Referendum* (London, 1976), 280. On the 1975 referendum see also B. Sarlvik *et al.* 'Britain's Membership of the EEC: A Profile of Electoral Opinions in the Spring of 1974—With a Postscript on the Referendum'. *European Journal of Political Research*, 4 (1976), 83–113; also the brief comments in D. Butler, 'Public Opinion and Community Membership', *Political Quarterly*, 50 (1979), 151–6.

TABLE 8.5 *British perceptions of the benefits of membership of the European Community, 1983–1990*

Taking everything into consideration, would you say that the United Kingdom has on balance benefited or not from being a member of the European Community (Common Market)? (%)

	1983	1984	1985	1986	1987	1988	1989	1990
Benefited	32	32	31	33	39	39	44	46
Not benefited	57	56	55	50	46	47	42	38
No opinion/No reply	11	12	11	17	15	14	14	16

Note: The spring 1989 poll was not the first *Eurobarometer* survey to find more respondents in the 'benefited' than in the 'non-benefited' column. In autumn 1987 the figures were 49 : 42, and in autumn 1988 were 47 : 40.

Source: compiled from *Eurobarometer* surveys.

Taking everything into consideration, would you say that the United Kingdom (your country) has on balance benefited or not from being a member of the European Community (Common Market)?

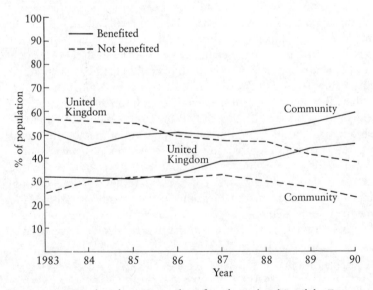

FIG. 8.3. Results of surveys on benefits of membership of the European Community, 1983–1990
Source: compiled from *Eurobarometer* surveys.

unenthusiastic about membership as the British, a majority of the population have, since the mid-1980s, consistently expressed the view that their country benefits from membership. Conversely, there has been a considerable measure of scepticism about the benefits of membership in some of those countries which are normally thought of as being amongst the most ardent Europeans: for example the percentage of the population believing their country has benefited from Community membership has, since the mid-1980s, only been in the mid- to high 50s in France, and the high 40s to mid-50s in Germany.

This scepticism in certain Community countries about the benefits of membership is as important as increasingly positive UK evaluations in helping to explain why the gap between UK attitudes and the average Community attitude has narrowed in recent years: as Figure 3 shows, from around 20 per cent in the 1983–6 period to around 10 per cent in the 1987–90 period.

4. Attitudes Towards Being 'a European' and Opinion on the Importance of Europe for Britain

In terms of personal identification the British have developed only a very limited 'European consciousness'. Certainly when the issue of nationality is raised in a direct manner—as it is, for example, in the question for which the findings are reported in Table 8.6—the British are more reluctant than the population of any other Community country to acknowledge that they may have not only a national, but also a European, identity.

When, however, the focus is shifted away from personal identity to an awareness of the current and potential importance of the European dimension for Britain, a clear majority of the population can be said to display at least some sense of a 'European consciousness'. That consciousness may be vague, its nature may be only partially understood, and the role of the Community may be confused with that of other international organizations, but that there is an increasing 'Europeanness' is seen in a number of different ways. In Table 8.7 it is seen in over 60 per cent of the population saying they are aware of an economic interdependence within the Community. In Table 8.8 it is seen in around 60 per cent of the population claiming to recognize a two-way influence between Britain and the Community—with the influence *on* Britain

TABLE 8.6 *Sense of European identity in member states of the European Community, June 1990*

Do you ever think of yourself as not only (nationality), but also European? (%)

	Belgium	Denmark	Germany	Greece	France	Ireland	Italy	Luxemburg	Netherlands	Portugal	Spain	UK	EC 12
Often	14	16	12	28	19	11	20	17	8	7	16	12	15
Sometimes	38	32	27	28	38	21	37	35	29	40	36	16	31
Never	46	50	53	41	41	67	43	42	60	45	47	71	51
No reply	2	2	7	3	2	2	1	6	3	7	2	1	3

Source: Eurobarometer, No. 33, June 1990.

TABLE 8.7 *British public awareness of Britain's economic interdependence with the rest of the European Community, 1989*

How closely would you say that the British economy is tied to or is dependent upon, that of the rest of the European Community? (%)

Very closely	18
Fairly closely	48
Not very closely	18
Not closely at all	5
Don't know	10

Source: Social Surveys (Gallup Poll) Ltd., *The Image of Europe*, 1989.

TABLE 8.8 *British public assessments of the influence of Britain and of the European Community on policy and development, 1989 (%)*

	Influence of Britain on the European Community	Influence of the European Community on Britain
A great deal	13	15
A fair amount	44	49
Not very much	32	26
None at all	4	3
Don't know	6	7

Source: Social Surveys (Gallup Poll) Ltd., *The Image of Europe*, 1989.

TABLE 8.9 *British opinion on which policies should be determined at European level, 1989 (1)*

Which policies do you think should be determined primarily at a European level? (%)*

Defence/nuclear arms	19
The environment/pollution	10
Trade/import and export control	10
Finance/monetary	9
Agriculture	5
Foreign relations	5
Employment	4
Health/social welfare	4
Education	3
Fight against drugs/terrorism	3
Other	26
None	8
Don't know	37

* All replies given on an unprompted basis. Multiple answers possible.
Source: Social Surveys (Gallup Poll) Ltd., *The Image of Europe*, 1989.

TABLE 8.10 *British opinion on which policies should be determined at European level, 1989 (2)*

Which of the following areas of policy do you think should be determined by the British Government, and which should be decided within the Community as a whole (%)

	By the British Government	Within the Community	Don't know
Broadcasting and press standards	67	24	9
Education standards	64	31	5
Currency	62	32	7
Protection of computer-based information on individuals	61	29	10
Standards for health and social welfare	55	41	4
Setting rates for VAT	53	38	9
Security and defence	49	47	4
Workers participation on company boards	45	40	15
Protection of the environment	38	59	3
Foreign policy with countries outside of the European Community	32	59	10
Scientific and technological research	28	65	8
Co-operation with developing countries/Third World	18	76	6

Source: Social Surveys (Gallup Poll) Ltd., *The Image of Europe*, 1989.

being perceived as slightly greater than that *of* Britain. In Table 8.9 it is seen in a majority of the population being able to name, on an unprompted basis, at least one policy issue which is best dealt with at the European, rather than the national, level. And in Table 8.10 it is seen in a majority of the population, when policy areas are placed before them, naming several important areas which should be determined at the Community level.

In attempting to summarize British opinion on Europe the most important point to make is that the British people are increasingly aware of, and supportive of, 'the European dimension'. At a minimum it seems fair to conclude that the public are far more positive about Europe and the Community than is commonly supposed to be the case.

At the same time, however, the extent to which the British are becoming 'good Europeans' must not be exaggerated. Although the size of the gaps has in most cases narrowed, the British still constantly fall well below the Community average on most indicators of 'European enthusiasm' and vie with the Danes for the description of 'most reluctant Community member'. Reluctance is seen most obviously in the large reservoirs of open opposition to, and reservations about, various aspects of European unity and the role of the Community. It is seen, too, in the way in which many of those who affirm the importance and benefit of Europe as a forum for policy action on key issues are often revealed, on closer examination, to be hesitant, divided, and confused in their views, and/or to be, at best, only dimly aware of what policy action at European level means and implies. Evidence of such hesitancy, division, confusion, and lack of basic knowledge is seen both in the way polls often display significantly different results depending on the way questions are phrased, and also in the difficulties which many survey respondents have when they are not prompted in their replies by lists but are required to provide the list entries themselves. (Compare, for example, Table 8.1 with Table 8.2, and Table 8.9 with Table 8.10.)

EXPLAINING BRITISH OPINION ON THE COMMUNITY

The formation of public opinion is a complex process, with many factors combining to mould beliefs, views, and prejudices. In seeking to explain British opinion on the Community, attention here will necessarily have to be restricted. There will not be any consideration of the complex mixture of 'general' cultural, social, and psychological factors which make most people in most parts of the world—not just Britain—subject to national attachments and loyalties. The focus will be on what appear to have been the principal factors in giving British opinion on the Community its particular shape.

The starting-point in explaining Britain's relatively high degree of 'Euro-scepticism' is usually located by observers in four inter-related historical factors:

(*a*) Britain has traditionally had strong political, economic, social, and cultural ties outside Europe: notably with the Empire and Commonwealth, and the United States. These ties have, in many respects, been stronger than European ties, as is evidenced by the fact that until well into the 1970s the British people consistently placed the United States, Australia, and Canada well above any European country when asked to name 'Britain's friends'.[7]

(*b*) Until the mid-1950s, and for longer in much of the public imagination, Britain was a world power of the first rank. There was no apparent need to integrate with other European countries.

(*c*) Western European countries have tended to be looked on with suspicion, and in some respects have been regarded as being second rate. Such attitudes, which have long historical roots, were encouraged by the experience of the Second World War.

(*d*) Britain has had a long and deep-seated tradition of independence and sovereignty. Whereas on the continent the Second World War had alerted publics to the frailty of their national institutions and so did something to prepare them for supranationalism, Britain's wartime experience seemingly served to emphasize the strength of her national structures.

It is clear that with the passage of time the importance of these 'historical' factors is now in decline. Doubtless they have left a legacy which still plays some part in helping to shape public attitudes—and they are, perhaps, of particular importance in explaining why the British are more concerned with preservation of sovereignty than any other Community country apart from Denmark—but changed circumstances have naturally brought new influencing factors forward. These factors can be divided into two categories: on the one hand, there are those which have tended to encourage a continued 'Euro-scepticism'; on the other hand, there are those which have tended to foster the development of more

[7] See Shepherd, *Public Opinion*, 87–9.

positive attitudes towards both Europe in general and the Community in particular.

Four principal factors have encouraged a continued 'Euro-scepticism':

(*a*) The early years of Community membership coincided with the post-1973–4 international economic recession and also with a range of serious domestic problems: inflation, rising unemployment, poor labour relations, and an increasingly sharp political polarization. The general pessimism this induced seems to have had some spill-over effect on to the Community, which assumed something of the role of a scapegoat for Britain's problems.

(*b*) Powerful political voices have been raised against both Community membership itself and particular aspects of Community membership. In the 1970s these voices came mainly from the Labour left and a small section of the Conservative right. In the early 1980s complete withdrawal from the Community became official Labour party policy for a period, whilst the Conservatives too were increasingly seen to be tinged with anti-Europeanism as Mrs Thatcher opened the decade demanding 'our money back' and closed it railing against the 'socialist excesses' of Brussels. With most voters largely uninterested in, and uninformed about, Community affairs it was inevitable that many should, on the Community issue, tend to follow the lead and reflect the views of their chosen political leaders and parties. Thus Labour voters were, until the late 1980s, much more hostile to the Community than Conservative voters, whilst Conservative voters did not regard the Community with as much favour as might have been expected.

(*c*) The information and images that have been carried by the media have hardly encouraged favourable attitudes towards the Community. Sections of the quality Press apart, European Community news has not figured prominently in the British media; indeed, the Community has tended to be covered only when highly important or controversial issues have featured. Frequently this coverage has been cast in terms of 'us' against 'them', or of the Community being in some way a problem for Britain. The tabloid press has been particularly culpable in this respect, with its treatment of the Community almost invariably being highly simplistic and misleading in manner: favourite themes have included the wastages and surpluses of the Common Agricultural Policy, the idiocy and meddling of overpaid Brussels bureaucrats, and—a theme much encouraged by the Government in the 1980s—Mrs Thatcher defiantly resisting the efforts of foreigners to undermine British independence and generally do Britain down. The 50 per cent or so of the British population who regularly read a daily tabloid have thus hardly been encouraged to see British interests as being served by Community membership.

(d) Governmental and public agencies in Britain have tended not to do so much as their continental counterparts to emphasize that Britain is an integrated part of the Community and reaps benefits from membership. There was, for example, very little governmental effort to stimulate awareness about Community issues until the Department of Trade and Industry's 'Europe—Open For Business' campaign got under way in the late 1980s. At the symbolic level, the European flag is a common sight in most member countries: in Britain it is rarely seen, except as a small insert on notices proclaiming that a development is being partly funded by the European Regional Development Fund.

Turning to the factors which explain the development in recent years of more positive attitudes towards Europe and the Community, the following have been particularly important:

(a) Changed political and economic circumstances have made people increasingly aware of the vulnerability and frailty of national institutions and, more especially, of the weakness of the national economy. The 1989 survey, *The Image of Europe*, contained the question: 'Do you believe that Britain has any other realistic alternatives but to participate fully in the European Community in order to safeguard its economic prosperity and position in the world?' Only 13 per cent said there were alternatives, 14 per cent did not know, and 72 per cent said there were no alternatives. In all gender, age, and class categories over 60 per cent recognized the necessity of full participation. Even amongst those who regard Community membership as a 'bad thing', only 32 per cent felt alternatives existed.[8]

(b) Following on from the previous point, Europe and the Community have increasingly been in the news and Britain's role in Europe has become increasingly difficult to ignore. Moreover, the view that Britain has a potentially important role to play in the 'new' Europe has come to be pressed from many varied, and in

---

[8] Social Surveys Ltd., *The Image of Europe: Summary Report*, 71–2.

TABLE 8.11 *British feelings of affinity towards Americans, people of the Commonwealth, and Europeans, June 1989*

Which of these groups do you feel closest to?
And which group would you say you felt next closest to? (%)

	Closest	Two Closest
Americans	21	47
People in countries like Australia, New Zealand, and Canada	31	60
People on the continent of Europe	31	52
Don't know	16	16

Source: Gallup Political Index, Report No. 346, June 1989.

some cases new, quarters: the Labour party, for example (attracted both by 'the social dimension' and by Conservative divisions on Europe); the trade union movement (attracted too by 'social Europe'); the business community (anxious to reap benefits from the 1992 programme); and the DTI (with its 'Europe—Open For Business' campaign).

(*c*) Increasing contact with, and awareness of, European countries—which has come about not only as a result of the consequences of Community membership but also as a result of non-political factors, such as the growth in foreign leisure travel and greater availability of continental food and drink—has helped to break down age-old barriers of distrust and suspicion. This has had the effect, when coupled with the loosening of the special ties that in the past have bound Britain to the Commonwealth and USA, of making the British feel increasingly close to the people of Europe. The attitudes suggested by Table 8.11 would have been inconceivable until relatively recently.

(*d*) The softening in the Labour party's opposition to Europe after 1983, and its development of a degree of enthusiasm after 1987, has been extremely important. Just as many Labour supporters followed their leadership's former 'anti'-Community stance, so have they followed the more pro-Community position: so much so that by the late 1980s there was no significant difference in attitudes on the general desirability of integration within the

Community (although there was on Community policy objectives) between the supporters of the Conservative and Labour parties.[9] As well as producing a direct increase in the number of 'pro-Europeans' amongst the British population, by bringing its supporters 'across', the change in Labour's position may also have had an indirect beneficial effect by virtually eliminating the question of whether Britain should or should not be a member of the Community from political debate, and thereby contributing to feelings that membership is inevitable and, on balance, desirable.

(e) Rising levels of affluence and of education have had some effect. This is because affluence and education have consistently been associated with pro-European views—in part, doubtless, because the affluent and the educated are more exposed to, and are more aware of, the political and economic realities and possibilities of international life. Two examples may be briefly cited to demonstrate the general consistency of this relationship over time. In 1975 a National Opinion Poll survey showed that 80 per cent of people in the AB socio-economic category were in favour of continued Community membership, 66 per cent of C1s were in favour, 50 per cent of C2s, and 41 per cent of DEs.[10] In 1989 *The Image of Europe* survey, on the much more specific issue of whether respondents were for or against the establishment of the Single European Market by 1992, found that 74 per cent of ABs were in favour, 60 per cent of C1s, 59 per cent of C2s, and 48 per cent of DEs.[11]

So as Britain as a whole has become more affluent, the development of more positive images of the Community has been facilitated.

PUBLIC OPINION ON THE COMMUNITY: ITS SIGNIFICANCE

In assessing the significance of British public opinion on the Community there are three main potential aspects: the significance for domestic politics; the significance for Britain's relations with the Community; and the significance for the overall viability and legitimacy of the Community.

[9] For further details see *The Image of Europe: Tabulated Results*, esp. pp. 32, 38.
[10] NOP, *The Common Market Referendum*, n.d.
[11] *The Image of Europe: Tabulated Results*, 31.

The Significance for Domestic Politics

Public opinion on the Community has affected domestic British politics in three principal ways.

First, it has helped to shape, as well as itself being shaped by, the policy positions on the Community of the major political parties. Developments in the Labour party are especially interesting in this regard. The anti-Community stance that was adopted by the party after its 1979 general election defeat was, if not caused by, at least greatly facilitated by, the then strong anti-Community feelings in the country. Similarly it was not coincidental that the virtual abandonment of the policy of hostility to the Community that followed the party's 1983 election defeat largely paralleled the increasingly favourable attitudes to the Community amongst the public that developed in the early to mid-1980s. These were attitudes that the party doubtless helped to create by its policy switch, but they were attitudes too that it was following—not least since the party's stance on Europe was portrayed in the early 1980s by the Conservatives and the SDP/Liberal Alliance as further evidence of Labour's extremism.

As for the Conservative party, it has never, since the first application to join the Community was made in 1961, been deflected from a basically pro-Community stance by periods of anti-Community majority opinion. That said, however, it has not been unaware of the public opinion implications of its policies, or—crucially important under Mrs Thatcher—the public presentation of those policies. There can, for example, be little doubt that whilst Mrs Thatcher's well-aired suspicions of the Community were genuine, she sought to tap nationalist sentiments and reap popular support from her stance of vigorously defending British interests in Community forums. Such, however, was the development of more positive attitudes towards the Community in the second half of the 1980s that by the end of the decade many senior Conservatives were beginning to wonder whether the Thatcher message and style was still striking an effective popular chord.

Secondly, changes in public opinion on the Community have been reflected in the nature and focus of political debate in Britain. This is most obviously seen in the way in which the question of membership has appeared on the political agenda: in the 1970s and early 1980s, when the opponents of membership normally outnumbered the supporters, the question featured prominently in political debate; since the mid-1980s, when supporters have been in an ever-increasing majority, the membership question has virtually disappeared and political debate has focused on what sort of European Community Britain should be helping to create.

Thirdly, public opinion has tempted and encouraged politicians to use patriotic and nationalistic political rhetoric. Aware of national suspicions and reservations about the Community, many politicians—above all Mrs Thatcher—have sought to emphasize the need, and their own capacity for being able, 'to stand up for Britain in Brussels'.

In addition to these three influences it might have been expected that public opinion on the Community would also have had a fourth influence: at the electoral level. In fact there is little evidence of much impact at all, other than in the highly negative sense of a lack of interest in, and knowledge about, the Community, providing a major part of the explanation for why the British turn-out in each of the three European Parliament elections (1979, 1984, 1989) was by far the lowest in the Community. At general elections there may have been a marginal benefit for the Labour party in February 1974, when Enoch Powell urged anti-Community Conservatives to vote Labour on the grounds that Labour was offering a referendum or a general election devoted to Community membership. There may too have been a marginal benefit for the Conservatives in 1983 when Labour campaigned for withdrawal from the Community and the Conservative lead over Labour as 'having the best policies on the Common Market' was 23 per cent by the end of the campaign.[12] These two possible exceptions apart, however, the role of the Community in general elections has been slight. The reason for this is that the Community has not satisfied the three conditions which Butler has suggested must each apply if an issue is to affect voting.[13] The three conditions are:

1. The electorate must have strong feelings on the issue. Clearly the Community has never ranked high amongst issues in the minds of the electorate. At no stage has it been of comparable importance to issues such as unemployment, inflation, or social service provi-

---

[12] D. Butler and D. Kavanagh, *The British General Election of 1983*, (London, 1984), 143.
[13] D. Butler, *British General Elections since 1945*, (Oxford, 1989), 89–90.

sion. For example, in a 1989 survey it ranked joint last—with private schools, and a long way behind issues such as the health service, the environment, and nuclear weapons—in a list of nine issues which respondents were asked to grade in terms of their significance regarding a possible switch in vote.[14]

2. The electorate must have a one-sided approach to the issue. Whilst never one-sided, this condition has partially applied, with a decided tilting of opinion at certain times: tending towards the hostile up to 1983–4, and becoming more favourable since.

3. The electorate must genuinely perceive a sharp contrast between the party stances. Apart from Labour's period of opposition to the Community in the early 1980s there can hardly be said to have been deep differences in the stances that the two major parties have adopted towards the Community.

The Significance for Britain's Relations with the Community

With the singular, but of course extremely important, exception of the 1975 referendum British policy towards the Community has never been much influenced, directly at least, by what the public thinks. Perhaps popular suspicion of the Community has encouraged Governments marginally to stiffen the stances of Britain's negotiators in the Council of Ministers—no Government, after all, wishes to be seen as a 'soft touch for foreigners'. For the most part, however, Britain's decision-makers have used their own judgements—subject to the usual accommodations to vested interests—on what British policy should be. In so far as public opinion has been noticed by decision-makers it has normally been judged to be too weak, too vague, or too confused to constitute much of a guide to, or restraint on, action. Arguably the only major instance when Britain's Community decision-makers have gone against their own natural instincts and preferences as a result of a contrary public opinion was when Mrs Thatcher, at the 1989 Madrid summit, agreed to Britain participating in the first stage of the Delors scheme for economic and monetary union: the summit was held shortly after the 1989 elections to the European Parliament in which the Conservative party had polled badly, and some had attributed the poor electoral performance to over-zealous 'Euro-bashing' by Mrs Thatcher.

[14] ICM survey conducted for the *Guardian* in September 1989. *Guardian*, 18 Sept. 1989.

To suggest that public opinion as a whole has not done much to help shape governmental attitudes and policies towards the Community is not, of course, to deny that particular sections of public opinion have sometimes exercised an influence. They have not done so, however as often or as much as is often suggested. Take, for example, the business community: for much of the 1980s its views on economic and monetary policy, and, in particular, on the question of the European Monetary System, were much more integrationist than those of the Government;[15] take trade-unionists: from 1986–7 polls showed them to be giving overwhelming support to the idea of a social dimension to 1992, but this left an ideologically unsympathetic Government unmoved; and take that section of society which is commonly thought to have exercised most influence—the farmers: in both the 1970s and the 1980s British Governments adopted fairly tough positions in Brussels in pressing for less Community expenditure on agriculture. It is beyond the scope of this chapter to detail why Governments have, for the most part, not been over responsive to sectional opinions, but three particularly important points might briefly be mentioned: many sectional opinions are fairly fixed in their party-political loyalties and are therefore poorly placed to be able to threaten a Government with withdrawal of support if sympathetic policy positions are not adopted; what is claimed and presented as sectional opinion is sometimes perceived by Governments as being no such thing but rather merely the opinion of sectional leaderships; and few numerically significant sections of society are sufficiently clear or cohesive in their views to warrant special notice on the part of Governments.

The Significance for the Overall Viability and Legitimacy of the Community

It has long been argued by those who wish to see further European integration that Community-building can benefit from favourable and supportive public opinion. Such benefit, it is argued, can take the form both of a general legitimization of Community processes, and pressure being placed on decision-makers to support policy integration.

[15] For a detailed analysis of business views see Social Surveys (Gallup Poll) Ltd., *Industrialists and City Survey: Tabulated Results*, June 1989.

There are few indications that public opinion in the Community has, as yet, had any such effect. What has been created in the Community has largely been the work of national and pan-European élites, subject usually only to the restraints and pressures exercised by powerful sectional interests. Public opinion across the Community has tended to be too diffuse, and insufficiently intense, to be capable of effective mobilization by the two institutions which would most like to use it for integrationist purposes: the Commission and the European Parliament. British opinion on the Community, as we have seen, has, along with Danish opinion, been particularly sluggish in developing an integrationist dynamism.

There is much in Robert Putnam's observation that public opinion will come to assist the process of European integration 'only insofar as European publics begin to define their interests in functional, ideological, or other pan-European terms instead of national terms'.[16] They can hardly be said to have done so as yet, although there are some indications that it is perhaps beginning to happen. In this connection Tables 8.9 and 8.10 are particularly interesting in the British context, showing, as they seemingly do, considerable support for Community decision-making powers in key policy areas.

CONCLUDING REMARKS

In their study of British attitudes on European integration in the 1970s Dalton and Duvall argued that public opinion is a consequence of two sorts of factors.[17] On the one hand there are long-term factors—such as values, cognitive mobilization, political partisanship, and other socio-political characteristics—which serve to create a sort of opinion 'norm'. On the other hand there are short-term factors—of which the most important are public events and media presentation of these events—which serve to produce 'deviations' from the 'norm'. As opinions are formed and become

---

[16] Comment by R. D. Putnam on the article by M. Slater 'Political Elites, Popular Indifference and Community Building', *Journal of Common Market Studies*, 21 (1983), 89.
[17] R. J. Dalton and R. Duvall, 'The Political Environment and Foreign Policy Opinions', *British Journal of Political Science*, 16 (1986), 113–34.

rooted in individual belief systems so does the relative importance of the long-term factors become more important and so does opinion become less sensitive to short-term shifts in events. This process of opinion formation and change is clearly seen in the more favourable attitudes towards European integration and the European Community that have been apparent in Britain since the early, and more especially the mid-1980s. Changes in some of the long-term factors have raised the 'norm' in each of the aspects of opinion that were considered in the earlier analysis: affective sentiment for European integration; support for Community membership; utilitarian calculation of the importance and advantages of the Community for Britain; and the identification of the British people with Europe and the Community. Of course, doubts, suspicions, and in some quarters hostility towards Europe and the Community remain, and ignorance about the nature and responsibilities of the Community is still widespread. But the reality and desirability of Community membership are increasingly accepted and the benefits that accrue from Community membership are increasingly recognized.

The gap between UK opinion and Community-wide opinion on European affairs has, of course, been an important aspect of Britain's semi-detached position *vis-à-vis* the Community: important in its own right, and important too as a contributory factor in explaining why politicians have often adopted negative, sometimes even bombastically hostile, stances on Community matters. The size of the gap, however, has narrowed as UK public opinion has slowly adapted to, or at least become reconciled to, the reality of Community membership. By the end of the 1980s the lag of public opinion behind governmental opinion, which at the beginning of the decade had seemingly been considerable, had virtually disappeared—indeed popular approval for Community action on social, environmental, and various other policy matters suggested that in certain respects the public were more integrationist than the Government.[18]

Whether support for the Community will continue to grow remains to be seen. Certainly there is nothing inevitable about such

---

[18] For example, in 1989–90, when the Government was vigorously campaigning against *The Community Charter of Fundamental Social Rights*, Eurobarometer polls consistently showed 65–70 per cent support for *The Charter* amongst the British people.

a process. Familiarization is no guarantee—as is demonstrated, for example, by stagnant, and in some respects slightly declining, support for the Community in West Germany in the 1980s. There are those who argue that generational change—and, in particular, the passing of the Second World War generation on the one hand, and the younger generation's increasing familiarization with Europe on the other—will guarantee increasing Euro-enthusiasm in Britain, but there is not much evidence to support this case: in most key respects there are, amongst the British people, few differences between the generations in their attitudes to Europe.[19]

In all probability two factors will be crucial in affecting the future evolution of opinion. First, national economic, and to a lesser extent political and social, performance, coupled with perceptions of the relationship between the Community and that performance. Secondly, general perceptions of the importance of the Community, and particular perceptions of its importance for Britain. It is no coincidence that support for the Community has usually grown when its saliency has increased or been emphasized: as during the Government's pro-Community publicity drive in 1972; as during the 1975 referendum campaign; as at the time of elections to the European Parliament; and, most importantly of all in terms of the future, as the importance of 1992 has been highlighted and come increasingly to be recognized.

[19] See, for example, Social Surveys (Gallup Poll) Ltd., *The Image of Europe: Tabulated Results*, 31.

9

Conclusion

Stephen George

IN 1973 Britain joined a Community that had already been in existence, in different forms, for over twenty years. The original member states had developed rules and ways of working together during that period. The rules were not all favourable towards the new member: for example, both the domination of the budget by the CAP and the system devised for funding the budget disadvantaged Britain. So far as the methods of working together were concerned, the British simply had a lot to learn, and that was bound to take time.

Both of these factors contributed to gaining Britain a reputation for being an awkward partner. Attempts by successive British Governments to find ways of removing the financial disadvantages of the budgetary arrangements led to a situation in which they were arguing against the representatives of the other member states, most of whom were net beneficiaries of the budget; and a certain clumsiness in pursuing their aims added to the impression of awkwardness, even though it was to some extent simply a consequence of the need to learn how the EC worked.

However, the impression that Britain was not whole-hearted in its membership of the EC, that it was a 'semi-detached' member, was heightened by the tone adopted in negotiations, particularly under Prime Ministers Harold Wilson and Margaret Thatcher. The rhetoric of the renegotiation of the terms of British entry in 1974–5 and of the negotiations over the size of British contributions to the Community budget between 1979 and 1984 was adversarial and nationalistic. Both Wilson and Thatcher spoke as though the issues under discussion were not problems for the EC as a whole, to be mutually and amicably resolved, but as though there was a battle between Britain and the 'Europeans', who were trying to cheat the British and who had to be put in their place by firmness and determination to protect the national interest.

It is not good enough, though, to explain such behaviour as the reflection of the personal predispositions of the Prime Ministers concerned. In this book we have tried to explain the image of Britain as a semi-detached member by disaggregating the concept of 'Britain'. We have looked at the influence of different elements in the pluralistic British political process on the content and tone of British policy in the EC. What conclusions can we draw from this examination?

First, there has been adaptation: a learning process has gone on at all levels of government and politics. However, the rate of adaptation seems to have varied according to the actor under consideration. Administratively there has been a steady adjustment to working within the EC, although this has not necessarily been the result of any conversion to support for the EC on the part of civil servants, who have adapted because they have had to do so at a variety of more or less technical levels. Much the same could be argued for pressure groups: for example, the TUC, whilst remaining for a long time officially opposed to British membership of the EC, was learning to be an effective actor in the Community political process through participation in the work of the Economic and Social Committee, the ETUC, and other Community bodies.

Against this steady adaptation at the technical level, politics seems to have adapted more slowly. Nigel Ashford and Neill Nugent provide an explanation for this in their chapters on political parties and public opinion. The whole basis for British political debate has rested on ideas of national sovereignty and the superiority of British political institutions. It took a tremendous effort to get the British public to approve membership of the EC, because of the lack of any sentiment of 'Europeanism'; and the leaders of the main parties (with the exception of the Liberals) made no effort to inculcate such attitudes. The evolution of opinion was therefore slow. Nugent has shown how public opinion has gradually become more favourable to the EC over a long period of time; but within the political parties the process has been a cause of considerable friction, as Ashford has demonstrated. Party leaders have had to move carefully to hold their parties together. This slow evolution of opinion within both the political parties and the general public has acted as a constraint on party leaders, and has contributed to the rather negative and anti-EC tone of some of their contributions to the Community policy debate.

Adaptation, then, has been irregular across the British administrative and political spectrum. It has also varied according to policy area. The less high-profile and politically sensitive the sector, the more smoothly has British policy adapted to working in a 'normal' Community manner. For example, in the case of the European Regional Development Fund, Britain has a good record on getting funds from the EC because the proposals that are submitted are well prepared. Because it is not a controversial subject, and because Britain benefits from working as a normal member of the EC in bidding for monies, the adaptation here has been relatively smooth and the learning process has been rapidly completed. In contrast, in the agricultural sector, where Britain has less of a vested interest in the CAP than have many other member states, and actually suffers from its distorting effect on the Community budget, the British Government has persistently argued for reform and frequently found itself in a minority of one. By attacking this 'sacred cow' of the original EC of six, one of its 'great achievements', the British enhanced their reputation for semi-detachment, and appeared to have been far from acting as a normal member.

The study-group at one stage considered including one or more case-studies of how British policy has been formulated in different policy areas, but eventually decided not to do so precisely because of this variation in adaptation by sector: there is no such thing as a typical area of policy. It is hoped eventually to follow the present volume with a set of case-studies which would apply the approach outlined here, and would illustrate this variability in adaptation.

A second conclusion from the present study is that British policy in the EC is the outcome of a variety of political influences and not as unified and internally consistent as it is sometimes presented as being. For example, as Geoffrey Edwards shows in his chapter on central government, there is an active process of bureaucratic politics that goes on before a policy is formulated.

The Foreign Office has a certain overall view of what it wants to see achieved within the EC, but the co-ordination of policy is done through the European Secretariat in the Cabinet Office, a small unit that cannot easily formulate an overall view because its very small size allows it too little time in which to do any forward thinking on policy. In consequence an active process of bureaucratic politics goes on to decide the stance that the British Government will take on any particular issue. In this process the view of the Foreign Office sometimes prevails: it does have considerable influence because of its synoptic view. On other occasions, though, the view of the Treasury prevails, and this was perhaps particularly frequently the case during Margaret Thatcher's premiership, because the view of the Prime Minister more frequently coincided with that of the Treasury than with that of the Foreign Office, which she suspected of being too pro-EC.

Not that the Treasury itself had a single synoptic view of EC policy to counterpose against that of the Foreign Office. On the contrary, the Treasury is a pluralistic government department in itself; nor does there seem to be any distinctively 'European' policy that has emerged from it. Rather, the Treasury view has been to judge particular issues by their effects on separate Treasury objectives. Thus, the dispute about the funding for the framework programme of technological research in 1986–7, which is reported in Chapter 2, can be seen as an example of natural Treasury parsimony over public spending, backed by the Prime Minister, and causing an impression of British semi-detachment from the EC which could only have been damaging to the goodwill that is needed to achieve other more positive objectives in the permanent diplomatic bargaining that goes on in Brussels.

Other government departments also have their say in this process of bureaucratic politics. The roles of the DTI and MAFF are both significant on issues which directly affect them. The appearance of semi-detachment from the EC that is sometimes given by British policy may therefore in part be a consequence of a degree of fragmentation in policy that is greater than one would expect given the very tight mandates that British negotiators have to work to in Brussels.

If this conclusion is surprising, it is partly because of the image that the British Government has given of keeping tight political control over the relations of Britain with the rest of the EC. Certainly a sustained attempt has been made by successive Governments of different political persuasions to play a 'gatekeeper' role, preventing the process of European integration from dissolving their control. But this has proved increasingly difficult. As Jill Preston has shown in her chapter, various local authority associations, and also some individual local authorities, have developed direct links with Brussels both in order to obtain grants under the ERDF, and to influence policy decisions. Alan Butt Philip has demonstrated the increasing links between British pressure groups and their European counterparts. In both these respects the Government's gatekeeper role is undermined.

From another direction, too, the gatekeeper role of the executive has come under increasing pressure. As has been explained in Chapter 4, Parliament has become increasingly concerned about its lack of control over Community legislation, and has been encroaching on the Government's freedom of action by demanding more effective procedures for scrutiny of such legislation. At the same time the tide of Community law has become a flood, significantly eroding sovereign parliamentary control over national law. Without increased powers over the increasingly extensive body of Community law, Parliament risks becoming marginalized in its primary legislative function.

As Nigel Ashford has shown, within the political parties, too, direct links have been forged with European counterparts below the level of the leadership, and this has led to a distinct evolution of opinion in some parts of each of the two major political parties, while other sections of the same parties have remained relatively insulated from the EC. This has made the process of party management on the issue of the EC very much more difficult.

Public opinion, also, has seen an evolution, which has been traced by Neill Nugent, and which owes little to any strong leadership given by the political parties. Thus both within their own parties and in the wider electorate the party leaders have found the European issue to have a life of its own, which comes to bind them rather than being controlled by them.

British policy in the EC is therefore a much more complex matter than simple representations of it as a rational and calculated strategy would lead us to believe. The 'realist' assumptions that underlay much of the analysis of the EC based on intergovernmental perspectives, such as frequently appear in the Press, give the impression that national negotiating positions represent a unified and reasoned calculation of what consitutes the national interest, and that the various positions taken up in negotiations are all part of a well-worked-out strategy. This book, and the book on the Federal Republic of Germany and the EC by Bulmer and Paterson,[1] indicate quite clearly that this is far too simple an explanation, and

---

[1] Simon Bulmer and William Paterson, *The Federal Republic of Germany and the European Community* (London, 1987).

therefore necessarily misleading. Governments have a vested interest in presenting their positions as coherent and rational, but the truth is that they represent the outcome of a domestic political process more than they do the outcome of a process of reasoning.

To understand the progress that the EC has made, and its prospects for further advance, it is necessary to begin from this understanding of how domestic policy-making processes operate. It is the hope of the members of the study-group that this type of analysis will now be applied to other member states so that a firmer foundation can be established for understanding politics and policy in the EC.

Index